INTEGRATED TALENT MANAGEMENT SCORECARDS

Insights From World-Class Organizations on Demonstrating Value

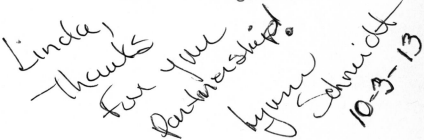

Toni Hodges DeTuncq and Lynn Schmidt, PhD

ASTD
PRESS

ASTD Press is an internationally renowned source of insightful and practical information on workplace learning, performance, and professional development.

ASTD Press
1640 King Street Box 1443
Alexandria, VA 22313-1443 USA

Ordering information: Books published by ASTD Press can be purchased by visiting ASTD's website at store.astd.org or by calling 800.628.2783 or 703.683.8100.

Library of Congress Control Number: 2012946150
ISBN-10: 1-56286-865-9
ISBN-13: 978-1-56286-865-9
e-ISBN: 978-1-60728-742-1

ASTD Press Editorial Staff:
Director: Glenn Saltzman
Manager, ASTD Press: Ashley McDonald
Community of Practice Manager, Human Capital: Ann Pace
Associate Editor: Stephanie Castellano
Editorial Assistant: Sarah Cough
Cover Design: Marisa Kelly
Text Design: Ana Foreman and Marisa Kelly

Printed by Versa Press, Inc., East Peoria, IL, www.versapress.com.

CONTENTS

FOREWORD

Kevin Oakes

When it comes to talent management, there's a four-letter word on the lips of human capital professionals everywhere—data. Consider this research from the Institute for Corporate Productivity (i4cp): When some of the world's top companies were asked what their biggest workforce planning challenges are, data-related challenges were the top two listed.

Workforce Planning Challenges for High-Performance Organizations	
1. Technologies that do not share data effectively	46%
2. Unreliable data	35%
6. Lack of data	32%

Source: 2012 Strategic Workforce Planning Survey. Institute for Corporate Productivity (i4cp).

Yet reliable and comprehensive data is crucial to effective talent management. While talent management is widely considered to begin with workforce planning, the workforce planning professionals who participated in the study confirmed that data problems are multifaceted, creating issues across the board for talent professionals. Data questions that are frequently asked include:

- Can we access the workforce data we need?

- Is our workforce data accurate?

- Do we know how to interpret the data effectively?

Easily accessing the right data is perplexing to most organizations. And many blame technology for that. Today, companies often resort to manual data analysis because automated processes aren't in place. Of the high-performing organizations (HPOs) studied, i4cp found that a full 37 percent lacked access to automated workforce data. Even among those with automated data, nearly half said it wasn't integrated across the organization. And among those who are able to access it, data accuracy is thrown into question. A third of those surveyed admitted that their organizations' workforce data wasn't reliable. Another i4cp report, *HR Analytics: Why We're Not There Yet* (2012), confirmed similar findings: About one in four respondents said they lacked confidence in their HR data, and nearly one in five said their organizations had no controls in place to ensure data accuracy.

Accuracy is more than "is-it-or-isn't-it-correct"; it is also about consistent understanding of data. Are definitions the same from one organizational department or function to the next? Take "turnover" for example. The different ways turnover is calculated both across and within companies is mindbog-gling. Studies show that top organizations are twice as likely to have company -wide standards for interpreting data as low-performance companies. Getting buy-in for consistent definitions of data is a fundamental step for effective measurement, yet too often this simple step is ignored or forgotten.

However, let's assume access to accurate data is easy. The next step—which can trip up even the most sophisticated companies—is finding individuals with the skills to organize, analyze, and interpret the data. In fact, well over half of low-performing companies cite lack of employees with the relevant skills and training as the biggest challenge they have in using data for decision-making. Finding HR professionals with the ability to tell the story behind the numbers and present data in ways that compel action—especially by senior leaders—has proven to be a rare skill. Yet it is this final storytelling piece that is so critical. The ability to connect the dots, which empowers leaders to use workforce data to positively affect business decision-making, is ultimately what it's all about.

Take heart, however. If you are reading this and thinking that forecasting, analytical, and statistical abilities are lacking on your team, you're not alone. Research shows that many companies face this obstacle, which is why borrowing best practices from others is so important today.

The scorecards and descriptions provided in this book should help close the gap on how to measure talent initiatives effectively. This is an important step for any company that either aspires to be, or wishes to remain, an HPO. The best companies are using data for strategic, long-term planning more than twice as much as low-performing organizations (LPOs) (96 percent compared to 47 percent); and are finding the talent and the processes in order to "tell the story."

The best organizations use data analysts and measurement tools for a more calculated outlook. This is supported by the survey participants' responses regarding the use of data for evaluating programs, or establishing the need for a future program, in which high performers again far outpaced low performers (91 percent and 59 percent, respectively). Top organizations are also far more focused on actively seeking information that improves the effectiveness of their planning and the performance of their programs and processes, while LPOs are more concerned about legal and compliance requirements.

The majority of companies are using workforce data as a way of keeping track of common measurements, such as performance ratings, headcount, turnover rate, and other housekeeping duties. These environmental scans are useful tools in any organization, provided they can be performed in ways that don't divert employees from other tasks that are tied to developing a more effective workforce.

Performance data is the most commonly collected type of data, with 91 percent of high performers reporting that their companies collect this information in some form or another. But training completed turnover rates, headcount, and time-to-fill, train, and onboard all scored high with top organizations.

What matters most, however, is what we refer to as "quality metrics." Top companies typically don't stop at measuring overarching items. Instead, they dig deep and examine workforce measures by specific demographics and root causes. For example, data may show that turnover rates have increased, but they can also tell us that a company is losing high-potential employees who were not provided with tailored development programs.

This example underscores the importance of tying workforce metrics to bottom-line business impact. The large gap between HPOs and LPOs in using data to show how HR programs generate measurable results is the single most important difference between the two. The ability of an organization to close that gap—to collect, analyze, and use data that can show the impact of human capital programs and talent initiatives—will be one sure way to help companies achieve high performance.

That's why integrated talent management scorecards are so critical. Not only will they help human capital professionals tell the story, they may help "data" become more than just a four-letter word.

Kevin Oakes

CEO, Institute for Corporate Productivity (i4cp)

INTRODUCTION

The term integrated talent management has been in vogue for about eight years, yet organizations are still trying to understand how to best integrate talent management functions to achieve business results. This book provides insights on integration techniques as well as ideas for designing and implementing talent management initiatives that affect the business. Even more importantly, the book provides techniques for measuring, evaluating, and demonstrating the impact of talent management initiatives at program, functional, and organizational levels.

There is increasing pressure from stakeholders on talent management functions to demonstrate their value to the business. Many organizations struggle to align their talent management initiatives with business strategies. It can be difficult to measure, evaluate, and demonstrate results. This collection of case studies demonstrates how talent management initiatives affect business results and contribute to organizational success. The case study authors, who represent various industries, all used scorecards as a framework for demonstrating the results of their talent management initiatives at the micro- and macro-levels. These cases are a rich source of information about the strategies, methods, and techniques of some of the best practitioners and consultants in the field. However, no case study necessarily represents the ideal textbook approach to talent management. In every case study it's possible to identify areas that could be improved upon. This is part of the learning experience—to build on the work of other people.

Table 1 contains an overview of the case studies by industry, type of talent management initiative, type of scorecard, and focus areas. It can serve as a quick reference for readers who want to examine the cases by particular audiences, industries, and program types.

Chapter	Industry	TM Initiative	Focus of Case Study
		Table 1. Overview of Case Studies	
3	Healthcare – Clinical and Insurance	Talent Acquisition (TA) and Recruiter Development / Micro Scorecard	Explains how to create value for the business by transforming recruiters into TA consultants and managing the recruiting of strategic positions internally versus externally, resulting in cost avoidance.
4	Government Healthcare	Competency Modeling and Employee Development / Micro Scorecard	Evaluates the impact of competency modeling for engineering professionals in a large government agency and demonstrates the resulting ROI.
5	Electronics	Customer Service Training and Coaching / Micro Scorecard	Shows how customer loyalty can be improved and sustained by transforming the way a global company's call center agents interact with customers.
6	Multiple Businesses, Including Sales and Healthcare	Employee Development and Stress Management / Micro Scorecard	Presents a unique employee development design that resulted in improved performance, where participants completed pre- and post-tests, attended training, and took part in a 30-minute individual tele-coaching session.
7	Banking	Mentoring of Sales Representatives / Micro Scorecard	Highlights a sales mentoring pilot program that contained unique design elements, which resulted in associates with mentors outperforming their peers by 55 percent over eight months.
8	Aerospace and Defense	Career Development for Emerging Leaders / Micro Scorecard	Demonstrates how a career development program can engage and retain high-potential leaders and be measured for impact.
9	Construction	Pre-Leadership Training / Micro Scorecard	Describes a talent management solution designed to prepare emerging leaders for future leadership roles, and the impact the program had on behavioral change.

10	Information Technology	Development of Sales Leaders Micro Scorecard	Demonstrates how a Fortune 500 company achieved increased revenue growth, improved customer satisfaction, and enhanced partner status by implementing a successful talent management program.
11	High Technology	Management Development and Leaders Teaching Leaders Micro Scorecard	Explains how to use several data collection methods to measure the impact of leaders teaching leaders. The benefits of this model include increasing managerial effectiveness and employee engagement.
12	Customer Communications Technologies	High-Potential Leadership Development Micro Scorecard	Describes how a CEO-sponsored leadership development program with a robust 18-month road map can be measured for impact.
13	Public Pension	360-Degree Feedback and Coaching Micro Scorecard	Explains how leaders were developed through a 360-degree feedback and coaching program. The evaluation metrics successfully demonstrated improvement in leadership effectiveness.
14	Biotechnology	Executive Coaching Micro Scorecard	Shows a unique approach to measuring the business impact and return-on-investment (ROI) of executive coaching.
15	Consumer Products	Succession Management and Job Movement Micro Scorecard	Explains how to assess the effectiveness of the talent movement aspect of the succession planning processes.
16	Fast-Food Restaurant	Employee Engagement Micro Scorecard	Provides an overview of how a national restaurant company tied employee engagement data to actual business outcomes.
17	Private Corporation	Retention and Engagement Micro Scorecard	Describes a successful organization-wide initiative to retain a short-term, high-performing workforce to stage the Olympic Winter Games.
18	Steel, Oil, Gas, Power, Shipping, and Ports	Talent Management System Implementation Micro Scorecard	Demonstrates how a global, diversified conglomerate approached the people and systemic challenges of a fast-growing enterprise, and went on to implement a complex SaaS in Asia.

19	Banking	Learning and Development Functional Macro Scorecard	Provides a look at how an international bank set up a learning and development macro scorecard to track its training programs across its organization.
20	Car Rental	Talent Management Organizational Macro Scorecard	Describes the merging of talent management functions into a fully integrated TM service unit that drives organizational effectiveness and market competitiveness.

It would be difficult to find a more impressive group of contributors to a publication of this nature than those included here. The case study authors are experienced professionals on the leading edge of talent management. Most are experts on the topic, and some are well known in their fields. A few are high-profile authors who have made tremendous contributions to their fields and have taken this opportunity to provide examples of their top-quality work. All have made significant contributions to the success of organizations and have shared examples of their work that can be implemented elsewhere.

As you review the cases, remember that each organization and its program are unique. What works well for one may not work for another without some modifications, even if both are in similar settings. The book offers various approaches and tools that you can adapt or build on to effectively demonstrate the value of talent management initiatives, functions, and organizations.

1

INTEGRATED TALENT MANAGEMENT: A BUSINESS IMPERATIVE

Lynn Schmidt, PhD

Integrated talent management (ITM) builds business capability by aligning the various talent management (TM) functions, so that they have a stronger impact on business results—the whole becomes greater than the individual parts. Alignment can lead to a stronger people strategy, eliminate redundancy, and create higher-performing individuals and businesses through increased efficiency and effectiveness. According to the Institute for Corporate Productivity (i4cp), high-performing businesses are twice as likely to have ITM strategies (2013).

But what is meant by the term "integrated talent management"? Although the term is used frequently, we seem to lack a common definition and agreement about what it means. According to the Merriam-Webster Dictionary (2013):

- *Integrate* can be defined as "to form, coordinate, or blend into a functioning or unified whole: unite."

- A definition of *talent* is "a person of talent or a group of persons of talent in a field or activity."

- *Management* can be defined as "judicious use of means to accomplish an end."

With those definitions in mind, the definition of integrated talent management, for the purposes of this book, is "United functions with a common goal of building employee capabilities to increase business performance." This may be easier said than done. A report from The Conference Board (Morton, 2004) states that while ITM in many businesses is aligned with strategic objectives, it is not often measured in terms that link to business results.

According to i4cp (2013), there are four characteristics related to ITM that separate high-performing businesses from those that are lower-performing:

- Leaders see ITM as vital to business success.

- Processes are in place to align ITM with business goals.

- Processes and policies support ITM.

- The components of TM are effectively integrated.

These requirements for successful ITM can be achieved through the use of scorecards, which will be explored later on in this chapter.

INTEGRATED TALENT MANAGEMENT FUNCTIONS

ITM functions are often referred to using different terminology. For the purposes of this book, the following six TM functions are considered the core functions within the ITM model, as illustrated in Figure 1-1. These six TM functions are found in the ITM organization and would drive its strategic TM initiatives.

1. **Workforce Planning:** This refers to the process of forecasting the talent needs of the business and creating plans that will ensure high performance. Strategic workforce planning (SWP) includes assessing the business direction, determining talent implications, identifying segmented roles, and defining the build or buy actions to be taken. The output of SWP assessments will influence the goals of the other TM functions.

2. **Talent Acquisition:** This involves attracting and selecting the talent that the business needs to accomplish its goals. The talent needs to be acquired at the right time, in the right place, and for the right price.

3. **Performance Management:** This includes how the business and individuals set goals, and how they manage and measure the performance

required to achieve individual and business success. The business goals cascade downward to achieve performance alignment.

4. Learning and Development: This is responsible for supplying the training and professional development opportunities required by individuals to successfully do their jobs. Other initiatives within this TM function are onboarding and mentoring.

5. Succession Management: This involves identifying high-potential employees, developing them, and transitioning them into key roles to ensure continued business success. Defining leadership competencies, executive development and coaching, 360-degree feedback, and job rotations are also within this TM function.

6. Engagement and Retention: This focuses on the TM activities that influence employee engagement and retention, such as employee surveys and related action planning. It also develops and implements tools and programs that reward and motivate individuals, such as diversity initiatives, employee resource groups, and recognition programs.

Figure 1-1. Integrated Talent Management Model

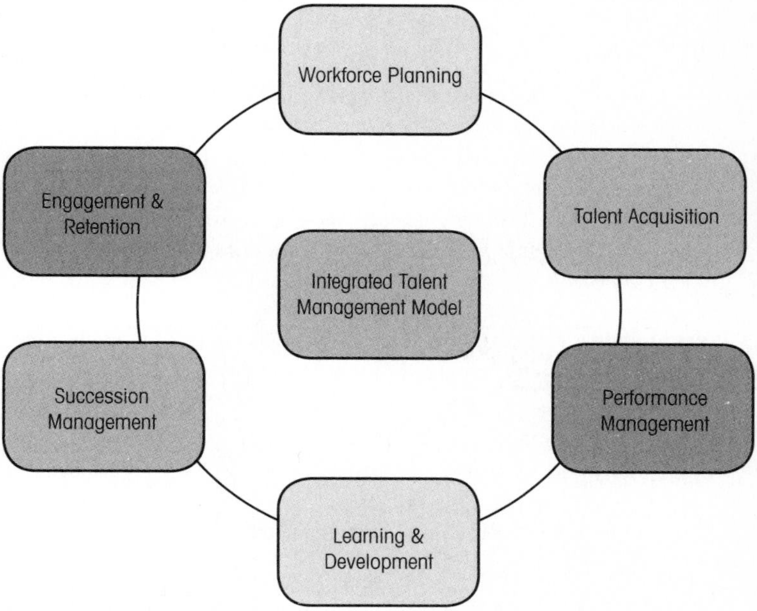

INTEGRATED TALENT MANAGEMENT SCORECARDS

Even when TM functions are integrated and aligned with strategic priorities, they often aren't able to demonstrate their contributions to business results. Yet the purpose of integrating TM functions is to achieve business results. In a study conducted by The Conference Board (Morton, 2005) it was found that mature ITM organizations collect and report on numerous metrics that are incorporated into their balanced scorecards. They collect activity, efficiency, and effectiveness metrics for TM initiatives and share results with their boards of directors. Integrated talent management scorecards enable ITM organizations to align TM initiatives with business goals, and collect data and report the business impact of those initiatives. As shown in Figure 1-2, there are three levels of integrated talent management scorecards:

1. **TM Organizational Macro Scorecard:** This scorecard is created at the ITM organization level and is directly aligned with business goals and measures, such as revenue, operational costs, customer satisfaction, product or service quality, employee engagement, and turnover. It contains a roll-up of the metrics for all TM functions within the ITM organization. This roll-up shows the overall ITM contribution to each business goal.

2. **TM Functional Macro Scorecard:** This scorecard is created at the TM functional level; the functions may include talent acquisition, learning and development, and succession management. The scorecard is aligned with the TM organizational macro scorecard, but would include additional activity, efficiency, and effectiveness measures specific to the TM function. It is a roll-up of measures from the TM initiative micro scorecards.

3. **TM Initiative Micro Scorecard:** This scorecard is aligned with the TM functional macro scorecard measures and may include additional activity, efficiency, and effectiveness measures of the initiative. Below are examples for TM initiatives that would each have their own micro scorecards with metrics including satisfaction, learning, application, and business impact and ROI data:

   » Workforce Planning: identification of strategic, key, core, and transitional roles and implementation of the action plans associated with each role

   » Talent Acquisition: executive recruiting, recruiting for strategic or key roles, internships, and college recruiting

» Performance Management: annual performance review process, quarterly performance review process, individual development plans, and performance improvement plans

» Learning and Development: onboarding program, sales training, mentoring programs, career development initiatives, and management development

» Succession Management: succession plans, 360-degree feedback, executive coaching, high-potential development program, and job rotations

» Engagement and Retention: employee engagement survey, employee resource groups, recognition program, and a diversity initiative.

The case studies in this book (found in chapters 3 through 20) present all three types of scorecards, with detailed descriptions of TM initiatives and scorecard implementation. Chapter 2 will provide more explanation on how to create these scorecards.

Figure 1-2. Integrated Talent Management Scorecards Model

TM Organizational Macro Scorecard	• Aligned with business-level measures, such as revenue, customer satisfaction, employee engagement, and turnover. • A roll-up of the metrics for all TM functions to show the overall TM contribution to each business goal.
TM Functional Macro Scorecard	• Aligned with the TM organizational macro scorecard measures. • A roll-up of TM initiative metrics by function; functions may include Talent Acquisition, Learning and Development, and Succession Management.
TM Initiative Micro Scorecard	• Aligned with the TM functional macro scorecard measures. • Examples of TM initiatives include executive recruiting, sales training, mentoring programs, executive coaching, and job rotations.

STRATEGIC WORKFORCE PLANNING

SWP helps to integrate the TM functions by providing the goals and metrics for the TM organizational and functional macro scorecards. SWP plays a critical role in assessing the current and future talent needs of the business and partnering with other TM functions to create action plans for addressing those needs. This section provides an overview of the SWP function and process. While SWP plays an important role in ITM, a study conducted by The Conference Board (Young, 2006) found that SWP was a new practice in many businesses; many were still in the process of realizing its potential. The majority of companies that participated in the study were either just getting started or had not fully implemented SWP. The six steps of the SWP process are outlined below.

Figure 1-3. Strategic Workforce Planning Process

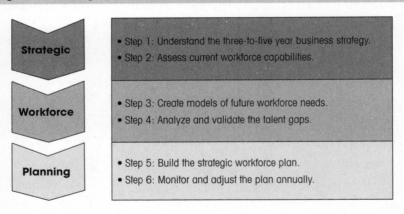

The first step in SWP involves understanding the business strategy. Often the SWP process will begin shortly after the annual business strategy is finalized. Business leaders are interviewed to gather data and to ensure that the SWP team fully understands the business strategy for the next three to five years. Once that data is collected, it is analyzed in step two to determine the current and future talent needs. The talent needs are then segmented into four specific roles:

- Strategic Roles: critical to creating a long-term advantage for the business

- Key Roles: critical to delivering results related to the current business strategy

- Core Roles: foundational roles that support and run the day-to-day business

- Transitional Roles: not critical to business strategies; have a transactional focus.

The third step is to assess the current workforce capability as compared to the roles identified. Do the roles and skills that were identified exist? Following this assessment, workforce modeling may be conducted to further assess the future talent needs and answer the question "How many individuals do we need in that role in one, two, three, four, and five years?" Once those analytics are complete, step four involves analyzing and validating the talent gaps that have been identified. There may not be enough individuals in the roles identified to meet current or future needs, or the skills may not currently exist in the business.

The fifth step is to build the strategic workforce plan based on the data gathered and the analysis conducted. These strategic workforce plans include buy, build, and transition action plans and influence the goals of the ITM organization and other TM functions. Buy plans—recruiting goals—would need to be incorporated into talent acquisition initiatives; build plans—plans to develop employees' skills—could be incorporated into performance management, learning and development, and succession management initiatives; and transition plans may call for a re-skilling initiative in the learning and development function. All of these initiatives combined may require new engagement and retention strategies. And they would all lead to the creation of new TM macro and micro scorecards. The sixth step of the SWP process is to monitor and adjust the plans on an annual basis to reflect changes to the strategic business plan.

As demonstrated, SWP drives the TM initiatives that are the focus of the other TM functions. SWP aligns ITM to the business goals and provides an avenue for ITM to demonstrate its value to the business. It's the glue that can hold the ITM functions together. For that reason, it's an important function to include in the ITM organization.

CONCLUSION

ITM can improve both individual and business performance and it is critical to the success of a business. An ITM organization aligns its TM function and initiatives with the business goals and demonstrates their value through TM macro- and micro-level scorecards. TM functions operating in silos will have difficulty with integration, which will affect the degree to which they can affect the business metrics.

Figure 1-4. Integrated Talent Management Functions and Scorecards

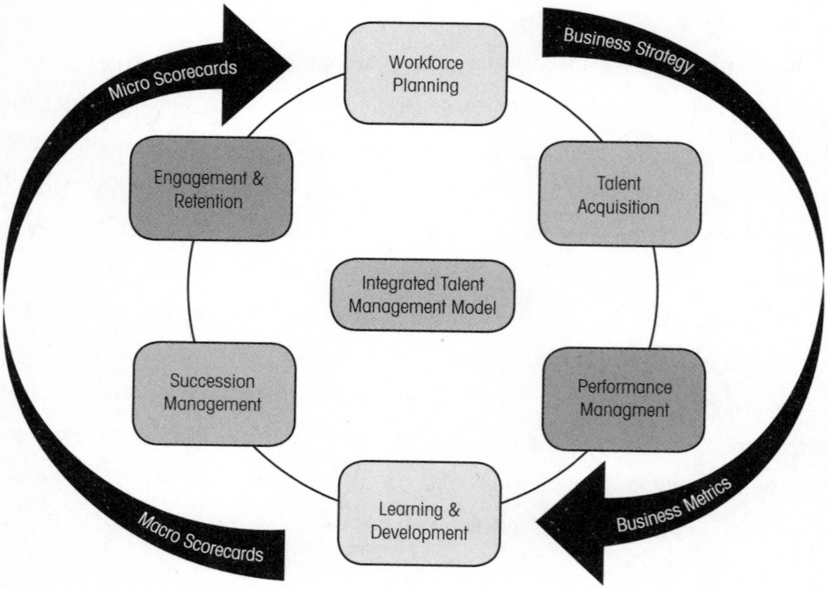

As Figure 1-4 illustrates, creating a viable TM organization requires the integration of the TM functions, alignment with the business strategy, and the implementation of TM macro and micro scorecards. The following chapters in the book will provide specific examples of how organizational, functional, and initiative TM scorecards have been created and implemented in businesses.

REFERENCES

i4cp. (2013). *Integrated Talent Management Strategies of High-Performance Organizations*. Talent Management Knowledge Center. Retrieved January 5, 2013 from http://i4cp.com/talent/talent-management.

Merriam-Webster. (2013). *Merriam-Webster's Dictionary*. Retrieved January 6, 2013 from www.merriam-webster.com.

Morton, L. (2004). *Integrated and Integrative Talent Management: A Strategic HR Framework*. Research Report R-1345-04. New York: The Conference Board.

Morton, L. (2005). *Talent Management Value Imperatives: Strategies for Execution*. Research Report R-1360-05-RR. New York: The Conference Board.

Young, M.B. (2006). *Strategic Workforce Planning: Forecasting Human Capital Needs to Execute Business Strategy*. Research Report R-1391-06-WG. New York: The Conference Board.

2

IMPLEMENTING INTEGRATED TALENT MANAGEMENT SCORECARDS

Toni DeTuncq

Many organizations use a balanced scorecard to track how they are progressing, as measured by key business success indicators such as revenue, customer satisfaction, employee satisfaction, and other organizational areas of desired success. Organizations providing TM initiatives would be wise to design separate TM scorecards to demonstrate the impact those initiatives are having on key business indicators. In order to do this, they must determine each program's objectives and how to measure the extent to which those objectives are being met. This chapter will provide the framework for evaluation and a look at the goals and methodologies for both micro and macro scorecards. It will describe the ITM scorecards model introduced in chapter 1, and the different components of TM initiative scorecards. Finally, a tool is offered for developing and linking the business, performance, and learning objectives needed for the TM initiative scorecards.

MEASUREMENT AND EVALUATION FRAMEWORK

Donald Kirkpatrick defined a framework for evaluation (Kirkpatrick, 1975) that was expanded by Jack Phillips (Phillips, 1997). This framework has proven helpful to the evaluation community because it provides a common language for us to use when we are determining and describing how to measure the extent to which program objectives have been met.

Briefly, the framework is as follows:

- Level 1—the reaction and perhaps planned actions, gathered from the participants at the completion of the initiative

- Level 2—the learning that took place as a result of the initiative

- Level 3—the performance improvement realized as a result of the initiative

- Level 4—the impact the initiative had on the business

- Level 5—the return-on-investment (ROI) realized as a result of the initiative.

The micro and macro scorecards described in this book utilize this framework in their evaluation processes.

TALENT MANAGEMENT SCORECARDS

We developed macro- and micro-learning scorecards to capture and display learning program results (Schmidt, 2003). We've presented these scorecards at presentations at several ASTD conferences. Both the macro- and micro-learning scorecards received praise at these sessions, with participants commenting that they could immediately be used back on the job. The learning scorecards have been used successfully in our own organizations and with clients. We have expanded our learning scorecards to "TM initiative scorecards," to capture the services that the entire performance improvement community is providing in addition to learning programs. The value of scorecards is that they:

- Provide a macro- and micro-level perspective of progress.

- Serve as a brief "at-a-glance" report, versus more detailed studies.

- Show the TM contribution to business objectives.

- Integrate various types of data.

- Demonstrate alignment between programs, strategic objectives, and operating goals.

Organizations can review their TM progress using the ITM scorecards model described in chapter 1.

TM Macro Scorecard

A macro scorecard tracks TM data throughout an organization, whether it is all of the TM initiatives the organization offers, or within one functional area of the organization. It can use the database software already used by the organization, or another kind of software. Organizations using macro scorecards often begin with an Excel spreadsheet and then advance to a more robust database software package, as more data is collected and more interaction with other organizational programs is required. An example of how one organization conceptualized and developed a TM organizational macro scorecard is included in chapter 20 of this book. The format of the TM organizational macro scorecard can be customized for each organization, but we suggest that it contains data aligned with the company's business goals.

The TM functional macro scorecard is also an overall look at how the organization is doing, but for only one particular TM function. It can be organized into two tiers. Tier 1 is the portion in which the data elements for that function are rolled up for the entire business; across business units, regions, or divisions. Tier 2 houses the data elements for that function, broken up across different lines of business, different regions, or other individual business units. Let's look at these different tiers of the TM functional macro scorecards.

TM Functional Macro Scorecard – Tier 1

Tier 1 data can be broken into three types of data elements:

1. Investment/efficiency data, which indicates how much of the initiative has taken place and its value to the organization.
2. Activity data, which indicates how often the initiative is taking place and its value to the organization.
3. Impact data, which indicates how effective the initiatives are in meeting their intended objectives. These can be broken down into the levels of evaluation discussed above.

Table 2-1 provides examples of data elements that could be included in Tier 1 of a macro scorecard.

Table 2-1. Example of Tier 1 Data Elements

Tier 1 Data Elements: Data Roll-Up From All Lines of Business
Investment/efficiency data, such as:
• dollars invested/employee
• L&D spending as % of overall operating expenditures (or as % of organizational payroll)
• number of employees trained (trend over past 12 months)
• training hours/employee/month (trend over past 12 months)
• cost of training/employee/day
• % of courses available via e-learning
Activity data, such as:
• % complete (trend over past 12 months)
• % course availability (trend over past 12 months)
• number of active courses (at least one session held in last 12 months)
• number of classroom sessions held (monthly)
• number of hours of training (monthly)
Impact data—overall averages for each line of business or business unit:
• Level 1 (Reaction/Satisfaction) data
• Level 2 (Learning) data (expressed as a % score)
• Level 3 (Job Performance) data (expressed as % score)
• Level 4 (Business Impact) data (expressed as % of objectives met)
• Level 5 (ROI) data (expressed as a %)

TM Functional Macro Scorecard – Tier 2

Tier 2 of the TM functional macro scorecard provides the same investment/ efficiency, activity, and impact data as the Tier 1 portion, but the data is provided for each individual part of the business, such as lines of business or regions. Also, for the impact data in Tier 2, each specific TM initiative is listed and its business objectives along with its alignment with the organizational strategy are documented. Then the results are expressed using the levels of evaluation. Table 2-2 provides an example of how this would look.

Table 2-2. Example of Tier 2 Data Elements

Tier 2 Data Elements: Data for Each Line of Business
Investment/efficiency data—same data elements listed in Tier 1
Activity data—same data elements listed in Tier 1
Impact data for each course or performance improvement program: • course title and applicable code • course business objective(s) • alignment with organizational strategy • current average Level 1 data results • current average Level 2 data results (expressed as a % score) • current average Level 3 data results where available (expressed as a % score) • current average Level 4 data results where available (expressed as % of objectives met) • current average Level 5 data results where available (expressed as a %)

This is a suggested format for a TM functional macro scorecard. But no matter the format, important principles should always be considered to enhance its value to the organization:

- The organization must be able to demonstrate how its programs are aligned with organizational strategy.

- Each program must have business objectives.

- Investment/efficiency and activity data will vary by organization but should be used to tell a story, and could be used to benchmark.

- The Level 1 instrument used must be standardized so the impact result scores can be compared.

- Level 2 instruments must be designed, validated, and scored consistently.

- Levels 3, 4, and 5 data must be collected using industry-accepted standards.

Chapter 19 provides an example of an organization's TM functional macro scorecard and illustrates these components and their value.

TM Initiative Micro Scorecards

The TM initiative micro scorecard provides detailed impact data for each TM initiative. This micro scorecard can provide, in a single table, all the data resulting from an impact study of a TM initiative (Schmidt, 2003). Figure 2-1 provides a template for a micro scorecard.

Figure 2-1. TM Initiative Micro Scorecard Template

TM Initiative Micro Scorecard Template				
Program Title:				
Target Audience:				
Number of Attendees:				
Duration:				
Business Objectives:				
Results				
Satisfaction	Learning	Application	Tangible Benefits	Intangible Benefits
Level 1	**Level 2**	**Level 3**	**Levels 4 & 5** **Business Impact** **ROI and BCR**	
Technique to Isolate Effects of Program:				
Technique to Convert Data to Monetary Value:				
Fully-Loaded Program Costs:				
Barriers to Application of Skills:				
Recommendations:				

The section under "Satisfaction" would include the extent to which the participants were satisfied with the initiative. These would be the results of a Level 1 analysis. Examples of what to include in this section would be

- relevance of the TM initiative to the job
- likelihood of recommending the initiative to others
- importance of the information received
- intention to use the initiative's offerings
- an overall rating from a satisfaction questionnaire.

The section under "Learning" would include the extent to which the learning objectives have been met. These would be the results of a Level 2 analysis. Examples of what to include in this section would be

- the participants' assessments of the initiative

- scores from any learning assessment that may have been conducted

- third-party observations.

The section under "Application" would include the extent to which the performance objectives were met. These would be the results of a Level 3 analysis. Examples of what to include in this section would be

- the importance of using the content from the initiative in the work environment

- the level of initiative adoption

- behavioral change or improvements in performance.

The section under "Tangible Benefits" would include the extent to which the impact objectives have been met. These would be impact data (Level 4 analysis) and possibly ROI data (Level 5 analysis) Examples of what to include in this section would include improvements in

- productivity and efficiency

- quality

- cost control

- customer satisfaction.

The section under "Intangible Benefits" would include those benefits discovered in the Level 4 analysis that could not be converted into a business measure, but are seen by the organization as providing value. The benefits might include

- improved customer satisfaction

- increased job satisfaction

- reduced conflicts

- reduced stress

- increased teamwork.

If performance and business impact were measured, the method used to isolate the impact of the TM initiative would be provided in the next section, such as a control group arrangement or participant or executive perceptions. If an ROI or benefit-cost ratio (BCR) analysis was conducted, the technique used to convert the impact data would be listed, as well as the fully loaded program costs. Barriers that impeded the success of the initiative would also be listed, as well as any recommendations that were made as a result of evaluating the TM initiative.

This book has 16 examples of TM micro scorecards from various organizations, presented in chapters 3 through 18. The TM initiative micro-scorecard format may vary by program or may have some elements missing if all levels of evaluation for that initiative were not conducted. Our chapters show examples in which not all levels of evaluation were conducted, but you will see that the scorecards still tell a story at a glance. No matter the format used or the levels of evaluation conducted, there are principles that should always be considered when building a TM initiative micro scorecard:

- Start building your TM initiative micro scorecards today—don't wait for someone to request it. They might request the data in a different format that would not be nearly as meaningful or concise (this is true for the macro scorecards as well).

- Begin with the end in mind—plan in advance so your method of evaluation will allow you to successfully complete a comprehensive scorecard.

- Always account for the influence of other factors.

- Be conservative when converting and isolating—consult the resources provided at the end of this chapter to learn how to do this credibly.

- Involve management in the process.

- Educate the TM initiative development and evaluation teams.

- Be prepared to educate the stakeholders of the program on the elements of the TM initiative micro scorecard.

- Use the scorecards to communicate the value of each TM initiative and to hold your team accountable for TM initiative results.

OBJECTIVE MAPPING

To ensure the TM functional macro scorecards effectively track the progress of TM initiatives, we need to define progress. Objective mapping is a technique for defining, linking, and documenting business objectives, performance objectives, and learning objectives (Hodges, 2002 and DeTuncq, 2012). The process allows us to determine the extent to which each objective is met.

Business Objectives

Business objectives are the goals for the organization. They include the metrics that determine the extent to which the objectives are met. Here are some examples of business objectives and their associated metrics:

- Increase sales revenue by 25 percent.

- Reduce overtime by 30 percent.

- Increase customer satisfaction index by 25 percent.

- Reduce turnover (or absenteeism) by 15 percent.

- Reduce waste by 35 percent.

Normally, business metrics fall into output, cost, time, or quality measures. Sometimes they can be soft data, such as work habits, the work climate, development, advancement, or some other area that may be unique to the organization. For example, an organization that works with the disabled community might be looking for an increase in resources, whereas a manufacturing company will be looking for increased revenue and reduced waste.

The objective-mapping process also requires the practitioner to determine potential enablers and barriers. Barriers are those factors that will inhibit or reduce the chances of meeting the objectives. Enablers are those factors that can be put into place to ensure the objectives are met or to mitigate the impact of the barriers. Table 2-3 provides examples of business objective enablers and barriers.

Table 2-3. Examples of Business Objective Enablers and Barriers

Example Enablers	Example Barriers
Incentive programs	Communication problems
New product line	Grievance process
Reorganization	Lack of personnel and material resources
Marketing programs	Appraisal process
Process improvements	Public perception

Performance Objectives

Performance objectives are the employee behaviors in the work environment that are necessary for meeting the business objectives. There must be at least one performance objective linked to each business objective, but usually there are many more. Performance objectives always begin with an action verb. Here are some examples of performance objectives:

- Use business language when communicating goals to executives, peers, and direct reports.

- Create a priority checklist for all meetings.

- Use the company's business framework to demonstrate value to clients.

- Resolve conflicts using the higher-conflict resolution approach.

- Provide coaching rather than orders to direct reports.

The objective-mapping process requires that a method is determined for measuring the extent to which each performance objective has been met. Examples of performance objective measurement methodologies are questionnaires, observations, action plans, interviews, and focus groups. Methods to isolate changes in performance that are due to the TM initiative must also be determined. These would include the use of control groups; trend-line analysis; participant, management, or customer estimates; and others. Just as with business objectives, barriers and enablers for meeting the performance objectives must be anticipated. Table 2-4 provides examples of enablers and barriers to meeting performance objectives.

Table 2-4. Examples of Performance Enablers and Barriers

Example Enablers	Example Barriers
Technology	Lack of technology
Job aids	Lack of management support
Supervisor reinforcement	Workload
Help lines	Insufficient time to use new skills
Performance reviews	Insufficient prerequisite skills

Learning Objectives

The learning objectives are those objectives required of the initiative to achieve the performance objectives. There must be at least one learning objective linked to each performance objective, but there are usually many more. These objectives should also begin with action verbs. Here are some examples of learning objectives:

- Use the recommended coaching skills for five typical situations.

- Select the steps to take for solving given problems.

- Become certified in the use of the new system.

- Develop and present an executive briefing to a class.

- Utilize the company's competency model to identify cultural differences between five typical diverse groups in the organization.

Although often challenging, developing methods to measure the extent to which each of the learning objectives has been met is a good idea. It will accurately demonstrate the extent to which the TM initiative was responsible for the improved performance. As with the business and performance objectives, barriers and enablers to meeting the learning objectives should be anticipated. Examples of those enablers and barriers are found in Table 2-5.

Table 2-5. Examples of Learning Objective Enablers and Barriers

Example Enablers	Example Barriers
Media type	Insufficient time
Knowledgeable instruction	Program materials too expensive
Supervisor support	Wrong audience
Exercises	Job distractions
Participant selection	Exercises not relevant or applicable

By doing this work up front, the TM initiatives will be targeted and focused on meeting the goals for the organization. This will yield greater results and waste less money. Each of the case studies in this book will reveal the steps that were taken to develop the business, performance, and learning objectives.

It may be desirable to document these objectives, metrics, measurement methodologies, and enablers and barriers. For example, many organizations are finding the use of an objective map helpful (Hodges, 2002, and DeTuncq, 2012). An example of a completed objective map that lists the three types of objectives, their enablers and barriers, and methods to measure each one, can be found in Table 2-6.

CONCLUSIONS

The TM macro and micro scorecards provide immense value in helping the organization see what the TM team is accomplishing with its programs. They demonstrate that the TM team is aligned with the goals of the business and is helping to achieve those goals. Money is being invested in talent management initiatives and that investment should be tracked and measured. Demonstrating that the TM team is just like any other business unit goes a long way in putting the TM team in a position to negotiate for funds and to request management involvement in their programs. Use the case studies provided in this book to see how the macro or micro scorecards have been adapted and used effectively to communicate the success of TM initiatives. You will learn many creative and powerful ways to develop scorecards for your organization.

Table 2-6. Example of an Objective Map

Business Objectives	Metric	Enablers/Barriers	Performance Objectives	Measurement Methodology	Enablers/Barriers	Learning Objectives	Measurement Methodology	Enablers/Barriers
1. Reduce turnover rate by 25%.	Cost savings due to reduction in turnover of subordinates	Barrier: Hiring competition	1. Communicate using positive language. 2. Determine when subordinates need assistance. 3. Conduct effective individual meetings.	One-shot program evaluation design Follow-up questionnaire and action plan Isolation technique: Participant estimates	Barrier: Workload Enabler: Meeting checklist	1. Distinguish between negative and positive phrases. 2. Provide examples of positive responses to different real-life scenarios. 3. Recognize different learning styles and personality types in others. 4. Learn your own learning style and personality type. 5. Recognize verbal cues indicating assistance is required. 6. Recognize non verbal cues indicating assistance is required. 7. Use active listening techniques.	Knowledge-based pre/post tests	Barrier: Insufficient time Enablers: 1. Online scenarios 2. Practice exercises
2. Increase individual efficiency and productivity.	Cost savings due to reduction in time spent in meetings Productivity increase (expressed as %)	Barrier: Overtime incentives Enabler: On-time completion incentives	1. Conduct productive team meetings. 2. Provide personality-type tests to team members. 3. Complete action plan.	Follow-up questionnaire and action plan Isolation technique: Participant estimates	Barrier: Transfer design	1. Open meetings with clearly stated goals. 2. Encourage group participation. 3. Keep discussion on track. 4. Close meetings with clearly stated follow-up actions. 5. Administer Myers-Briggs Personality Indicator Tests. 6. Explain the meaning of the results. 7. Explain the importance of the results for team effectiveness. 8. Determine areas for improvement. 9. List specific goals to ensure improvement of determined areas. 10. List resources required for goal completion. 11. List deadlines for meeting goals listed. 12. Communicate action plan to supervisor.	Performance-based simulated proficiency	Enablers: 1. Online scenarios 2. Practice exercises

REFERENCES

DeTuncq, T. (2012). "Demystifying Measurement and Evaluation." *Infoline,* no. 1211. Alexandria, VA: ASTD Press.

Hodges, T.K. (2002). *Linking Learning and Performance: A Practical Guide to Measuring Learning and On-the-Job Application.* Woburn, Massachusetts: Butterworth-Heinemann.

Kirkpatrick, D.L. (1975). *Evaluating Training Programs.* Alexandria, VA: ASTD Press.

Phillips, J.J. (2003). *Return On Investment in Training and Performance Improvement Programs,* 2nd edition. Woburn, Massachusetts: Butterworth-Heinemann.

Schmidt, L., ed. (2003). *In Action: Implementing Training Scorecards.* Alexandria, VA: ASTD Press.

3

TRANSFORMING TALENT ACQUISITION: DEVELOPING THE CONSULTANT RECRUITER

Karen Fenstermacher

INTRODUCTION

Today's recruiter is very different from the recruiter of five years ago. The days of pushing résumés are in the past. Since recruiting top talent has never been more important, recruiter roles, functions, and competencies are evolving. This case study is about the pilot of an initiative to develop the consultative skills of recruiters within a healthcare organization. The project was extremely successful, not only from a skill-building perspective, but also because it resulted in a $400,000 cost avoidance. The pilot was created to be the precursor to a larger initiative and helped build the case to move forward.

BACKGROUND

Group Health Cooperative (GHC) is a consumer-governed, nonprofit healthcare system that coordinates care delivery and insurance plan coverage. Based in Seattle, Washington, GHC and its subsidiary health carriers serve more than half a million plan members in the state of Washington. Group Health's mission is to design, finance, and deliver high-quality healthcare.

GHC began in 1947 as a community coalition. Its defining purpose was to make quality healthcare available and affordable. Today GHC is one of the few healthcare organizations in the country governed by consumers—its plan members. The Board of Trustees is composed of health-plan members elected by other plan members. The Board works closely with management and medical staff to maintain company policies and a patient-centered focus.

GHC has more than 9,000 employees, 25 facilities in Washington, and $3.5 billion in revenue. As a model for innovative patient care, GHC attracts world-class healthcare professionals. From primary and specialty care to surgical, maternal, and urgent care services, GHC boasts a nationally respected integrated healthcare delivery system.

GHC has an attractive employment brand that typically draws a steady flow of applicants to its employment website. However, despite the recession that led to hundreds of skilled workers applying for relatively few positions, GHC found that it still had an abundance of positions that were proving difficult to fill. From 2009 to 2011, GHC averaged about 450 open jobs at any one time, with approximately 100 of the 450 (22 percent) defined as "hard-to-fill" positions. These positions were often open for as long as six months. Some took more than a year to fill. GHC often turned to employment agencies for help, incurring costly agency recruiting fees.

In the healthcare industry, positions that are often in short supply include physical therapists, pharmacy informatics, nurse practitioners, and clinical operations management staff. Healthcare technology positions have also become increasingly difficult to fill, due to the rise of the Internet and information technology-based processes, such as the use of electronic patient records and escalating Medicare and Medicaid government reporting requirements. GHC has traditionally been ahead of the curve in implementing such innovations as web-enabled electronic patient records, iPhone application appointment scheduling, and business intelligence marketing strategies. Yet talent in these technology areas is in high demand and also scarce.

Every industry has its own positions for which the talent pool is smaller than the demand, and companies will continue to compete for the top skills in these areas. Because of this, this case study is applicable to a wide range of industries and professions.

GHC's situation created an opportunity to re-evaluate its recruiting process and develop a pilot program that could be the basis of a new recruiter development program. One recruiter was selected to participate in this pilot. This recruiter was charged with documenting the process that would model current recruiting best practices.

A model to demonstrate evolution toward best practices in recruiting is outlined in the book *RecruitCONSULT!* by Jeremy Eskenazi (2011). A similar model was created to reflect GHC strategies and focus on Lean processes. This model is presented in Figure 3-1 in this case study.

Although few measures and metrics were applied during the pilot project, performance surveys and actual costs against projected market-based costs demonstrated the value of creating the larger initiative that would achieve Phase IV, Strategic Recruiting, as outlined in the Talent Acquisition Evolution Model. The pilot project also helped inform the decisions of which metrics and measures would be applied to the larger initiative.

TALENT MANAGEMENT INITIATIVE

Group Health recruiters were performing at Phase II in the Talent Acquisition Evolution Model. Recruiters had a full recruiting load to fill positions that were not classified as hard-to-fill, which they could typically fill within 60 days. However, high-volume requisition loads of 30 to 50 open jobs per recruiter allowed little time to serve as client-facing consultative recruiting partners to their hiring managers, or to conduct sourcing and research to head-hunt talent. Recruiters primarily functioned as order-takers to fill jobs for their client hiring managers, responding to large numbers of candidate applications from advertising channels. The current recruiters also did not have research and sourcing skills to headhunt talent for hard-to-fill positions.

Figure 3-1. GHC Talent Acquisition Evolution Model: A Continuous Improvement Journey

▼ GROUP HEALTH IS HERE

PHASES I-II Active Applicant Recruiting	PHASES II-III Recruiting Both Active Applicants and Passive Prospects	PHASE III Creating Process Improvement	PHASE IV Strategic Recruiting
• Recruiters rely on active applicant recruiting and occasional searching for résumés on job boards such as Monster and Career Builder.	• The **shift** to Phases II-III not initially understood by stakeholders.	• Create strategic position forecasting.	• Established strategic recruiting plan.
• Hiring managers rely on their personal networks, referrals, and résumés forwarded from recruiters from advertising on the GHC website, in newspapers, and job board postings (such as Monster).	• Begin to transform recruiting philosophy to hiring the **best candidate** for the business need.	• Create sustainable employment brand.	• Defined mission-critical, tactical jobs aligned with business.
• Hiring managers rely on search firms, costs in the 20-33% of base annual salary per hire.	• Re-engineer recruiters to serve as client-facing consulting partners.	• Recruiters become consultants – informed and aligned with business needs.	• Position forecasting.
• Little or no candidate pipelines are developed for standard position profiles.	• Begin to integrate sourcing partners into process improvement initiatives.	• Recruiting/sourcing process flows are designed, documented, and communicated.	• Established position recruiting strategies and timelines.
• Recruiting outcomes are not measured.	• Begin to create standard position profiles to focus pipeline efforts.	• Initiate candidate experience standards.	• Mature hiring manager relationships.
	• Current recruiting is transactional – little position forecasting.	• Analyze current/future states and gap analysis.	• Regular tracking and reporting against goals and SLAs.
	• Hiring managers to be trained on approach to passive prospects.	• Begin benchmark metrics and ROI.	• Strategic, cost-effective sourcing.
	• Acclimate hiring managers to making decisions on vetted candidates vs. reading résumés.	• Internal education and training takes place.	• Collaboration with related HR functions.
	• Hiring managers continue to utilize outside employment agencies.	• Applicant tracking is used throughout the organization.	• Continuous disciplined and iterative planning cycles.
	• Technologies and resources are not leveraged fully.	• Solid relationships formed with vendors, associations, and so on.	• Bottom-line results are captured.
	• Prospect and candidate pipelines underutilized.	• Utilize talent community (pipelines) in ongoing recruiting efforts.	• Lean process improvement and standard workflow definition.
			• Utilizing active and passive recruiting.
			• Robust use of highly developed talent community (pipelines).
			• Quality new-hire experience.

The result for GHC was long-term openings for key hard-to-fill positions, resulting in business and opportunity losses and delayed initiatives. Many of these positions were critical for driving growth initiatives and positioning GHC in the market.

Hiring managers and department leaders became frustrated as they missed goals and deadlines due to lack of proper staffing. If a department decided not to pay agency fees to hire for these hard-to-fill jobs, positions often remained open up to nine months or more before a suitable applicant would apply. These vacancies created business opportunity losses, employee morale and engagement issues, and stalled initiatives.

Prior to 2010, GHC regularly paid fees to employment agencies to hire for hard-to-fill positions. Department leaders would take the recruiting of difficult positions into their own hands and often incur, to their own budgets, the significant costs of utilizing outside employment agencies to fill their positions. Thus, attempts by the talent acquisition division to control, monitor, and calculate agency utilization and costs were unsuccessful.

Contingency fees average between 20 to 25 percent of annualized compensation. Executive-level retained search fees can cost up to 33 percent of annualized compensation. Neither solution guaranteed a shorter time to fill.

The key elements of the problem can be summarized in five points:

1. Timeline: Filling hard-to-fill positions took a long time. Hiring managers tended to focus on hard-to-fill positions. Perception of recruiter effectiveness and efficiency suffered.

2. Consulting skills: Consulting skills were not well developed among most recruiters. Recruiters functioned as order-takers versus client-facing recruiting consultant partners to their hiring managers. This contributed to lack of hiring manager satisfaction with the recruiting services provided.

3. Recruiter overload: Responding to large numbers of applicants for high-volume requisition loads prevented recruiters from serving as consultative partners or sourcing for hard-to-fill positions.

4. Sourcing skills: Recruiters did not have well-developed research and sourcing skills to headhunt talent. Hard-to-fill positions did not typically attract applicants from advertising.

5.   Cost containment: Controlling costs from employment agency utilization was difficult. Budgets for agency use were not centralized and were therefore difficult to control.

The Needs Assessment

In 2010, GHC's talent acquisition management determined that recruiting was not keeping up with a supply-and-demand imperative for key hard-to-fill positions. It became increasingly apparent that it was important to consider alternatives to mitigate costly agency fees and curb business opportunity losses created by extended position vacancies. To do this, an assessment was conducted of the current GHC recruiting processes and recruiter roles. Recruiting best practices were explored and compared to this assessment. The assessment was conducted using the following methods.

- A Lean problem-solving exercise allowed the team to:
  » Understand the current situation and issues.
  » Identify the gap(s) and areas for improvement.
  » Brainstorm ideas.
  » Consider target outcomes.

- Team meetings were held with recruiters to determine:
  » What are GHC recruiting priorities?
  » What processes and functions do recruiters consider most important?
  » What are the current recruiting functions and what is the time required for these activities?
  » What recruiting processes ended up being sacrificed to time limitations?

- Sources for recruiting best practices were examined. These included:
  » "Building Next-Generation Recruiter Capabilities" whitepaper by the Corporate Leadership Council (2010)
  » *2011 Healthcare Recruitment Benchmark Study* by Lean Human Capital (2011).
  » Active and passive recruiting strategies were examined and ideas for measures and metrics were explored.

As a result of comparing GHC's current recruiting processes to the industry best practices, it became evident that GHC needed to redefine its processes.

This would require a shift in talent acquisition philosophy from order-taking to a more consultative approach to recruiting. It was also becoming increasingly clear that this was to be a multiple-phase, multi-year journey to Phase IV, Strategic Recruiting.

The assessment sparked the creation of the pilot program. The pilot helped inform a larger future initiative and created the basis for an overall shift in talent acquisition philosophy. This shift included a consultative recruiting model that not only responded to applicants from advertising, but also created a headhunting model to find passive candidates for hard-to-fill positions. Initially, the pilot project addressed hard-to-fill positions in the technology division. It also addressed the five key issues with the current recruiting process:

1. Shorten time to fill for hard-to-fill technical positions.
2. Create two recruiting roles: the consultant and the "sourcer."
3. Redesign the technology recruiter role as a consultative recruiting partner role.
4. Engage a contract talent sourcer to headhunt technical talent.
5. Decrease or eliminate the use of employment agencies for technical hiring.

The Pilot Project and the Shift in GHC Talent Acquisition Philosophy

The pilot project was a year-long recruiting project that covered three technology areas reporting up to the chief technology officer. The pilot project expected outcome was to create an integrated recruiting process between two new recruiting roles: the client-facing recruiting consultant and the talent sourcer. The intended result of this process was to deliver key information technology talent to support business initiatives in a timely and cost-effective manner, without incurring employment agency fees.

After evaluating best-practice talent acquisition models, the talent acquisition manager defined core competencies needed in the new recruiting structure. The new recruiting structure would not only require additional recruiter skills, but collaboration between two very different recruiter roles and a reorientation of the approach to client hiring managers. The two-pronged approach, outlined below, is further defined in a whitepaper by the Corporate Executive Board Company, "CLC Recruiting" (2010).

- Client-facing recruiter consultants are "decision influencers, not order-takers. They earn the right to influence by informing staffing decisions with acute knowledge of the organization."

- Talent-sourcing experts are creative researchers and experts at locating passive talent prospects. They manage pipelines of both active and passive candidates and develop deep understanding of external markets.

This approach is also described in a process-flow diagram (Figure 3-2) from the Lean Human Capital presentation on the *Healthcare Recruitment Benchmark Study* (2011).

For the pilot project, talent acquisition management applied this approach to filling the competency gap:

- A current GHC recruiter was identified to be coached, mentored, and trained to function in the client-facing recruiter consultant role for the technical division.

- A contract technical-recruiting talent sourcer was engaged to source and locate passive talent prospects.

Because the contract recruiting talent sourcer would be hired with the specific technical recruiting competencies to find hard-to-fill technical talent, the talent acquisition manager chose a highly-regarded senior recruiting staff member to act as the client-facing recruiter for the technical division. This recruiter did not have a background in technology. She did, however, have an excellent reputation, had been with the company six years, understood the company's mission and vision, and was well-known as a high performer. This recruiter was also chosen because she would be critical in helping to develop and document the larger initiative beyond the pilot.

Talent acquisition management engaged a coach to mentor and train the recruiter with the following learning and development goals and the pilot project outcomes in mind:

- Learning about technology at GHC. The curriculum would include an introduction to the technology life cycle. The curriculum would also

Figure 3-2. GHC Consultative Recruiter and Talent-Sourcer Model

GHC has adopted Lean process-improvement strategies to create recruiting efficiencies. The pilot sourcing model splits the role of the existing recruiting function between a consulting recruiter and talent sourcer. This model provides an excellent experience for both the hiring manager and the candidate. It drives a lean, cost-effective staffing process that can be scaled to business needs.

BUSINESS FOCUS

- Business Knowledge
- Consulting Relationship With Hiring Manager
- Process Improvement
- Service-Level Agreements
- Candidate Experience
- Negotiation/Close

CONSULTING RECRUITER

Consultative process and collaboration lead to tangible results. The magic happens in the middle!

- Strategic Recruiting. Building Relationships and Partnership. Consultative Communication. Shared Project Management Timelines, Milestones, and Goal Achievement. Shared Accountability. Shared Learning.
- Creating the Magic in the Middle: Build a trust relationship between recruiter and sourcer to create full partnership. Understanding and appreciation of unique roles and responsibilities.
- Defining the job beyond the job description, including soft skills, intangibles, and nuances. Establishing recruiting strategies.
- Leveraging the partnership model to create a competitive edge in the market.

SOURCING EXPERT

- Understand the Market
- Name Generation and Prospect Database Management
- Candidate Development
- Talent Community Development and Pipeline Creation
- Search Engine Optimization Strategies
- Social Networking Strategies

MARKETPLACE

Adapted for GHC from the Lean Human Capital presentation on the *Healthcare Recruitment Metrics Benchmark Study* (2011).

include learning about each client hiring manager's business by attending departmental meetings, shadowing managers, and ultimately becoming recognized as a consultative recruiting partner for the client organization.

- Successfully conducting recruiting-strategy meetings with client hiring managers. These meetings would not only address current position-vacancy discussions, but would also address future vacancies and long-term sourcing strategies to reduce time-to-fill.

- Partnering with client hiring managers to develop their understanding of recruiting concepts, including understanding the new talent acquisition approach.

- Creating client and recruiter collaborative strategies, including developing recruiting timelines, service-level agreements, search strategies, and referral networks.

- Creating a project management approach to include change order management, setting expectations for roles and agreements, and creating milestones and metrics.

- Developing listening skills; for example, re-articulating client statements for clarification, listening to understand, and asking questions.

- Developing recruiting communication behaviors as a toolkit of practice; for example, influencing, utilizing concepts of the fierce conversation, promoting candidate advocacy strategies, and honing negotiating skills.

- Integrating the talent sourcer into the recruiting process; for example, defining the recruiter and sourcer relationship, developing a two-way accountability process, and creating a quality candidate experience.

Table 3-1 is a description of the objectives for developing the client-facing consultative recruiting partner.

Recruiter Development Methodology

There were three steps utilized in the coaching process:

1. assessment of recruiter
2. coaching and training of recruiter
3. monitoring results of recruiter training and coaching.

Table 3-1. Objectives for Recruiter Development in the Pilot Project
Level 2 Learning Objectives
After completing this development program, the recruiter will:
• Uncover skill and behavioral gaps.
• Translate coaching and training feedback into daily information feedback loops and process improvement.
• Collaborate with client hiring managers—involve them in pilot project goals.
• Communicate effectively—strengthen listening and influencing skills.
Level 3 Application Objectives
After completing this development program, the recruiter will:
• Incorporate training and coaching feedback into standard work processes for the pilot project.
• Shift behavior to client-facing consulting versus "order-taking."
• Establish collaborative partnership with talent sourcer to include shared goals, shared learning, and shared accountability.
• Continually improve work processes for the pilot project and make recommendations for the future initiative.
Level 4 Impact Objectives
Measurable process improvements will occur in the following areas:
• cost-savings for recruiting hard-to-fill positions
• recruitment strategies aligned with business needs of technology division
• more efficient recruiting processes
• improved client hiring-manager satisfaction.

Assessment

The recruiter was performing at a very high level in her current position as program manager for recruiting operations. Her enthusiasm and motivation to take on the pilot project and help develop a new talent acquisition approach was a benefit to the undertaking. However, she did have skill and knowledge gaps to overcome. These gaps included lack of knowledge of information technology, lack of knowledge of the business initiatives associated with information technology, and she had no current partner relationships with technology client hiring managers. In addition, the recruiter would need to collaborate with the talent sourcer and develop a process between them, which had never been done before. The recruiter had also been functioning in the existing order-taker recruiting paradigm. Building skills as a client-facing recruiting consultant would be a key part of her journey.

Coaching, Mentoring, and Training

Weekly coaching, mentoring, and training included:

- training in information-technology life cycle concepts

- coach shadowing recruiter at client meetings to observe her behaviors

- recruiter shadowing client managers to learn their business

- coach using role-modeling and situational learning techniques to develop recruiter's listening, influencing, and negotiating skills

- coach mentoring recruiter on using consulting methods and a coaching approach with clients

- developing a standard work process and accountability framework for relationship with talent sourcer.

EVALUATION METHODOLOGY AND RESULTS

Soliciting ad-hoc information from client hiring managers on a weekly basis proved to be the most valuable measure of the recruiter's learning. Much of this was done through informal conversations. Table 3-2 describes the Level 2 learning results, Level 3 application objectives, and Level 4 business impact objectives.

Level 2 Learning Results: Monitoring Recruiter's Results

The recruiter quickly grasped technology concepts, as was observed and reported by client hiring managers to both the talent acquisition management and coach. The survey of client hiring managers indicated that the recruiter had become an invaluable member of their team. The recruiter had developed mature client relationships.

The recruiter not only became familiar with her clients' business, she embraced their strategies and helped them design a SharePoint site to forecast recruiting needs through the use of sourcing pipelines and other high-level recruiting strategies.

Table 3-2. Results of Recruiter Development in the Pilot Project

Level 2 Learning Results

After completing this development program, the recruiter:

- Demonstrated superior performance of the skills and behaviors for new client-facing recruiter role.
- Documented processes for a service-level agreement between the client-facing recruiter and the talent sourcer.
- Developed mature client relationships; helped client hiring managers establish a SharePoint site to forecast recruiting needs; and coached client hiring managers on interviewing skills and managing candidate expectations.

Level 3 Application Objectives

After completing this development program, the recruiter:

- Developed the new process for filling hard-to-fill positions, so that there was no longer a need to use outside employment agencies.
- Shifted behavior to that of a client-facing consultant.
- Developed two distinct recruiting roles: a consulting recruiter and a talent sourcer.
- Created collaborative processes to manage workflow between consultative client-facing functions and sourcing functions.
- Partnered with technology division hiring managers to forecast hard-to-fill staffing needs.

Level 4 Impact Objectives

After completing the pilot project and recruiter coaching, improvement occurred in the following areas:

- cost savings resulting from using contract talent sourcers to fill hard-to-fill positions (see Table 3-3)
- recruitment strategies aligned with business needs of the technology division
- recruiting efficiencies observed and time-to-fill metrics improved—22 hard-to-fill technology positions filled without using external employment agency
- improved candidate quality
- improved retention of new hires in hard-to-fill positions
- improved client hiring manager satisfaction.

The recruiter began coaching client hiring managers on interviewing skills and managing candidate expectations. Her managers began active participation in creating candidate referral networks. This was an unexpected benefit to the client managers and they were very pleased.

The recruiter documented processes for a service-level agreement between herself as the client-facing recruiter and the talent sourcer. This partnership allowed for an efficient hand-off of recruited talent and an effective hiring process.

Level 3 Application Objectives: The Tangible Benefits of Recruiter Results

The tangible benefits of the recruiter's development results addressed the five key elements of the GHC's business problem:

1. Timeline: Combining a consultative recruiter with a skilled sourcer significantly reduced the time-to-fill for difficult positions.

2. Consulting skills: The recruiter modeled the client-facing recruiter consultant as described in both the GHC Talent Acquisition Evolution Model and the Corporate Leadership Council's best-practice guidelines and, consequently, hiring manager satisfaction and trust improved.

3. Recruiter overload: Recruiter workload was reduced by incorporating two distinct roles—a consulting recruiter collaborating with an experienced sourcer who targeted the hard-to-fill positions.

4. Sourcing skills: Urgently needed research and sourcing skills were obtained using experienced sourcers rather than attempting to create an intensive sourcing training program.

5. Cost containment: Recruiter partnered with the technology division's client hiring managers to anticipate hard-to-fill staffing needs. Because of this practice, as well as the shorter time-to-fill and improved communication, hiring managers no longer felt the need to utilize outside employment agencies. Costs for recruiting hard-to-fill technology positions could be controlled by talent acquisition. Talent acquisition sparingly approved agency use, and costs were reduced significantly.

Level 4 Impact Objectives: Pilot Project Results and Tangible Benefits

The business impact of the pilot project was demonstrated by the successful hiring for 22 hard-to-fill technology positions without utilizing an outside employment agency. Actual cost savings from not utilizing employment agencies could not be calculated, because prior agency use by the technology department was not managed by talent acquisition and thus costs were not captured. However, the cost of using a contract talent sourcer was far less than the cost of using an employment agency to fill similar hard-to-fill jobs. That comparison is demonstrated in Table 3-3.

Table 3-3. Technology Pilot Recruiting Projected Cost Savings					
22 Hard-to-Fill Positions	Total Compensation	Total Billed by Contract Talent Sourcer	% Cost per Hire	Projected Agency Cost at 20%	Projected Savings
IT Recruiting Year End 2010	$2,593,980.00	$114,630.00	4.42%	$518,796.00	$404,166.00

TM INITIATIVE MICRO SCORECARD

By virtue of the accolades received by hiring managers, recruiter engagement, and senior management satisfaction, anecdotally, the pilot recruiting project had paved the way for the larger recruiting initiative. But one of the biggest lessons learned was that hard data measurements had not been captured. Surveys and measurement capabilities had not been set up to truly showcase the project's ROI.

The TM micro scorecard in Table 3-4 demonstrates how to measure application and business impact. If this scorecard had been used to plan and implement this pilot project, it would have been rich with statistics and monetary results that would have demonstrated both performance efficiencies and significant cost savings. It has been used in this case study to organize the results of the pilot project and serve as a foundation for measuring the results of the larger initiative.

Beyond the Pilot: The Future GHC Initiative to Phase IV— Strategic Recruiting

When talent acquisition management held the initial team meetings with recruiters to determine how they spent their time, what they considered to be important to their success, and what they wanted to do versus what they had time to do, they discovered some important information. Most of the recruiters felt that their current work did not allow them the opportunity to do their best work.

A table of objectives for development of recruiters to Phase IV might look like Table 3-5 on page 41.

Table 3-4. TM Initiative Micro Scorecard

Program Title: Pilot Program: The Consultative Recruiting Approach

Target Audience: Recruiters

Cost of Hire Metrics: Hard-to-fill Jobs

Duration: 2010-2011

Business Objectives: Decrease time-to-fill on hard-to-fill technology positions. Save costs of using external recruiting agencies for hard-to-fill technical jobs. Pilot a larger change management initiative.

	Results			
Satisfaction	Learning	Application	Tangible Benefits	Intangible Benefits
Recruiter: Includes coaching and training to change behaviors and integrate functional competencies. No quantitative measurements were utilized but satisfaction with results was high.	Recruiter: Talent-sourcing model implemented and integrated On-the-job recruiter training Behaviors and functional competencies integrated into the pilot area	Recruiter: • Incorporated a consultative approach with hiring managers • Expanded intake sessions to include recruiter and sourcer • Aligned with client business by attending department meetings • Utilized a service-level agreement (SLA) with sourcer to pipeline for finalist candidate slate	Level 4: Successful filling of 22 "hard-to-fill" positions in IT 95% retention rate for filled "hard-to-fill" positions $404,166 saved versus cost of using external agencies for some positions Extremely low cost-to-hire ratio for filled "hard-to-fill" positions: 4.42% Level 5: ROI not determined	Increased candidate quality Recruiting partnerships with hiring managers well established Feedback loops and process improvement opportunities created Hiring manager satisfaction high when model utilized

Technique to Isolate Effects of Program: Applicant tracking system data, HR leadership input

Technique to Convert Data to Monetary Value: Comparison of using hourly contract sourcer to costs of utilizing external agencies that charge a fee equal to 20% of annual salary

Fully-Loaded Program Costs: Not utilized in this pilot – but recommended for full implementation

Barriers to Application of Skills: Current administrative duties create demand on time

Recommendations: Program to be continued as designed

Table 3-5. Objectives for Recruiters to Perform at Phase IV of the Strategic Recruiting Model

Level 1 Reaction Objectives

After participating in the development program, the recruiter will complete a survey to evaluate perceptions of the recruiter development for the strategic recruiting initiative:

- Perceive the development program to be relevant to the recruiting initiative.
- Perceive the development program to be important to achieving the skills and behaviors needed to be a client-facing consulting recruiter.
- Perceive the development program to have achieved the goals relative to time and funds invested.
- Communication with hiring managers will be undertaken and their partnership solicited as stakeholders in the strategic recruiting initiative. Hiring manager surveys will be created to measure performance to objectives.

Level 2 Learning Objectives

After completing this development program, recruiters will:

- Uncover skills and behavioral gaps in their current recruiting abilities to function in the new consultative recruiting paradigm as client-facing recruiters.
- Shift behavior to client-facing consulting versus "order-taker."
- Translate development program feedback into daily information feedback loops and process improvement.
- Involve their recruiting team members in adjusting and fine-tuning new recruiting processes.
- Collaborate with client hiring managers—involve them in goal-setting and planning of recruiting strategies.
- Collaborate with talent sourcers to create recruiting strategies and results.
- Communicate effectively—strengthen listening and influencing skills.
- Participate in the design and capture of meaningful quantitative and qualitative measures and metrics for new recruiting processes. Metrics to be tied to cost-savings dollars, such as time-to-fill and cost-to-hire.

Level 3 Application Objectives

After completing this development program, the recruiters will:

- Have incorporated development feedback into standard work processes for the implementation of the initiative.
- Partner with client hiring managers to align recruiting with business strategies, forecast future openings, pipeline talent, and influence hiring decisions.
- Have established collaborative partnership with talent sourcers to include shared goals, shared learning, and shared accountability.
- Show continuous improvement in incorporating learning from identified skill and behavioral gaps (such as listening, influencing, and negotiating) into standard work processes.
- Use defined quantitative and qualitative measures and metrics for new recruiting processes.
- Record recruiting data transactions to support monthly metrics reporting on time-to-fill and cost-to hire.

Level 4 Impact Objectives
After completing the project and recruiter development goals, improvement will occur in the following areas: • more cost-effective recruiting processes for filling "hard-to-fill" positions • recruiting strategies aligned with business needs of each business division of GHC • quantitative and qualitative measures and metrics captured for the new recruiting processes • increased recruiting efficiencies • improved client hiring manager satisfaction levels.
Level 5 ROI Objective
A projected ROI value of the strategic recruiting model will be defined by cost savings from quantitative measures divided by the cost of the development program.

CONCLUSIONS

The pilot project has been an inspiration for the Group Health talent acquisition department to take the next steps in its journey to Phase IV, Strategic Recruiting. The results encouraged some of the recruiters on the team to begin stepping into consultative client-facing roles even before a formal initiative had been launched. The benefits of a more consultative partnering with hiring managers began to be noticed—and hiring managers began requesting a higher level of service. The new approach is allowing talent acquisition at GHC to evolve.

Any large initiative for recruiter development, like the one described in this case study, will need to be justified to senior management. A pilot is helpful for gaining practical experience, but even a pilot has more credibility if measures are in place to evaluate its effectiveness. Here are steps to create a formal measurement plan:

- Create satisfaction-measurement tools, such as surveys, for recruiters.

- Design a thorough plan for collaborating with hiring managers.

- Carefully consider the cost, complexity, and structure of a recruiter development program.

- Align the effort with the business goals to keep the initiative on senior management's radar.

- And finally—the key lesson learned: Set up a micro scorecard that pre-establishes the fully-loaded program costs as well as the predicted ROI, to create substantive justification for moving forward with the full initiative.

ABOUT THE AUTHOR

Karen Fenstermacher is an ICF-credentialed coach, and has a master's in business administration and more than 20 years of experience in human resources for the entertainment, information technology, healthcare, and pharmaceutical industries.

Karen is the president of NorthWest Recruiting Professionals and actively manages a team of senior recruiting consultants. Her corporate management and consulting experience includes both human resources and talent acquisition roles for clients and employers, including the Gates Foundation, Paramount Pictures, Sony Pictures, Yahoo, Path, the Carson Companies, and Bullock's Federated Department Stores.

Karen currently serves on the board of the ICF Washington State Coaches Association and is the Seattle Society of Human Resources Management (SHRM) leader for the Coaching in Organizations Special Interest Group. She was the 2009 president of the Seattle SHRM and past chair of the South Bay Los Angeles Chapter of SHRM.

REFERENCES

Eskenazi, J. (2011). *RecruitCONSULT! Leadership: The Corporate Talent Acquisition Leader's Fieldbook.* Long Beach, CA: STARoundtable Press.

Corporate Leadership Council. (2010). *Building Next-Generation Recruiter Capabilities,* Executive Summary. CLC Recruiting. Accessible at www.executiveboard.com/exbd-resources/pdf/human-resources/recruiting/rr-building-nexgen-recruiter-capabilities.pdf.

Lean Human Capital. (2011). *Healthcare Recruitment Benchmark Study.* Accessible at www.leanhumancapital.com/blog/wp-content/uploads/2012/01/LEAN-Healthcare-Recruitment-Metrics-Benchmark-Study.pdf.

Phillips, J., and L. Schmidt. (2004). *The Leadership Scorecard.* Burlington, MA: Elsevier Butterworth-Heinemann.

4

MEASURING THE IMPACT OF USING JOB-SPECIFIC COMPETENCY MODELS TO DETERMINE PROFESSIONAL DEVELOPMENT NEEDS

J. Patrick Whalen, PhD

INTRODUCTION

This case study investigates the overall effectiveness and impact on organizational performance metrics of one facet of a talent management initiative. It concerns engineering professionals in a large government agency. By using a comprehensive yet practical evaluation process, it was discovered that competency modeling can provide a positive ROI.

BACKGROUND

Like many private organizations, the public sector is facing a human-capital management challenge as the need for continuous performance improvement increases. The Government Healthcare Organization (GHO) is one of those federal agencies going through a dramatic period of change and it faces many of the challenges that private-sector organizations are facing, such as hiring, developing, and retaining a quality and adaptive workforce that can meet the challenges of a continually changing healthcare environment. GHO is one of the largest healthcare providers in the world with more than 235,000 employees and five represented unions located in all 50 states, the District of Columbia, Puerto Rico, Guam, and other U.S. territories, as well as the Philippine Islands and South Korea. The primary employees of GHO are the healthcare professionals in 158 GHO medical centers, 854 clinics, and 21 regional offices. GHO employs more than 14,700 physicians and 51,000 registered nurses, nurse anesthetists, practical nurses, and licensed practical nurses, all highly trained and dedicated to providing top-quality healthcare.

A department within GHO, the construction and facilities management (CFM) function, supports GHO's overall mission by delivering high-quality and cost-effective facilities construction and maintenance in support of our nation's military and veterans. CFM accomplishes this through GHO's major construction programs, which include property acquisition, new construction, additions, and renovations through an allocation of $8 billion in funding. CFM is currently comprised of approximately 995 employees and it is anticipated that it will need an additional 540 professionals over the next several years.

CFM professional positions require extensive technical knowledge and a complex mix of skills. Knowledge requirements include engineering fundamentals related to design and construction of specialized healthcare environments and infrastructure, as well as the ability to collaborate with senior officials at local facilities, other professional engineers, and representatives from firms and companies that provide specific work products associated with the construction process.

TALENT MANAGEMENT INITIATIVE

To manage the predicted rapid growth, CFM decided to undertake an extensive competency modeling, assessment, and development effort as part of a larger talent management initiative. The competency framework and development process enabled CFM to attract new talent, retain key employees, and ensure that appropriate skill levels are developed and maintained. This was accomplished through the alignment of performance plans with organizational objectives, identifying current skill gaps, the use of succession planning, and meeting workforce development needs.

Internal studies and organizational performance reports showed that the skills and competencies of CFM professionals needed to be documented and performance gaps identified. While other non-training system interventions were implemented, developing a competency model, conducting an assessment, implementing needed training, and evaluating the results was the charge given to the educational department of the organization.

The process began by forming a steering committee that included representation from senior management, educational professionals, CFM managers and supervisors, subject matter experts from various disciplines, and human resources representatives. CFM applied a participatory competency-model development approach by having key staff work with senior managers to identify a consistent set of definitions of effective performance. It also generated acceptance and buy-in from all levels of the organization.

Next, the committee met to identify the organization's strategy and expected performance outcomes for CFM professionals. These included key CFM measures such as hiring strategies, turnover and retention, cost reduction, customer service, quality, performance of staff, and employee development. Identifying these measures was essential in aligning the competency project to the organization's most critical performance needs.

Once the organizational outcomes were clarified, other key decisions were made, including the agreement that the model would be a general competency model with behavioral indicators describing each critical competency and the expected performance standards and behavior. Then the competency development process began with the identification of critical skills and competencies for CFM professionals, based on the identified outcomes and tasks. Several groups of high-performing CFM professionals were identified in each region and asked to participate in one of the focus groups. High-performing CFM professionals were defined by the team as those who are (a) consistently exceeding expectations and achieving excellent ratings on performance reviews, (b) consistently meeting or exceeding business or unit objectives, (c) informally labeled "masters" or experts by their peers and managers or are sought out for their knowledge of or expertise in a particular subject, (d) like what they are doing, and (e) are respected by others.

Led by trained facilitators, the groups went through a structured discussion and identified the critical and most common tasks, skills, and competencies. The output was a draft competency model that was then validated by using an online survey of all CFM professionals across GHO, to determine its applicability, and relevance. It was also shared with senior management and the steering committee to ensure alignment with current and future strategic objectives of the organization. After minor adjustments, the final CFM professional competency model (14 core competencies, and varying function-specific models) was approved by the project committee.

Once the competency model was finalized, a competency-assessment process was developed and made available online as part of their CFM-PM system. The purpose of this assessment was to evaluate current versus expected competency levels in an effort to identify priority development needs. Each of the 998 CFM professionals was given an opportunity to participate in the online competency assessment as part of their development planning process. It was offered as a multi-rater assessment so that they had the option of allowing their managers as well as subordinates and peers to offer feedback on the functional competency categories. The multi-rater assessment was to be used only for development purposes in this initial phase, although plans were made to align it with the performance management system in the future. One of the benefits the committee felt the multi-rater assessment offered was to provide more open and honest feedback than a traditional performance appraisal process or self-assessment. The assessment also provided a more complete picture of skill performance based on feedback from multiple sources and different levels of the organization. The assessment had a response rate of 46 percent. The staff analyzed accumulated data grouped by category or topic, discussion points, and presented the final analysis and report to the committee.

Following the skills assessment, an aggregated report of prioritized competency development needs was made available. The committee used the reports to charter targeted training and development initiatives across CFM. The individuals used their personal skill-gaps reports to begin their online development planning process (Whalen, 2011).

EVALUATION METHODOLOGY AND RESULTS

Data Collection

For this evaluation study, data was collected through several types of instruments at various stages of the program implementation. Methods used included pre-post assessments, an online observation by administrators of use of system discussions, an online questionnaire, action plans, and personal development plans. The impact of using competency models for CFM professionals was evaluated using a comprehensive evaluative framework that links evaluative criteria of participant satisfaction and planned action, to learning and knowledge acquisition, to job application, to tangible/intangible business impact variables, to calculating return-on-investment (Phillips and Whalen, 2000). To accomplish this measurement methodology, data was captured through several sources including participants, faculty, subject matter experts, mentors, and CFM coordinators. Data was also collected from the participants regarding their functional action plans, and submitted by managers who implemented projects that addressed actual CFM issues. The principle means of capturing the business impact and ROI was a follow-up questionnaire administered to the CFM participants the final month of the program. The follow-up survey was used to gather participant's application of skills and the business impact data that resulted from that application. In addition, data was collected to do a cost comparison of promoting from within, and using a blended learning approach to training.

Techniques to Isolate Effects of Program

Three primary techniques were used to isolate the effects from other factors of this program:

- individual and team estimates of performance improvements, provided through performance improvement worksheets

- internal experts' estimates of cost savings and performance improvements, which provided data on actual values of performance, cost avoidance, employee costs, and other influences that teams may not consider

- comparative analysis and general accounting data to determine actual dollar values and expenditures related to cost savings and performance improvements.

It is important to note that specific guidelines were established to produce more realistic and conservative estimates of performance improvements with the team performance outcome worksheets. The outcome worksheets included a question regarding "percent of outcome as a result of this program" and a question requiring them to place a confidence value of the data they provided to allow for a further conservative adjustment. Equally important was that all data-collection methods, timing, isolation factors, and expected outcome data were agreed on by senior management and the steering committee prior to project launch, to avoid data discrepancies and encourage buy-in.

The Conservative Approach for Data Conversion

This measurement study included high-level business impact data and the necessity to convert data to monetary values; therefore, a conservative approach to data analysis was adopted. The total benefits are based only on the data furnished by the participants and other appropriate organization resources. As suggested by Phillips and Whalen (2000), participants who did not furnish data are assumed to have no improvement. Participants who did not return monetary data or who only provided partial data are not included in the benefits portion of the ROI calculation, but all participants are included in the cost component of the formula.

The costs are fully loaded and include values for all participants. Estimated salaries and benefits for each participant are included for the time the participants spent "in program." The value of improvements is reduced to reflect the percentage that participants link directly to this program. Where estimates are used, the values are adjusted to reflect the confidence each respondent felt about his estimates (confidence level). Each value is multiplied by the respective confidence percentage. For example, if a participant reports a $20,000 improvement with an 80 percent confidence level, the participant is suggesting a potential 20 percent error in the estimation. The value could be in the range of $16,000 to $24,000. The $16,000 value is used to be conservative. Additionally, only the first-year values for benefits are used, although there are clearly second- and third-year benefits. With these adjustments and considerations, it is highly probable that the ROI for this project is understated.

Results and Findings

The ultimate challenge of this impact study was to determine the business impact of participants' application of skills taught, and to calculate the ROI to CFM for implementing this program.

The steering committee developed an evaluation plan to monitor and measure the competency project over the course of a year. For the purpose of this measurement the CFM core competency model was used as the baseline data collection. Data from the function-specific models are not reported in this case study. Data was gathered to measure the effectiveness of the initiative at all five levels of evaluation.

Level 1: Reaction and Satisfaction

Level 1 (reaction) data was very positive and improvements suggested by participants were made immediately by the design team. The steering committee identified three Level 1 reaction and satisfaction measures:

- Satisfaction with the competency identification and assessment process received a score of 4.7 out of 5.

- Satisfaction with the personal development planning process received a score of 4.8 out of 5.

- Overall satisfaction with this initiative received a score of 4.0 out of 5.

Level 2: Knowledge Acquisition

The Level 2 pre- and post-process implementation data demonstrated knowledge enhancements of the CFM-PM process, and individual skill-gap identification as a result of the employee training and focus group participation. It was also determined through specific exercises in the PM system that each participant had to demonstrate knowledge acquisition to move to subsequent sections of the process. All participants satisfied these requirements.

Level 3: Application of Skills

The Level 3 evaluation data was obtained by the use of follow-up surveys, action plans, human resource data, and system monitoring. CFM professionals were given an online survey six months following the training to ask about performance improvements, examples of how they have applied what they learned, and examples of how their competencies have improved. Participants were also asked to record any job changes or leadership opportunities they experienced as a result of their participation in CFM-PM.

- Forty-five percent of participants took on new responsibilities in their current jobs as a result of proper matching of skills with departmental needs.

- Seventy-seven percent of participants worked on a special project or assignment as part of their development process after identifying skill gaps.

- Twenty-seven percent of the participants applied for a new job promotion, and of this 27 percent, 23 percent received a job promotion.

- Twenty-seven percent of participants had a job change or lateral move to better match their experience or skill sets.

- Ninety-five percent of all CFM professionals demonstrated ability to use the system and entered their personal profile information.

- Sixty-seven percent of participants completed competency assessments.

Additionally, application measures were captured and monitored throughout the process with various system checkpoints and usage statistics.

One of the higher Level 3 measures included the development of a process for identifying and prioritizing CFM development needs. The results of this data suggested that the majority of the 14 core competencies were rated higher than 3.5 (on a 5-point scale) of perceived importance, and above a 3.0 in the amount of development needed by participants. There was little difference between the ratings for each competency, making it more difficult to prioritize them. However, combining the various data points (level of importance, performance gaps, and development needed) for each competency allows for easier prioritization. Thus the top three development needs based on these data points are

1. Organizational, Enterprise, and Trade Knowledge (3.91 importance, -0.65 performance gap, and 3.05 development need)
2. Technical Expertise and Consultation (3.79 importance, -0.59 performance gap, and 2.98 development need)
3. Data Collection, Analysis, and Reporting (3.86 importance, -0.55 performance gap, and 3.02 development need).

This data was reported and used as part of the Level 4 evaluation regarding cost savings in prioritized development for CFM.

Due to the large scope of the overall talent management initiative, a primary part of the measurement plan was to determine which components were successfully implemented. Thus the steering committee and senior leadership agreed that participants be asked to respond to questionnaires, focus groups, and interviews throughout the process. They were asked to provide data and comments on the barriers that they felt interfered with successful implementation of this initiative and competency skill development. The data were grouped and placed into four categories, listed in order of influence:

1. **Lack of resources and tools.** Participants suggested that insufficient staffing might be requiring work to be performed at levels below expected performance standards just to get the job done. Lack of educational or development opportunities and up-to-date resources and equipment was hindering performance. The budget did not allow

for adequate application of newer technologies and tools needed to meet performance expectations.

2. **Lack of role clarity, capability, and development.** Participants stated that they are being asked to play the role of project managers rather than engineering consultants. Moving into a PM role will require a cultural shift of both those in the CFM-professional role as well as managers supporting the role. Participants noted there was confusion regarding the roles of CFM professional and engineering roles. Senior managers did not understand a performance culture and the CFM professional role. There was a lack of mentoring or coaching programs for new CFM professionals.

3. **Lack of support, structure, and communication.** Data suggested that the infrastructure and systems for CFM professionals' skills development are stuck in the traditional model of "command and control" rather than an employee-driven performance framework. Lack of communication of organizational goals by leadership renders alignment difficult and de-emphasizes the need for coordinated team efforts that support the strategic mission. Participants also commented that there is a view that strategic planning is the sole responsibility of the leadership team, and they do not want input from other levels and functions. This contributes to internal silos with competing priorities and goals.

4. **Insufficient time, excessive workload, and having to perform multiple roles.** Fourth, barriers were related to time and workloads, as well as the reality of playing multiple roles. Performing quality project-management work is difficult when you have to also be the subject matter expert, train new employees, and work with a multitude of contractors. It was reported that CFM professionals are well-trained individuals who possess the general professional skills necessary to do their jobs. The problem is that additional duties are piled on, and these collateral duties are insufficiently supported. As a result, performance of the primary CFM-professional role suffers.

This barrier data was reported to the steering committee and senior leadership, and project plans were developed to address these barriers.

Level 4: Tangible and Intangible Business Impact

Level 4, organizational improvement data, was monitored primarily through the GHO performance-tracking system and through the surveys and action plans. While improvements were taken at the one-year mark, long-term results are expected to be tracked over time.

Tangible business impact outcomes include the following:

- CFM team performance improvements. The improvement of specific team performance measures was demonstrated by identification of current job skills, competencies, and the linkage to organizational goals. The steering committee and leadership team agreed to utilize these three tangible data components to determine the business impact. The data compiled from participants suggests very positive results of business impacts and savings to the organization.

- In addition to the follow-up survey, participants were asked to complete a comprehensive action plan to determine the business impact data as a result of the skills they were able to apply on the job. Although it is sometimes difficult to provide data that reveal a dollar value, six team leaders provided specific tangible data that they converted to monetary values. It is important to note that the data were provided by the team leaders based on their completion of projects or changed business procedures. A set of "credibility criteria" was created to determine if the action plans included the conservative calculations based on what was agreed upon as tangible verifiable conservative data. If participants did not fully meet the criteria for completing this component of the survey, then the data was recorded and presented as intangible data.

- The conservative guiding principles and credibility criteria were utilized to determine a more realistic view of benefits as a result of the action plans. The team-leader action plans were reviewed by an evaluation team and had to meet specified criteria agreed to by senior management. Those that did not meet specified criteria were simply reported as intangibles. The above conversions include the participant's estimate of value of the business improvement multiplied by the percent of value they felt the program influenced that variable. This was then multiplied by the percent of value of confidence they had in that value being realized or accurate. The example depicted in Figure 4-1 is one of the six action plans that was received and is provided to illustrate how the data was accumulated and conservative adjustments made.

Figure 4-1. Participant-Specific Application Plans

Participant individual application plan #1:

As part of a 15-person staff office of CFM, we're always looking for ways to consolidate the workload and keep costs down. We had a need for someone to do webpage monitoring and design for our functional website. As a result of the competency identification process, we were able to identify a team member who had those skill sets within our team, and assigned them this duty, which resulted in cost savings for the office.

How the dollar value was determined:

Cost savings of avoiding contracting a part-time position to manage this work was calculated. Average salary of a part-time external contractor was estimated to begin at $32,000.

Estimated percent of this business outcome being a direct result of your participation in the CFM-PM program?	70%
Confidence in the estimate provided above?	70%

Conservative adjustment of business impact value:

$32,000 annual benefit	X	70% result of CFM-PM	X	70% confidence estimate	=	$15,680

- The summary of the action plans agreed upon as credible is as follows:
  - » Cost savings of not hiring outside contractor: $32,000 x 0.7 x 0.7= $15,680
  - » Performance improvements of staff as a result of new skills development: $9,000 (savings) x 0.5 (% attributed to PM) x 1 (% of confidence) = $4,500
  - » Reduction in unnecessary general engineer skills training in favor of targeted project management training: $372,192 (savings) x 0.8 (% attributed to PM) x 0.9 (% of confidence) = $267,978
  - » Staffing/workload restructuring of new skills development: $6,500 (savings) x 0.2 (% attributed to PM) x 1 (% of confidence) = $1,300
  - » Performance improvements as result of focusing on functional goals: $1,000,000 (savings) x 0.1 (% attributed to PM) x 0.7 (% of confidence) = $70,000
  - » Staffing/workload restructuring: $360,000 (savings) x 0.5 (% attributed to PM) x 1 (% of confidence) = $180,000

  The total improvements or savings value from the six team-leader application plans totaled $1,777,192, with the conservative adjusted improvements or savings totaling $539,458.

- Cost savings resulting from prioritized development. A cost savings was realized through performance enhancements and development programs that are specifically targeted to the identified need, based on the competency skill prioritization process. The cost-savings data is based on the CFM core competency skills assessments as tracked through the CFM-PM electronic process. Utilizing competency assessment data allows for the prioritization of training needs at organizational, functional, and individual levels. CFM-determined development needs was based on a traditional "wish-list" training and development process. The competency modeling process was a shift to a more comprehensive and targeted approach that enabled real-time skill development. To determine the benefit factor, a comparison of the costs of travel, facility, design, and delivery was conducted. A cost comparison between pre-project scheduled programs that were cancelled and replaced with post-project, shorter, more targeted development activities was conducted. This does not include the cost of employee time spent as this was already captured in the overall costs of the program. Participants further stated that this targeted skills approach to learning was conducive to their needs, and all the components of the learning programs scored high satisfaction ratings. The results of the prioritized competency/skills development data was a savings of $89,700. Previously scheduled training program costs were calculated at $174,500. The new targeted skills courses were actually $84,800. This is a total difference in cost of $89,700.

- Reduced costs of staffing and hiring. The CFM-PM was implemented because of a critical shortage of leaders and key professionals within the department, with a projected 45 percent eligible for retirement within the next five years. CFM-PM has a candidate replacement or readiness pool for these open positions. CFM-PM provides learning opportunities for a diverse group of employees to prepare them for expanded roles as they compete for future vacancies.

The cost-savings data for CFM primarily includes the savings generated by promoting from within. The basis for this calculation is derived from the stated purpose of the program in creating a candidate readiness pool. Currently there are 78 GS-12s eligible for retirement. The midpoint salary for GS-12 is $61,500.

The internal HR data on turnover costs shows the replacement cost for this level to be 125 to 200 percent of this annual salary. Since the primary purpose of CFM-PM is to develop a replacement pool for CFM positions, it is appropriate to capture the benefits of promoting from within as compared to hiring externally. This is the essence of the GHO succession planning and it is one way it pays for itself.

To determine the replacement costs or savings from promoting from within, it is necessary to look at what the difference in replacement costs are for the promotion position, if it is assumed that a typical promotion is from a GS-11 to a GS-12. (Note this is a conservative promotion stepping in grade; according to GHO data, promotion stepping typically comprises two to three grades.)

If the average salary of GS-11 is $51,500 and replacement costs are typically 1.25 times a person's salary, then the average replacement costs total about $64,375. If the average salary of a GS-12 position is $61,500 and that figure is multiplied again by 1.25, the replacement costs total $76,875. The difference in replacement costs for the GS-12 position is $12,500.

Thus, the result of the using the competency and skills identification process in CFM was reduced costs associated with staffing due to internal job transfers and promotions. According to HR records, six CFM participants received internal promotions. The internal promotion of six people produced approximately $75,000 (conservatively adjusted $12,500 x 6) of savings in hiring costs. It is suggested that in the future, supportive data of potential internal and external hiring costs is needed from HR in order to calculate the true savings to CFM. However, this data was not available for this program so the assumptions listed above illustrate a conservative outcome measure.

The participants provided their perceptions of the application of knowledge or skills learned from CFM-PM that had a positive influence on key business measures. The following are intangible business impact outcomes.

- Created a line of sight: As a result of participation in this process, employees and managers reported in the follow-up surveys and focus groups that they developed a line of sight from the performance expectations of their team or role, to the tasks that need to be completed, to the competencies and skills they need to perform successfully. Participants stated improved work performance and more focused goals.

- Personal development: Participants acknowledged that this initiative significantly enhanced their skills. The creation of personal development plans also assisted them in overall education and training needs identification.

- Understanding of job roles and enhanced bench strength: Participants stated that they understand the enterprise view and know which skills they need to develop to enhance their suitability for future promotions.

- Understanding of job roles and skill-gap development: Participants demonstrated improved understanding of job roles, performance expectations, tasks, and competency development needs. Managers report that they can easily determine the development priorities of their employees as well as match skills and competencies on necessary project teams.

- One hundred percent of participants reported that CFM-PM improved employee satisfaction, and strengthened teamwork and individual relationships.

- Ninety-six percent of participants reported that CFM-PM improved their ability to deliver internal and external customer service.

- Eighty-seven percent of the participants reported that CFM-PM improved the "service delivery promise" in general.

Additionally, only the first-year values for benefits are used, although there are clearly second- and third-year benefits. With these adjustments and considerations, it is highly probable that the ROI is understated.

Level 5: ROI Calculation

Fully-loaded program costs include:

- **CFM-PM Consulting, Materials, System, and Travel Costs = $246,220.00**
  This cost category includes all fully-loaded costs associated with developing and implementing this project, as recorded in the CFM Account Tracking System.

- **Participant Time Associated With Participation in CFM-PM = $209,767.22**
  This cost category includes fully-loaded employee costs (including salary and benefits) of time spent in CFM-PM and related activities.

- **Management and Administrative Staff Time Associated With Participation in CFM-PM = $39,955.78**
  This cost category includes fully-loaded employee costs (including salary and benefits) of time spent in CFM-PM and related activities.

- **Prorated Program Evaluation Costs = $10,000.00**
  This cost category includes a prorated cost of evaluation that is allocated and applied to all GHA programs and initiatives.

- **Total costs for CFM-PM = $505,943.00**

- **Cost Benefit and ROI Conversion Based on Conservative Adjustments:**
  Program Costs = $505,943.00   Program Benefits = $704,158.00

  Benefit-Cost Ratio = $704,158/$505,943 = 1.39
  ROI = $704,158 - $505,943 = $198,215 = 39%

TM INITIATIVE MICRO SCORECARD

Table 4-1 illustrates how the results data have been inserted into a micro scorecard.

Table 4-1. TM Initiative Micro Scorecard

Talent Management Initiative: Using Job-Specific Competency Models to Determine Prioritized Professional Development Needs

Target Audience: Engineering/Construction and Facilities Management Professionals (n=998)

Duration: 1 year

Business Objectives:

1. Organizational improvements
2. Effectiveness of competency process in prioritizing development needs
3. Cost savings through prioritizing programs
4. Improved employee selection and hiring process

			Results	
Reaction	Learning	Application	Tangible Benefits	Intangible Benefits
Level 1	**Level 2**	**Level 3**	**Level 4**	• Created a line of sight of performance to goals
• Satisfaction with the competency identification and assessment process received a 4.7 out of 5.	• All participants demonstrated knowledge acquisition through required documentation and system participation checkpoints.	• 45% of participants took on new responsibilities in current job.	• Specific team performance improvements based on identification of current job skills, competencies, and the linkage to organizational goals: $539,458	• Personal development
• Satisfaction with the personal development planning process received 4.8 out of 5.		• 77% of participants worked on a special project or assignment.	• Cost savings through performance enhancements or development programs that are specifically targeted to the identified need, based on the competency skill prioritization process: $89,700	• Understanding of job roles and enhanced bench strength
• Overall satisfaction to the support for this initiative received a 4.0 out of 5.		• 23% of the participants received a job promotion.	• Cost savings in staffing/hiring due to internal job transfers and promotions as a result of job skills identification: $75,000	• Understanding of job roles and identification of skill gaps
		• 27% of participants had a lateral job change.	**Level 5**	
		• The system and processes were utilized by 95% of participants.	Cost Benefit and ROI Conversion BCR = $704,158/$505,943=1.39 ROI ($704,158 - $505,943)/$505,943= 39%	

Technique to Isolate Effects of Program:

- Participant/team estimates of performance improvements
- Internal experts' estimates of cost savings and performance improvements
- Comparative analysis and general accounting data

Technique to Convert Data to Monetary Value: 1) Team leader's submission of action plan; 2) Cost savings of targeted and prioritized training; 3) Cost savings for internal promotions or reallocation of participants' duties.

Fully-Loaded Program Costs:

Item	Total Cost
CFM-PM consulting, materials, system, and travel costs	$246,220.00
Participant time associated with participation in CFM-PM	$209,767.22
Management and administrative time	$39,955.78
Prorated program evaluation costs	$10,000.00
Total costs for CFM-PM	$505,943.00

Barriers to Application of Skills:

- Lack of resources and tools
- Role clarity, capability, and development
- Support, structure, and communication
- Time, workload, and multiple roles

Recommendations:

Continued utilization of the CFM professional competency model for hiring and retention, training and development, succession planning, and other relevant human capital workforce needs

CONCLUSIONS

The following are conclusions and recommended next steps for implementing the CFM professional competency model:

- This project was a part of a very large-scale talent management initiative throughout GHO. The data presented are only the findings for the CFM-PM component of that larger initiative.

- The data presented in this study were intentionally kept as conservative as possible, per management request, as management was somewhat skeptical as to how business impact data can be found in generally "soft" HR programs like competency modeling. CFM management agreed to evaluation methodology and all data findings and methodology, prior to the final presentation.

- The findings from this study support recommending that CFM continue to communicate and share the CFM professional competency model with the project stakeholders, CFM professionals, and their managers.

- The findings from this study support recommending that CFM develop training initiatives using the "Training and Development Priorities" list and other findings in the competency validation survey.

- The findings from this study support recommending that CFM consider developing and utilizing a multi-rater competency assessment as a development tool for CFM professionals.

- It is also suggested that better clarification of actual needs or discrepancies between manager and CFM professional ratings be done to ensure they are aligned between managers and CFM professionals (to ensure that managers are defining "development" in the same way as CFM professionals, and so forth).

- Utilize focus group and interview feedback to address the barriers to performance as reported by managers and CFM professionals.

ABOUT THE AUTHOR

J. Patrick Whalen, PhD, PHR, is an experienced training, consulting, and human resource professional with expertise in management, performance and succession management, competency modeling, facilitation, employee development, needs analysis, evaluation methods, and program design and development. Dr. Whalen is currently the senior director of global consulting for the International Center for Performance Improvement (ICPI). He is also the managing director for TeamEffective. He consults with a broad range of clients and organizations on talent management, performance analysis, organizational development, strategic planning, needs analysis, measurement, and evaluation.

REFERENCES

Phillips, J.J. and J.P. Whalen. (2000). "Return-on-Investment for Technology-Based Training." In *The ASTD Handbook of Training Design and Delivery*, eds. G.M. Piskurich, P. Beckschi, and B. Hall. New York: McGraw-Hill.

Whalen, J. P. (2011). *CFM Competency-Based Performance Improvement Initiative Measurement Report FY2010*. Unpublished internal company report and research study of the International Center for Performance Improvement (ICPI).

5

TRANSFORMING THE CUSTOMER EXPERIENCE THROUGH A NEW CONVERSATION

Scott A. Heitland and Dr. John R. Miller

INTRODUCTION

This case study shows how customer loyalty can be improved on a sustained basis by transforming the way a company's call center agents interact with customers. It introduces a new approach to customer service, one that is effective in multilingual, multicultural, and multi-geographical customer populations, and it demonstrates the coaching and other supervisor skills necessary to support and sustain the improved customer interactions. It also discusses the tools used for measuring the success of the new approach.

BACKGROUND

Royal Philips Electronics is a multinational electronics company headquartered in Amsterdam, and employs approximately 122,000 people in more than 60 countries. The consumer lifestyle division of Philips manufactures and distributes a wide range of consumer products, ranging from household appliances and personal care items to sophisticated electronics such as interactive flat-screen TVs and audio systems.

In 2011, Royal Philips Electronics engaged Pretium Solutions, a United States-based global customer experience consulting firm, to work with the customer service organization inside Philips's consumer lifestyle division in an initiative to improve customer loyalty and satisfaction, which Philips measures and tracks using the Net Promoter System (NPS). Many Philips customers contact Philips directly by phone, live online chat, and email for after-sale questions, concerns, complaints, and problem resolution. For this purpose, Philips operates numerous call centers throughout Europe, India, Asia, and the Americas.

NPS measures customer loyalty based on a simple survey of customers' willingness to recommend a company's products and services to friends and family. At Philips, NPS scores not only drive awareness of the current state of customer loyalty, but also serve as a key component of management compensation. At the time of the engagement, NPS scores in Philips call centers had reached plateaus in some territories, had been unstable in others, and generally had not been hitting desired targets.

TALENT MANAGEMENT INITIATIVE

The primary goal of the Golden Touchpoint™ initiative was to strengthen customer loyalty by creating sustainable change in the way call center agents interacted with Philips customers. Pretium developed a talent management process for Philips, including leadership and agent training, post-training calibration, and extended follow-up and measurement to ensure that learned behaviors were engrained in the Philips call center culture on a sustained basis.

When Philips contacted Pretium, the customer service operations inside the consumer lifestyle division were solidly mired in a typical call center conversation. Like so many other companies' service representatives, the great majority of Philips customer service agents were polite, professional, knowledgeable, and well intentioned. However, they were not engaging in conversations that were strategically crafted to create sustainable customer loyalty. Rather, agents had a reactive approach: They answered customers' questions, addressed their concerns, and solved their problems quickly and often robotically. Agents were not adequately focusing on and anchoring the interactions in customers' true needs, concerns, and feelings.

The more Pretium worked with Philips customer care leadership, the more it became clear to all stakeholders that Philips needed to engage in a powerful new conversation with its customers, one that aligns the company with the customer. This new conversation, which Pretium calls the Golden Touchpoint™, would accomplish four goals and allow Philips to generate greater customer loyalty and promotion.

First, and most obviously, the Philips service agent must solve the customer's practical need, the primary reason for the interaction. Second, the agent must also actively identify and address the customer's emotional need tied to the practical need. If the agent fails to uncover the emotional dimension of the customer's story and address that aspect as an important reason to fix the practical problem, the customer will have difficulty believing the company cares enough about him to earn his loyalty.

Third, the Philips agent must provide a low-effort solution for the customer, one that demonstrates to the customer that the company is actually working to align its resources to the customer's practical and emotional needs. Finally, only after addressing the customer's practical and emotional needs and offering a low-effort solution, the Philips agent must then proactively build the positive, value-plus emotions into the customer experience that lead to loyalty. These include all of the value-added benefits Philips products offer to build confidence, trust, and goodwill, ultimately leading to a relationship that generates loyalty and promotion.

Figure 5-1 depicts a complete process map to the Golden Touchpoint™ as implemented for Philips, beginning with a robust discovery process, which included specific questions and honest dialogue about whether existing customer service systems and processes actually supported the creation of loyal promoters of Philips brand and products. Any effort to change agent behaviors during the customer interaction would fail if the supporting systems and processes were not aligned with the desired outcomes. For the Golden

Touchpoint™ initiative, discovery proved to be an ongoing process with leadership continually asking itself whether existing systems and processes support new conversations that build loyalty and promotion.

Figure 5-1. Golden Touchpoint™ Process Map

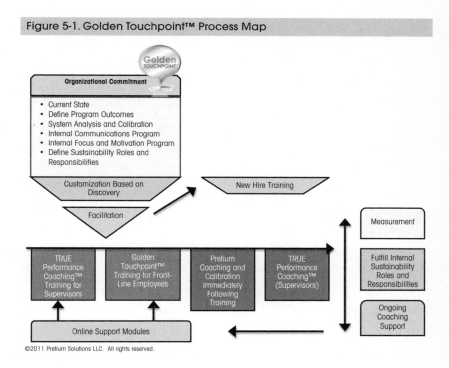

Discovery was followed by the development phase at each Philips call center location in Europe, beginning with the site in Eindhoven, Netherlands, followed by sites in Barcelona, Spain, Kingston, U.K., and Warsaw, Poland. Service agents, along with leadership and quality teams, were trained and coached on-site in the behaviors and skills necessary to engage in and support the new conversation. Each site was truly global in nature, supporting multicultural and multi-geographical customer populations. Classroom development was conducted entirely in English and was provided by a team of Pretium expert facilitators and coaches. In some cases, translators assisted in facilitating discussions and role plays.

Training

The development phase began at each site with a general management kick-off meeting, which served both as a program overview and a platform to challenge local call center management to wholeheartedly commit to and support the program. Training then began with leadership and coaching classes. Philips leadership understood that supervisors play a critical role in the success of any change initiative, especially one involving front-line behaviors with customers. Supervisors must be able to support the front-line employees in their growth toward implementing the Golden Touchpoint™ and creating loyal promoters.

Although Pretium provided follow-up support, it was incumbent on supervisors to ensure the sustainability of the program by consistently leading and coaching their direct-reporting service agents. Each leadership class (12 hours in total duration) included a deep dive into the Golden Touch-point™ from a leadership perspective, as well as extensive development using Pretium's TRUE Performance Coaching™ model (The acronym TRUE standing for timely, real, unique, and effective). Supervisors learned the skills to evaluate an agent's Golden Touchpoint™ skills, provide effective feedback, engage in role plays, gain commitment from their teams to performance improvement, and instill the proper levels of personal and managerial accountability. Pretium designed highly interactive leadership sessions with extensive use of exercises and role plays. These exercises provided Pretium with excellent Level 2 evaluation feedback.

The next component of the Golden Touchpoint™ process was training for the call center agents. Call center training is a unique challenge. Experienced agents have likely seen a few training iterations; therefore, they tend to approach any new class with a set of expectations that are not always positive. Understanding this dynamic, the Pretium development and facilitation team knew they would need to make this day-long session fast-paced, highly interactive, and focused on everyday real-life situations. With that in mind, Pretium used recorded calls from actual interactions between Philips agents and customers. Every Golden Touchpoint™ principle taught was connected to an actual call in which the agent either exemplified the principle, or more often, demonstrated behaviors which ran counter to the principle.

The training with the materials guided the call-center agents through the four keys of the Golden Touchpoint™:

1. Own the interaction: Pretium challenged agents' purpose, passion, and professionalism to motivate them to take ownership of and be held accountable for the customer experience.

2. Blend your skills: In this section of the training, Pretium assisted agents in understanding the scope of the skills they needed to be successful. In addition to the product and system skills, they needed skills to be able to transform an ordinary customer into a promoter. While traditional soft skills play a role in this process, the ability to be polite or pleasant would not be enough to facilitate this transformation. Pretium taught the following concepts to transform customer interactions:

   » Engage the customer: Help the customer understand from the very first moment of the interaction that you are there to help him and provide a solution that meets his needs.

   » Discover the customer's story: Pretium taught the Philips agents how to identify the customer's emotional need, in addition to the practical need. When you solve a customer's practical need, you gain a satisfied customer. When you satisfy both his practical need *and* his emotional need, you build his loyalty.

   » Align your own behaviors and responses to the customer's story: Pretium emphasized the importance of the agents aligning their own words and behaviors to the customer's story, so the customer begins to realize he has an advocate on the other end, one who actually cares about meeting his needs.

   » Respond: Once the agent was able to engage, discover, and align with the customer's practical and emotional needs, he could then use his product and system skills to develop a solution that meets the customer's practical and emotional needs and requires the lowest-possible customer effort.

3. Build a great call flow: Many companies determine call flow for the agents by way of a script or strict processes or procedures. The need for personal and product data is obviously critical; however, it should never short-circuit or undermine the customer's need to tell his story or the agent's ability to engage the customer. With this in mind and with Philips's permission, Pretium trained the agents to be flexible in terms of the point of interaction where they asked for data, and to gain information in a way which would not disrupt the engage, discover, and align approach. The best way to approach this was to propose a brief agenda for the inter-action with the customer, and gain the customer's consent to that agenda,

as early in the interaction as possible. The agenda informs the customer what the agent intends to do to solve the customer's problem and meet his needs, *and* creates customer *buy-in* to the manner in which the interaction will unfold. The agenda includes an opportunity for the agent to gather relevant personal and product information, but does so only as part of an overall plan crafted by the agent to set expectations and create value for the customer.

4. Apply the value-added close: The final piece of the Golden Touchpoint™ puzzle was to train the agents to understand that they should never just say "goodbye" at the end of a call. Instead, they must always look to confirm, restore, increase, and entrench value. This *confirm, restore, increase, and entrench* value cycle helps the customer tie value to the Philips brand.

On-Site Coaching and Calibration

Upon completion of their individual training sessions, Philips supervisors and agents connected immediately with an on-site Pretium coach. The coach worked directly with the agents immediately before and after live customer interactions to assist the agents in their execution of the Golden Touchpoint™ skills, methods, and techniques while the learning remained fresh. The coach also actively participated in call quality calibrations, a standard call center process designed to limit variation in the way agent performance criteria are interpreted.

The format of the coaching and calibration sessions ranged from individual feedback sessions to small huddle-style meetings, to large group meetings where agents and supervisors shared their successes and challenges with the Golden Touchpoint™ process. The purpose of coaching and calibration was to ensure that the Golden Touchpoint™ approach was engrained throughout the Philips customer service culture and that it meshed with both the environmental and individual nuances to fill gaps in learning and improve the new conversation model in each customer interaction.

The development phase in any one Philips call center, which included Golden Touchpoint™ and coaching development for supervisors, Golden Touchpoint™ development for service representatives, and coaching and calibration support, lasted between one and three weeks, depending on the size of the particular service center population.

Ongoing Support

Following the formal development phase, Pretium provided ongoing support to Philips supervisors, including weekly teleconferences for the first month after training completion at a particular site and monthly teleconferences thereafter. These support calls, which were scheduled with each site, featured a combination of sharing success stories, short development discussions which would help them as they engaged agents in coaching sessions, and opportunities to discuss challenges they were experiencing on site. In addition, Philips supervisors received a copy of a coaching support booklet entitled *The Big Idea*. This document offered supervisors a complete guide to their first six coaching sessions after the training.

Pretium also provided a series of five online review modules to support Philips agents as they continued to apply their Golden Touchpoint™ skills. These modules offered a concise summary of Golden Touchpoint™ principles, along with helpful tips for agents as they interacted with Philips customers. Each online module included a summary of important Golden Touchpoint™ principles, a quiz to ensure participants fully understood the review principle, and a list of questions for supervisors to use in post-module one-on-one sessions to stimulate discussion and application.

EVALUATION METHODOLOGY AND RESULTS

Pretium measured the effectiveness and results of the Golden Touchpoint™ program for Philips by using the Kirkpatrick Levels of Evaluation (Kirkpatrick and Kirkpatrick, 2006). Pretium did not conduct a Level 5 evaluation (return-on-investment), as this was outside the scope of Pretium's engagement with Philips.

Level 1

Pretium obtained Level 1 data from a standard reaction survey (see Table 5-1) given at the end of each training session. The same tool was used for both supervisors and call center agents.

Table 5-1. Standard Reaction Survey

Your feedback on today's training session is very important in helping us know what improvements could be made for future groups. We ask that you take some time to think over and complete this evaluation.

Name (Optional) _____ Department (Optional) _____

Please rate the following on a scale of 1-5, with "5" being the highest score.

I found the content of the class helpful.	1	2	3	4	5
The pacing of the training session was good.	1	2	3	4	5
The facilitators knew the material.	1	2	3	4	5
The material was presented in a clear and understandable manner.	1	2	3	4	5
There was appropriate opportunity for participation.	1	2	3	4	5
Our discussion in class was relevant to my job.	1	2	3	4	5
The examples the facilitators used were real and easy to understand.	1	2	3	4	5
The exercises used in today's session helped me understand the principles.	1	2	3	4	5
I would be interested in attending future sessions presented by these facilitators.	1	2	3	4	5

In addition to the standard survey questions, participants were also invited to provide comments on their classroom experience. The following two questions were asked:

1. What did you find most helpful about today's session?
2. What would you have changed about today's session?

When results were combined across Philips' European call centers, Pretium found that 92 percent of the agents indicated they were either satisfied or extremely satisfied (indicated by average scores of 4.0 and above) with the training, while 98 percent of the supervisors indicated they were either satisfied or extremely satisfied with the training. The comments were uniformly consistent in praise for both the facilitation and the materials.

Both the scores and the comments showed stability across the Philips call center population. One reason for this stability was Pretium's deployment of the same facilitation and coaching team for the entirety of this project, meaning there was no variation in the level of presentation and facilitation skills; the groups in Barcelona received the same experience as the groups in Eindhoven, Kingston, and Warsaw. This proved to be a great advantage because of this facilitation team's ability to establish immediate and credible connections with participants.

Level 2

The central focus of the Golden Touchpoint™ training is customer service agents' application of new skills and behaviors, not just agents' knowledge of a new customer service training product or program. An innovative measurement approach was required to ensure participants received the information in an immediately usable way, and to ensure they knew how to customize their communication with customers to meet each customer's specific need. A generic or academic use of the skills would sound scripted, which was not a desired or intended result. Therefore, a standard Level 2-type test would not be effective.

With this in mind, Pretium implemented a systematic observation process for Level 2, starting in the classroom and finishing after the participants emerged from the training session and had used their learned skills and techniques during actual customer interactions. The evaluation process began during training as the Pretium facilitators played actual recorded calls between Philips agents and customers and asked participants to identify the customer's practical and emotional needs. The facilitators then initiated both large- and small-group discussions to understand how well each of the participants was able to identify and assess the customer's true needs, from both a practical and emotional viewpoint. In this discussion, the facilitators were particularly interested in gauging participants' knowledge of the emotional dimension. Since many of the participants were fairly seasoned call center agents, they were accustomed to listening for a customer's practical need; however, very rarely had they been concerned about understanding the customer's emotional needs. This was a seminal point in the training and in the eventual application of the Golden Touchpoint™ back on the job. For this reason, the Pretium facilitation team had to make sure each participant had a firm grasp of the emotional-need concept. They accomplished this by moving throughout the classroom, listening intently to the small-group discussions, and making sure each participant was called upon throughout the course of the day to answer out loud in class. In some of the small groups, various discussions would take place in non-English conversations, and the facilitators had to check with participants who spoke both languages well to ensure the participants were actually demonstrating proficiency.

Next, the facilitators tested the participants on how they would create a low-effort experience for this particular customer. The Philips customer service agent must make Philips easy to do business with, or at least create this perception. This methodology was repeated throughout the training in the rest of the Golden Touchpoint™ principles and concepts. As each participant responded, the facilitation team assessed his learning and understanding of the Golden Touchpoint™ principles and concepts, and demonstrated them in front of the class to generate greater depth of learning.

After participants had completed the training, they returned to the call center floor, where a Pretium coach continued the observation process. The coach evaluated the extent to which each agent understood the training material, assessed the agent's proficiency in applying the methods and skills during live customer interactions, and coached individuals as needed, to further engrain the learning and assist the agents in improving their proficiency. The coach also met with the supervisors, team leaders, and quality assurance personnel to make sure that they had adopted the training principles and skills and were able to coach front-line employees as needed. Direct observation and immediate assessment and coaching helped the agents to understand and adopt the training principles and skills on a sustained basis, because they viewed them as a systemic change in how agents should listen to and work with their customers, not a "flavor-of-the-month" training to which many agents had become accustomed.

Pretium has found this methodology of assessing learning to be much more practical and useful than testing or other Level 2 methods, especially in dealing with front-line workers, many of whom are either not accustomed to on-the-job testing protocols or who are not accustomed to test-taking. In addition, this real-time observation method allows Level 2 evaluation to bridge to further explanations, reinforcement, and course improvements while the participants are still learning the material. This transforms Level 2 from a process of what happened to a process of what is happening.

Because of the nature of Pretium's Level 2 evaluation, they were able to confirm the extent to which each front-line and supervisor participant understood the Golden Touchpoint™ principles and skills. Combining results across Philips' European call centers, Pretium found that 88 percent of the agents demonstrated learning of the primary front-line skills, while 100 percent of the supervisors demonstrated learning of the coaching skills. Twenty-two percent of the agents demonstrated proficiency with the skills immediately after training. The proficiency rate increased significantly in the weeks to follow.

Level 3

Pretium's assessment of application of the Golden Touchpoint™ skills came from live observations in each of the call centers. During the discovery phase, Pretium and Philips leadership worked to overhaul the call quality monitoring form to track, assess, and optimize the results of agents' customer interactions and the sustainability of the Golden Touchpoint™ methods and techniques inside the Philips call center environment. This accomplished three important dynamics. First, the call center agents were being measured and graded on predetermined elements that would be most successful in achieving high NPS scores. During the due-diligence process, Pretium specifically defined the new behaviors which would lead to sustained higher NPS scores. It made sense there would be a new set of criteria to judge the success of a customer interaction. In other words, there was not a gap between the intended training outcomes and what the agents were being held accountable for from a quality perspective.

Second, the new call quality monitoring form sent a positive message to agents, indicating that Philips leadership believed in the new conversation and was willing to validate their support by changing the metrics. As a result, agents realized management was committed. Third and most importantly, the new call quality monitoring form measured application of skills learned in the training. Because the call quality monitoring form measured completely different skills than the pre-existing form, measurement was not a matter of determining whether an agent was doing something more or better, but rather, whether that agent was applying the new skill at all. For example, if the agent listened to the customer's story and responded in a way that aligned with the story on both a practical and emotional level, it was agreed that the agent had successfully applied this new, never-before-measured skill.

Using the new call quality monitoring form, team leaders and managers were able to determine whether agents' performance and the quality of the customer interactions were improving. The anecdotal evidence, such as Pretium's personal observations of call calibrations, and informal feedback from and discussions with quality personnel, team leaders, supervisors, and managers, indicated a noticeable increase in agent performance and quality of the customer interaction. As the micro talent management scorecard in the next section indicates, there was steady growth over the first 90 days in the application of Golden Touchpoint™ skills. The proficiency rate reached 64 percent after four weeks and 81 percent after 90 days. This not only was an indication of the agents applying the skills they learned in training, but of the success of the overall follow-up programs as described earlier.

Level 4

The Level 2 personal observations for learning, understanding, and application combined with the Level 3 call quality performance measurement were critical in creating meaningful behavioral change to drive business results. As stated earlier, the entire purpose of the Golden Touchpoint™ was to drive higher NPS scores across the European call center platform. This, then, became the sole determinant as to whether increased business results were achieved.

After implementing the Golden Touchpoint™, the interactions between Philips customer-service representatives and Philips customers were transformed, and NPS increased dramatically and sustainably across the Philips customer-care units in Europe. Table 5-2 summarizes these results.

Table 5-2. NPS Increases After Implementation of the Golden Touchpoint™

Territory	Channel	Pre-GTP NPS	Post-GTP NPS	% Increase	Period
Benelux[1]	Phone	29.7	36.2	21.9%	5 months
	Email	15.6	18.0	15.4%	5 months
	Live Chat	25.7	40.6	58.0%	5 months
Germany	Phone	40.1	46.8	16.7%	2 months
	Email	30.7	36.8	19.9%	2 months
Spain	Email	48.1	49.9	3.7%	4 months
	Live Chat	43.7	60.8	39.1%	4 months

Italy	Live Chat	46.3	55.3	19.4%	4 months
France	Phone	30.9	37.2	20.4%	3 months
	Email	26.7	45.9	71.9%	3 months
UK	Email	39.2	47.8	21.9%	2 months
	Live Chat	36.5	43.2	18.4%	2 months
Nordic[2]	Phone	50.1	56.8	13.4%	2 months
	Email	35.8	48.9	36.6%	2 months
Poland	Phone	50.3	59.1	17.5%	2 months
	Email	36.8	69.9	89.9%	2 months

[1] Benelux Countries = Belgium, Netherlands, and Luxembourg
[2] Nordic Countries = Denmark, Finland, Norway, and Sweden

Philips management was particularly focused on improving NPS for its customer support in France. NPS scores for France had been mired in the 20s to low 30s for well over a year prior to the implementation of the Golden Touchpoint™. Within one month after implementation, the aggregate NPS score for France had reached 42.4, the first time that Philips's NPS for France had ever reached 40 or higher.

The NPS score for call center support of Philips customers in Belgium, Netherlands, and Luxembourg increased from 30 to 44, an increase of 47 percent, within the first month after implementation of the Golden Touchpoint™. The NPS score of 44 marked the highest NPS score in the history of Philips customer support in these countries.

NPS scores for email and live-chat interactions skyrocketed: a 58 percent increase for live-chat support in Belgium, Netherlands, and Luxembourg, a 90 percent increase for email support in Poland, a 72 percent increase for email support in France, and a 39 percent increase for live-chat support in Spain.

An NPS score compares the number of promoters (those who are highly likely to recommend a company and its products) to the number of detractors (those who are unlikely to do so) within an organization's customer universe. Those customers who fall in between the most loyal customers (promoters) and the least loyal customers (detractors) are referred to as passives. NPS scores rise if and to the extent that the number of detractors decreases and the number of promoters increases.

The link between NPS scores and financial success has gained acceptance and credibility as NPS has become widely adopted as a customer loyalty metric. Satmetrix, the co-developer of NPS, has attempted to quantify the worth of promoters and detractors in an industry segment similar to the Philips consumer-lifestyle line of business—high technology, business-to-consumer computer manufacturers (Nowinski, 2009).

Financial Impact

According to this research, based on an average annual spend on computer products by customers of $1,615, promoters spent $203 more (for a total of $1,818), while detractors spent $158 less (for a total of $1,457). However, it was also determined that every promoter created an additional $816 of annual worth to the company through positive word-of-mouth. Detractors, on the other hand, were found to have created a hidden annual cost of $1,352 through negative word-of-mouth. Based on these numbers, the difference between the total annual customer worth of a promoter ($2,634) and the total annual customer worth of detractor ($105) is more than $2,500.

TM INITIATIVE MICRO SCORECARD

Pretium delivered the Golden Touchpoint™ training to 352 agents and 48 supervisors and measured the results over a five-month period. Ninety-two percent of the agent participants and 98 percent of the supervisor participants indicated they were either satisfied or extremely satisfied with the Golden Touchpoint™ training. Eighty-eight percent of the agents demonstrated learning of the primary front-line skills, and 100 percent of the supervisors demonstrated learning of the coaching skills.

Table 5-3. TM Initiative Micro Scorecard

Program Title: Golden Touchpoint™ Program

Target Audience: Call Center Supervisors and Agents

Number of Participants: 48 Supervisors and 352 Agents

Duration: 5 Months

Business Objectives: To raise individual agent and call center NPS scores across all Philips consumer-lifestyle European call centers

Results				
Reaction	Learning	Application	Tangible Benefits	Intangible Benefits
Level 1 92% of the call center agents indicated they were either satisfied or extremely satisfied with the training. 98% of the call center supervisors indicated they were either satisfied or extremely satisfied with the training.	**Level 2** 88% of the call center agents clearly demonstrated learning of the four primary Golden Touchpoint™ skills through success in diagramming and analyzing recorded calls and other interactive exercises. 100% of the call center supervisors demonstrated a solid learning of the Golden Touchpoint™ coaching skills through success in role plays and other interactive exercises. Upon completion of the training, there was a 22% proficiency in meeting or completing the standards on the Golden Touchpoint™ call quality monitoring form.	**Level 3** After 4 weeks, there was a 64% proficiency in meeting or completing the standards on the Golden Touchpoint™ call quality monitoring form. After 90 days, there was an 81% proficiency in meeting or completing the standards on the Golden Touchpoint™ call quality monitoring form.	**Level 4** **Level 5: N/A** Business Impact Converting NPS improvements to monetary value Across all 8 training populations, NPS scores on phone service increased by an average of 16.9%. This means that for every 100 callers, 16.9 chose to be Promoters. The increased value of a Promoter over a Detractor = $2,519. Therefore, for every 100 callers, revenue increased by $42,571.	From direct comments from both call center agents and supervisors: • Greater motivation; greater job satisfaction • Participants were able to see the Golden Touchpoint™ skills as life skills, not just skills for their current job • Greater employee engagement • Participants were happier with the new call quality monitoring form • The changes took scripts away and gave them skills they could personalize for their customers

> **Technique to Isolate Effects of Program:** There were no other operational, system, or training initiatives in place during this period that would have positively affected NPS scores. When surveyed, Philips management indicated that 100% of the increases in NPS scores and attendant positive business impact were attributable solely and directly to the Golden Touchpoint™ initiative.
>
> **Technique to Convert Data to Monetary Value:** The dollar value of incremental increase in NPS scores
>
> **Barriers to Application of Skills:** Culture, system, process, and policy
>
> **Recommendations:** Continued training, coaching, and application of the Golden Touchpoint™ leader and agent skills

Evaluated against the standards of the new call quality monitoring form, 22 percent of the agents demonstrated proficiency upon completion of the training sessions. Four weeks after the training sessions, the agent proficiency rate increased to 64 percent, and after 90 days, the agent proficiency rate increased to 81 percent.

Across all training populations, NPS scores for phone service, the primary channel for customer interactions, increased by an average of 16.9 percent, which translates to a revenue increase of $42,571 for every 100 callers. In addition to monetary impact, the Golden Touchpoint™ program produced increased employee motivation, job satisfaction, and on-the-job engagement. Perhaps most importantly, participants indicated that the Golden Touchpoint™ skills were life skills, not just skills useful in their current employment.

The Golden Touchpoint™ skills, methods, and techniques have been adapted in over two dozen European languages and across various geographic customer populations.

CONCLUSIONS

- Customer service agents built customer loyalty and improved NPS scores by solving the customer's practical problem, identifying and addressing the customer's emotional need, and creating a low-effort experience for the customer.

- Customer service agents learned and applied skills, methods, and techniques that transformed their interactions with customers, increased customer loyalty, and improved NPS scores dramatically and sustainably across the Philips customer care footprint in Europe.

- The call quality monitoring form used to monitor and assess agent performance during the customer interaction must properly align with the Golden Touchpoint™ approach to encourage and incentivize loyalty-generating agent behaviors. Any gaps between the Golden Touchpoint™ skills and what agents are held accountable for from a call quality standpoint must be minimized.

- The sustainability of the Golden Touchpoint™ program relies in part on company leadership's commitment and willingness to support fundamental changes in agent, supervisor, and manager behaviors, and to address system and process issues that may inhibit or conflict with Golden Touchpoint™ principles.

- Effective coaching and calibration sessions with agents and supervisors are critical to ensuring that Golden Touchpoint™ principles, skills, and methods are engrained in the crucial days immediately following the classroom training experience.

- Effective learning and application of the Golden Touchpoint™ skills increase sales revenues and also create intangible benefits for the company's employees, both personally and professionally.

ABOUT THE AUTHORS

Scott A. Heitland is the Chief Operating Officer and General Counsel of Pretium Solutions. Scott also designs and directs the TRUE Performance Coaching™ component of the Golden Touchpoint™, which is in active use in approximately 50 countries and more than two dozen languages. Scott received his JD from Georgetown University Law Center and graduated Phi Beta Kappa from the University of Virginia.

Dr. John R. Miller is an organization development expert with extensive experience in strategic development, performance management, leadership, team-building and employee engagement programs. John worked with Pretium on the Philips engagement and has worked on other Pretium engagements with Thomson Reuters, Anheuser-Busch, MasterCard, and Nestlé

Purina. John has a master's degree in organizational communication from Lindenwood University and a doctorate in international management from Nova Southeastern University.

REFERENCES

Kirkpatrick, D., and J. Kirkpatrick (2006). *Evaluating Training Programs*, 3rd edition. San Francisco, CA: Berrett-Koehler.

Nowinski, V. (2009). *Exploring the Relationship Between Net Promoter and Word of Mouth in the Computer Hardware Industry*. Satmetrix.

6

PROVEN STRATEGIES FOR ENHANCING PERFORMANCE: A NOVEL APPROACH

Dr. Deborah Bright

INTRODUCTION

The Strategies for Enhancing Performance program is designed to increase workplace performance levels by managing team and individual stress. The eight-week program uses a unique learning design in which participants complete pre- and post-test forms, attend four hours of training followed by one 30-minute individual tele-coaching session three to four weeks after the training. The program was evaluated using an experimental and control design where 115 participants showed significant positive gains in numerous work-related areas, including overall job performance. The program's evaluative design also demonstrates that assessment is possible in soft-skill areas.

BACKGROUND

Workplace stress and its effects on job performance have been a concern within organizations for years from both an economic and human perspective (Noblet and LaMontagne, 2006). Recent reports show that three out of every four American workers describe their work as stressful (Maxon, 2011). Alarmingly, workplace stress for U.S. companies is costing employers an estimated $200 billion per year in absenteeism, lower productivity, staff turnover, workers compensation, medical insurance, and related expenses associated with mistakes and errors (Maxon, 2011). The pressures for workers to perform at higher levels so that they can compete globally are only intensifying.

Although there have been numerous studies conducted on stress, very few studies have been conducted on the specific behavioral and cognitive skills associated with the management of stress and performance. One explanation for this lack of a controlled exploration in this area is that job performance is a complex variable (Jex, 1998).

Despite concerns about complexity issues involving job performance, it was decided to pursue the simultaneous development and evaluation of the Strategies for Enhancing Performance program for the purpose of better equipping employees to perform at higher levels and direct their stress in more positive ways.

The Strategies for Enhancing Performance program focuses on identifying, isolating, testing, and measuring the effectiveness of certain "performance-control practices" (behavioral and cognitive skills) in enhancing workplace performance; while simultaneously mitigating the negative effects of stress.

To assess the value of the specific performance-control practices identified, many employees, managers, executives, and sales professionals from various service industries participated in the program's evaluation process.

TALENT MANAGEMENT INITIATIVE

The program was designed based on current research methods, including the use of experimental and control groups. This approach was chosen over the customary route of developing a training program where specific needs of a particular audience are identified, the program is designed to meet those needs, and then is typically marketed to client companies.

Before describing the program, it is necessary to make note of how stress is being defined here. For the purpose of this program's design, the definition adopted (proposed by Richard Lazarus and Susan Folkman in 1984 in their book *Stress, Appraisal, and Coping*) states: "Stress is depicted as pressure arising from an event external to us. The situation could involve demands to achieve, to engage in some kind of frightening social interaction, or any experience that might result in our feelings of anxiety. This 'external' event, however, does not comprise stress in and of itself. Rather, our interpretation and response must occur before we call an event stressful and it is our response to potential threats that the psychological description of coping processes originates" (Lazarus and Folkman, 1984).

In essence, stress is viewed as a coping strategy.

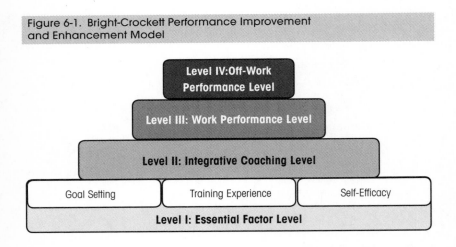

Figure 6-1. Bright-Crockett Performance Improvement and Enhancement Model

The Bright-Crockett Performance Improvement and Enhancement Model builds upon the theoretical work that has been done over the years and attempts to address what Kirkpatrick refers to as the "realities of the new workplace with its emphasis on self-directed work teams and greater personal autonomy" (Kirkpatrick, 1996). The model visually represents the key aspects of adult learners and forms the basis for the Strategies for Enhancing Performance program's design. In this model, we define performance improvement as the occurrence of an individual perceiving his performance to be less than effective, whereas performance enhancement refers to those individuals who believe their performance meets expectations but could do even better. The Essential Factor Level (Level I) identifies three essential factors linked to the transfer of learning to the workplace: self efficacy, goal setting, and the training experience. The Integrative Coaching Level (Level II) is the needed repetition and personal interaction that coaching provides. Coaching is the integration component that has repeatedly been credited to bring about behavioral changes in a variety of settings. The length of time does not always guarantee linear progression. The model leaves room for individuals to progress at their own pace—an important component of adult learning principles. Level III, or the Work Performance Level, creates the expectation of the need and the opportunity to apply the skills for performance improvement and enhancement on the job. The Off-Work Performance Level in this model states that performance improvement and enhancement would result off the job. While off-work performance was not the main focus of the program, it is an important consideration given the amount of emphasis placed on work-life balance. This transference builds upon the same set of assumptions and theoretical framework that occurs when newly acquired skills introduced during training are transferred to the workplace (Bright and Crockett, 2012).

What's important to emphasize is that the Strategies for Enhancing Performance program is not another stress-management program where attendees learn to recognize the signs of stress and identify its sources. Rather, the Strategies for Enhancing Performance program focused on how to manage that stress through behavioral and cognitive skills (performance-control practices), in a way that enhanced individual performance and mitigated the negative effects of stress.

The Strategies for Enhancing Performance program's design is streamlined and easily implemented. Over an eight-week period, participants attended four hours of training followed by one 30-minute tele-coaching session three to four weeks later. Participants completed their own individualized approaches for bringing about behavioral change using the performance-control plan. Their plans included the use of the cognitive and behavioral skills introduced during the training but were not limited to these skills. The individualized tele-coaching calls focused primarily on what participants identified in their performance-control plans. Participants also completed pre- and post-test questionnaires.

Figure 6-2. Learning Design for the Experimental Group

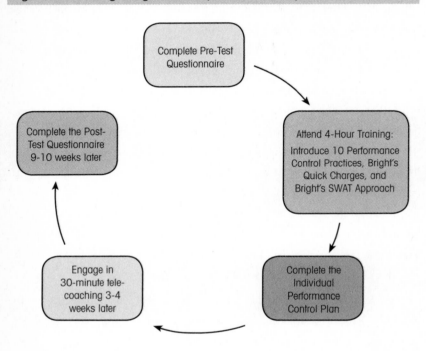

The Strategies for Enhancing Performance program also included a mechanism to ensure that a transfer of learning occurred, and the participant's newly acquired skills were applied back in the workplace. In this process two talent management categories, training and coaching, were coupled.

Objectives of the four-hour training were as follows:

- Participants clearly understood the relationship of control to high performance.

- Participants accurately assessed where their control lies in any given situation.

- Participants effectively utilized Bright's SWAT Approach.

- Participants developed a performance-control plan for bringing about changes in their own behavior.

The four-hour training took place in a highly-interactive setting in which participants engaged in a performance test designed by Dr. Bright, which proved unequivocally to the audience that when stress reaches particular levels, performance diminishes. After participants completed this quick-paced, highly-competitive exercise they readily concluded that the adage "individuals work best under pressure" was a myth!

Throughout the four-hour training participants were introduced to ten performance-control practices that were designed to serve two purposes: enhance performance and mitigate the negative effects of stress. These 10 behavioral and cognitive skills resulted from survey findings from more than 1,000 workers living and working in the Northeast. The purpose of the survey was to identify and isolate the most effective skills and techniques these workers used on a frequent basis to enhance workplace performance while simultaneously mitigating the negative effects of stress. Over the years workers have been bombarded with hundreds of books and thousands of newspaper and magazine articles on the subjects of stress and performance. The survey attempted to isolate what employees were currently using and benefiting from the most.

A unique aspect of the program's design was that the learning experience was customized for each participant, through the use of their performance-control plans. Training typically operates with a one-size-fits-all approach. While staying within the economy of scale that training offers, the Strategies for Enhancing Performance program was able to create an individualized approach for each participant.

Another element of the program that ensured its success was the tele-coaching session. The single coaching session helped to overcome a faulty assumption that self-motivation and personal commitment are enough to override the difficulties participants encounter after training when trying to implement new knowledge and work behaviors.

A particularly distinctive aspect of the program's learning design resulted from analyzing the top three most effective skills identified when surveying Northeast workers. These are referred to as the Three Underlying Elements for Behavior Change. Similar to Bandura's Self-Efficacy Theory, which states that adherence to new behaviors is the result of one's ability to self-regulate and persist despite potential difficulties or impediments (Davis, et. al. 2007), the findings revealed that for behavioral change to occur, participants needed to

- have a plan in place for implementation

- be primarily in control of this plan

- identify milestones of achievement along the way to serve as motivators.

The Three Underlying Elements for Behavior Change were incorporated in the entire program's design. Participants also learned about them through Bright's SWAT Approach, which was one of the 10 behavioral and cognitive skills introduced in the four-hour training. Also introduced in the training were Bright's Quick Charges: stress-reduction techniques designed to be implemented instantly without detection from others. The following Quick Charge techniques were introduced: Bright's 2M Simultaneous Focus Quick Charge, Bright's Wastepaper Basket Quick Charge, Bright's So What Quick Charge, and Bright's Anchor Quick Charge. Additional skills that were also included in the training design besides Bright's SWAT Approach and Quick Charges included building to-do lists, setting goals, breaking larger tasks into smaller parts, instilling personal confidence, and receiving criticism. Individual control was the operative concept of the training.

The training also touched on specific stressful situations that were identified in the survey of Northeast workers. For instance, according to survey results, receiving criticism was the second greatest producer of stress. As a result, the training included simulations in which participants received criticism.

Other stressful situations identified from the survey and incorporated in the training included having too much to do and too little time to do it, being unable to mentally disengage at the end of the day, and having to deal with co-workers who do not deliver what they promised. Throughout the training, the instructor emphasized the importance of using the behavioral and cognitive skills, as opposed to merely learning about them.

EVALUATION METHODOLOGY AND RESULTS

Method

The purpose of evaluating the Strategies for Enhancing Performance program was to assess individual outcomes in job performance, job satisfaction, and work relationships using experimental and control groups. To ensure that the program ultimately contributed to the body of knowledge already established in the field of stress and performance, the survey portion of the research design received Institutional Review Board (IRB) approval from New York Presbyterian Hospital Cornell Medical Center. IRB approval signifies that the study is in compliance with certain standards and that it meets certain requirements.

Participants in the experimental and control design came from various businesses in the service sector and were randomly assigned to either the experimental or control group. The experimental group participated in the program that consisted of a four-hour traditional classroom training experience, followed by one 30-minute individual tele-coaching session three to four weeks after the training. Data using pre-and post-test questionnaires were gathered prior to the training and then again eight to 10 weeks later.

Experimental group participants noted that what they liked most about the 10 performance-enhancing and stress-coping techniques, which were introduced in the four-hour training, was that they were easily utilized throughout their working day.

Control group participants completed pre- and post- test questionnaires over the same eight to 10 weeks. During that period, however, no contact was made with the control group.

Because participants in the control group were employees from actual organizations striving to achieve real goals, at the conclusion of the study, they wanted to receive the four-hour classroom training experience followed by the tele-coaching session. No data was collected to measure any changes after they were scheduled to partake in the actual learning experience.

Sample

The population used to measure the program's effectiveness consisted of 115 adults, 18 years of age and older, who were working full-time in either profit or nonprofit organizations. In general, participants in the study were sales professionals, managers, executives, nurses, and other professionals from various businesses. It is important to note that all participants came from the service sector. Attempts were made to engage as many sales managers and sales representatives in the sample population as possible because their results (in the form of sales) are readily evident and more easily measured. See Table 6-1 for a demographic breakdown of the experimental and control groups.

Participation in the evaluation was all voluntary. Because this sample was limited in size and does not reflect the larger business community, it is difficult to make generalizations with regards to other work populations.

Measures

To ensure that objectivity was maintained when analyzing and interpreting data, Technometrica, a New Jersey-based market intelligence firm, was used. Below are the methods used to collect the data for the different evaluation levels (Phillips and Schmidt, 2004).

Level 1: Reaction

At the conclusion of the four-hour training, experimental group participants were asked to complete an evaluation form that assessed their overall level of satisfaction with the program on a one-to-10 Likert scale. The questionnaire also asked questions regarding key areas of learning gained and areas where content needed clarification. The questionnaires were tabulated and summarized. Results revealed that 65 percent of participants reported that the four-hour training exceeded their expectations. Another 35 percent of attendees indicated that the four-hour training met their expectations. The summary findings from the questionnaires were used as supplemental information when conducting the 30-minute one-on-one coaching calls.

Table 6-1. Description of Experimental and Control Group

Experimental Group	Control Group
Age	
85% between 25 - 54 years of age 18% over 55 years of age	68% between 25 - 54 years of age 27% over 55 years of age
Education	
81% had a four-year degree or more	93% had a four-year degree or more
Gender	
56% male, 44% female	54% male, 46% female
Marital Status	
58% were married	70% were married
Ethnicity	
77% White non-Hispanic	86% White non-Hispanic
9% Hispanic or Latino	14% Hispanic or Latino
15% were Black non-Hispanic, Asian, Pacific Islander, American Indian, or Alaskan native	

Level 2: Learning

To ensure that learning was taking place, experimental group participants had an opportunity to address specific workplace situations. Various group exercises and role-plays were included in the training. Observation and coaching throughout the four-hour classroom training program helped with determining the use of the performance-control practices. The performance-control plan was used to document what participants learned and planned to integrate into their workday following the training.

Level 3: Application

The Performance Strategy Inventory (PSI) was developed and validated explicitly for the program's evaluation and was used as part of the pre- and post-tests for both the experimental and control groups. Personal and demographic data were collected relating to participants' age, gender, educational level, and general health conditions for both experimental and control group volunteers using the Performance Strategy Inventory (PSI). Besides gathering demographic information, the PSI instrument was designed specifically to collect subjective data on participants' effectiveness in handling typical work-related stressful situations, in addition to recording how stress affected their day-to-day performance levels. Responses were on a five-point Likert scale, ranging from "not effective" to "very effective," or from "no effect" to "great effect." The measure included 13 typical work-related stressful situations where perceived effectiveness in handling the situation was assessed. Additional questions assessed perceived stress and the effects of stress on job performance.

For content validity, experts from education, research, practice, stress, and job performance, as well as survey design, were consulted. To measure the internal consistency, Cronbach's alpha was used, which "determines the internal consistency or average correlation of items in a survey instrument to gauge its reliability" (Santos, 1999). The alpha coefficient was a coefficient of 0.81 (a reliability coefficient of 0.70 or higher is considered "acceptable" in most social-science research situations).

As mentioned, an unbiased market intelligence research firm, Technometrica, tabulated the results. To assess whether experimental group participants benefited from the program when compared to the control group, and that the benefits they experienced were solely the result of attending the program, the data was analyzed using statistical hypothesis z- and t-tests. The t-test and z-test compared the groups to see if one is significantly higher than the other at the standard 90 percent confidence levels. The population of 115 participants was broken down into 73 participants comprising the experimental group, whereas 42 were from the control group.

Results
Level 3: Application

When considering t-test results, significance at the 0.05 level was found for the experimental group with regard to their ability to more effectively deal with changing priorities and tight deadlines, as well as their effectiveness at turning around assignments so they met the expectations of others (including supervisors, peers, and customers). Significance was also found at the 0.05 level when examining how the experimental group handled situations that involved negativity. Significant differences were found at the 0.05 level for their effectiveness at being criticized. When examining the negative effects of stress on an individual's ability to function effectively while engaging with others or when simply working on tasks, significance was found at the 0.05 level for the experimental group. Furthermore, experimental group participants were significantly better (0.5 level) at identifying solutions and at articulating ideas more clearly and concisely when compared to the control group. It is important to note, even though it is not statistically significant, that at the 0.05 level gains were made to mitigate the negative effects of stress on the ability to recall vital information, to the point of being educationally significant.

When using a z-test to compare differences between experimental and control group participants, experimental group participants showed a significant improvement (at the 0.05 level) in their ability to rebound effectively from disappointments, mistakes, and setbacks. Experimental participants also showed significance (at the 0.10 level) at being more effective at giving criticism and leaving "work problems" at the office. Experimental group participants also reported significant improvement at the 0.05 level in their overall performance during the past six weeks and a heightened level of job satisfaction (significance at the 0.05 level).

No significant difference was found between experimental and control groups in their effectiveness in handling more tasks and responsibilities within an insufficient timeframe. There was also no significant difference between experimental and control group participants' ability to listen, concentrate, or complete tasks at certain standards.

Level 4: Business Impact

This particular measurement was not factored into the original design. When considering the potential organizational impact of implementing the skills and behaviors from the Strategies for Enhancing Performance program, it might be valuable to collect data on sales numbers, patient and customer satisfaction scores, number of HR interventions concerning employee-related matters, and organizational, attitudinal, or employee satisfaction survey ratings.

What is noteworthy and where the study's evaluative design differs from other studies is the one-time coaching experience. Results showed that positive outcomes resulted from participants engaging in only one coaching session versus numerous coaching sessions over an extended period of time. This finding has important implications for organizations where time as well as costs are at a premium. Another noteworthy consideration is that coaching and the benefits accompanying the coaching can be used to reach a broader audience as opposed to being limited to middle and senior levels within organizations.

Another recommendation is to collect data as part of a one- to two-year follow-up effort. With one subset of the experimental group population, a simple two-year random follow-up effort was conducted by phone. After reaching out to more than 50 percent of the experimental group participants, results showed that 100 percent of the participants recalled the Strategies for Enhancing Performance program, and 100 percent cited specific situations in which they were continuing to use the 10 performance-control practices intro-duced in the four-hour training. What follow-up participants were unable to do was provide the names of these skills. Another subset of the population tracked sales results for one year. The findings following the implementation of the Strategies for Enhancing Performance program were noteworthy but not conclusive. In particular, the sales manager noted that the sales team was spending more time in front of the customer and that their daily sales-call activity was greater. Overall, team sales consistently improved, and the regional sales manager received a promotion.

In the service sector, where subjective- or perception-based measurements are acceptable, it might be valuable to obtain management observations at three stages: prior to the introduction of the program (pre-test); at the conclusion of the eight- to 10-week period or post-test; and then again, one to two years later as part of a longer-term follow-up effort. The subjective data could be correlated with employee's performance-review ratings, promotions, and job satisfaction levels as part of an overall employee retention or job satisfaction effort.

Level 5: ROI

Measuring the financial benefits of the program compared to the costs associated with implementing the program was outside the scope of the evaluation's design. It would be valuable, especially in a sales organization, to gather such measurements; however, one can never be sure that the positive sales gains could be attributed solely to the program.

Another valuable insight gained from evaluating the Strategies for Enhancing Performance program was specifically how stress affected workers' daily performance. A noteworthy intangible benefit was that experimental group participants showed significant improvements in their ability to overcome the negative effects of stress particularly as it relates to identifying solutions and articulating ideas clearly and concisely. Think of the positive implications to businesses from a performance and cost perspective if employees are more effective in these two areas.

What's clear from the benefits resulting from the Strategies for Enhancing Performance program is that rather than assume that workers are equipped to handle today's high-pressured work environment, managers, leaders, and HR professionals may want to invest in ensuring that workers have the behavioral and cognitive skills necessary to manage stress, perform optimally, and gain satisfaction from their work. The research findings suggest they are in need of the 10 performance-control practices covered in the program.

TM INITIATIVE MICRO SCORECARD

Table 6-2 illustrates how the evaluation data were integrated into the micro scorecard to demonstrate the value of the program.

Table 6-2. TM Initiative Micro Scorecard

Talent Management Initiative: "A Proven Streamlined Approach for Building Talent: The Strategies for Enhancing Performance Program"

Target Audience: 320 participants, with a total of 115 who completed all aspects of the program as part of experimental or control groups

Duration: 4 hours of training followed by a 30-minute one-on-one tele-coaching session that took place 3-4 weeks later, as part of an 8-week effort

Business Objectives: Increase employee satisfaction and performance.

Reaction	Learning	Results			
		Application	Tangible Benefits	Intangible Benefits
Level 1	**Level 2**	**Level 3**	**Level 4**	
Using paper questionnaires, the experimental group attendees rated their satisfaction with the class. 65% of attendees said the program exceeded their expectations. 35% of attendees said the program met their expectations. 0% of attendees rated the program as not meeting expectations.	Observation and coaching, combined with various activities including real-time role plays, were used to ensure that learning was taking place. Learning Objectives: 1) Clearly understand the relationship of control to high performance. 2) Accurately assess where their control lies in any given situation. 3) Effectively utilize Bright's SWAT Approach. 4) Develop a clear plan for bringing about changes in their own behavior through the accurate completion of their performance-control plans.	Using a t-test: • Ability to more effectively deal with changing priorities (significance at the 0.05 level). • Ability to more effectively deal with tight deadlines (significance at the 0.05 level). • Ability to more effectively turn around assignments so they meet the expectations of others (managers, peers, customers) (significance at the 0.05 level). • Being more effective when on the receiving end of criticism (significance at the 0.05 level). • Ability to identify solutions that positively affect the work to be done (significance at the 0.05 level). • Ability to articulate ideas clearly and concisely (significance at the 0.05 level).	**Business Impact** Not part of original program's design **Level 5** **ROI or Cost/Benefit** Not part of original program's design	Experimental group attendees showed significant differences in their ability to overcome the negative effects of stress as it relates to identifying solutions to issues and articulating ideas clearly and concisely.

Using a z-test:

- Ability to rebound effectively from setbacks, disappointments, and mistakes (significance was found at the 0.05 level).

- More effective at having to give another person criticism (significance was found at the 0.10 level).

- Leaving "work problems" at the office (significance was found at the 0.10 level).

- Improvement in overall performance during the past 6 weeks (significance at the 0.05 level).

- Heightened levels of job satisfaction (significance at the 0.05 level).

Technique to Isolate Effects of Program: Experimental/control research design

Technique to Convert Data to Monetary Value: Calculation of monetary gains was outside the scope of this research project.

Fully-Loaded Program Costs: Not available

Barriers to Application of Skills: None apparent. Important to emphasize to audience that the focus of the program is on application of skills as opposed to the acquisition of skills.

Recommendations: Program is easily implemented, time efficient, and lends itself to a licensed program.

CONCLUSIONS

- The intended audience is broader than expected. At the onset, it was anticipated that supervisory and possibly mid-level managers would be best suited for the program. However, executive- and senior-level leaders, as well as seasoned sales representatives, benefited greatly from the program. Two criteria proved to be of greatest importance when selecting participants for the program:

  » need to work with and through others in order to achieve their goals

  » are engaged in multitasking throughout their work day.

- Explanation of what to expect from the Strategies for Enhancing Performance program is valuable when seeking to gain participant commitment. Participants learn up front that the purpose of the program is the effective implementation of specific behavioral and cognitive skills, even though they may already be familiar with these proven skills and techniques. Participants are advised that they need to understand and buy into the requirements of the program, which includes the need to:

  » Complete pre- and post-test forms.

  » Attend a four-hour training program.

  » Develop their performance control plans, or personalized road maps for enhancing their performance.

  » Engage in a one-time 30-minute individual coaching session.

- Minor customization is required: In order to appeal to a diverse audience, it is preferred that trainers customize certain agenda topics. For example, it's valuable to link to situations within their organizations when discussing the topic of making control operative. Another topic area where customization is necessary is during the discussion on key aspects about human performance.

- The trainer needs to periodically reinforce the purpose of the program to ensure that participants are properly focused.

- The timing of passing out the performance-control plan is important to set the stage for the upcoming one-on-one tele-coaching call. To ensure that the performance-control plan reflects areas of performance enhancement that are meaningful to participants, the entire group was offered the opportunity to return their completed plans three to five days following the completion of the four-hour training program.

- Expand the pre- and post-test forms. It may prove valuable for learning and development departments to include additional metrics, such as:

  » improvement in participants' effectiveness when interacting with others

» the number of employee complaints to HR, sales performance, 360-degree feedback, customer satisfaction scores, and other existing pertinent external metrics.

ABOUT THE AUTHOR

Dr. Deborah Bright is the founder and president of Bright Enterprises, Inc., a consulting firm whose sole mission is the design of human technologies for enhanced performance. In addition to speaking professionally at conferences worldwide, Dr. Bright customizes licensed programs for major companies such as NYSE Euronext, IBM, Chase, and Morgan Stanley in an effort to help their leaders achieve consistent results. As a bestselling author, Dr. Bright has published five books with major publishers on performance enhancement, leadership, communication, and the handling of stress.

REFERENCES

Bright, D., and A. Crockett. (2012). "Training Combined With Coaching Can Make a Significant Difference in Job Performance and Satisfaction." *Coaching: An International Journal of Theory, Research and Practice* 5(1): 4-21.

Bright, D. (2004). "2003-2004 Quantitative Stress Control Study" whitepaper. Unpublished. Tucson, AZ.

Davis, A.H.T., A.J. Figueredo, B.F. Fahy, and T. Rawiworrakul. (2007). "Reliability and Validity of the Exercise Self-Efficacy Scale for Individuals With Chronic Obstructive Pulmonary Disease." *Heart and Lung* 36(3): 205-216.

Jex, S.M. (1998). *Stress and Job Performance: Theory, Research and Implications for Managerial Practice.* Thousand Oaks, CA: Sage Publications.

Kirkpatrick, D. (1996). "Great Ideas Revisited." *Training and Development* 50(1): 54-59.

Lazarus, R.S., and S. Folkman. (1984). *Stress, Appraisal, and Coping.* New York: Springer.

Maxon, R. (1999). "Stress in the Workplace: A Costly Epidemic." *Fairleigh Dickinson University* Magazine. Accessed at www.fdu.edu/newspubs/magazine/99su/stress.html.

Noblet, A., and A.D. LaMontagne. "The Role of Workplace Health Promotion in Addressing Job Stress." *Health Promotion International 2006* 21(4): 346-353.

Phillips, J., and L. Schmidt. (2004). *The Leadership Scorecard.* New York: Elsevier.

Santos, J.R.A. (1999). "Cronbach's Alpha: A Tool for Assessing the Reliability of Scales." *Journal of Extension* 37(2). Accessed at www.joe.org/joe/1999april/tt3.php.

Scott, W. (1966). "Activation Theory and Task Design." *Organizational Behavior and Human Performance* (1): 3-30.

Snyder, C.R., and H.M. Lefcourt. (2001). *Coping With Stress: Effective People and Processes.* New York: Oxford University Press.

7

MEASURING THE EFFECTIVENESS OF MENTORING PROGRAMS

Michele Beane Ricchiuto

INTRODUCTION

This case study demonstrates how nontraditional learning initiatives, like mentoring programs, can be successfully designed and evaluated using Six-Sigma methodology, statistical analysis, and traditional learning evaluation methods. This case highlights a sales mentoring pilot program that contained unique design elements, which resulted in mentored associates statistically outperforming their peers by 55 percent over eight months.

BACKGROUND

Bank of America is one of the world's largest financial institutions, serving individual consumers, small- and middle-market businesses, and large corporations through operations in more than 40 countries. The organization employs a large salesforce with a variety of specialty sales roles designed to serve each customer segment. For sales organizations like Bank of America, the turnover of top-performing sales associates not only negatively affects revenue but also the customer experience.

This case study begins in 2005, a year with a competitive job market, in one of Bank of America's smaller sales divisions. This division, with 1,500 sales associates and 150 sales managers, had a problem with turnover rates of the new-hire population. Almost 70 percent of associates who left did so within their first year on the job. Additionally, the division's new management team had plans to expand its sales force, objectives now complicated by this problem.

The management team, looking for opportunities to improve retention, reviewed associates' exit interviews, which led them to focus on the onboarding process. Over half of departing associates told recruiters that they had wanted a "coach" or mentor during the onboarding process. These associates felt that having a mentor would have helped them ramp up their sales production more quickly. The finding surprised the management team because a mentoring program already existed within the division.

Prompted by this discovery, the management team distributed a survey to the entire workforce inquiring about the efficiency of the onboarding process and mentoring program. The survey findings further validated the problem uncovered in the exit interviews. Approximately 70 percent of those surveyed said they were not assigned a mentor and of the one-third that were, only 62 percent were satisfied with the level of support the mentor provided. Furthermore, associates told management that a mentoring program would make the biggest overall improvement to onboarding. The team realized that the mentoring program needed to be redesigned if it were going to be effective.

TALENT MANAGEMENT INITIATIVE

The decision to expand the salesforce intensified the need for effective programs that would help new hires quickly achieve their sales targets, defined as six units per month. On average it took new hires 17 months to achieve these sales targets, because establishing and cultivating business leads was a time-consuming process. This ramp-up period was largely seen as too lengthy by both the associates (who were paid on commission) and by the management team. Not only would an effective mentoring program help associates become productive more quickly, they suspected that associates would be less inclined to become discouraged and leave within the first year. A mentoring program also had the added benefit of providing an opportunity for senior sales associates to develop their coaching skills, a must-have if they wanted to advance into a sales management position.

The management team wanted to design a mentoring program that would be effective and beneficial to associates. To do this they used the feedback from associates to create a set of requirements for the new program design. The new mentoring program, with some unusual design components, was deployed as a test to a small group of associates in a pilot. Partnering for Success was the new name given to this program. The goal of the pilot was twofold.

The first goal was to ensure that associates actually adopted the program. To accomplish this, the team put in place a clear set of expectations, process controls, and inspection points for the program. Mentor and mentee adoption was measured by the frequency in which these partners met for the purpose of associate development.

The second and most important objective of the program was to build partnerships between the mentors and mentees that translated to an increase in sales production. Clearly, this could not occur if associates did not first adopt the program, so both components (adoption and sales production) were evaluated due to their interdependency on one another. The performance of the mentees in the program was measured through the use of a pilot and control group and statistical analysis. Specifically, the sales production or number of units sold each month for new hires enrolled in Partnering for Success program was compared to a control group of new hires who were not enrolled in the program. This approach helped the management team answer the fundamental question: Was the Partnering for Success program effective at increasing new-hire sales production?

Building an Effective Mentoring Program

Before the management team could design a more effective mentoring program, they needed to understand why the current program was unsuccessful. The management team held three focus group sessions with sales managers, senior sales associates, and selected new hires to answer two important questions. The first focus group session asked participants why mentoring was not occurring. The second and third focus groups asked participants to identify the factors that were critical to a successful mentoring program from both a mentor and a mentee's perspective.

By using the Six Sigma "Five Why's" tool, the team was able to tease out four main reasons that the current mentoring program was not successful. Six Sigma is a business management strategy, originally developed by Motorola in 1986, and seeks to improve the quality of a process by identifying and removing the causes of defects (errors) and minimizing variability in the business processes. It uses a set of quality management methods, including statistical methods. The Five Why's tool is an effective facilitation guide for asking questions that will ultimately identify root causes to problems.

The somewhat surprising finding from these focus groups was that senior sales associates really wanted to mentor new hires. They saw this as a way to build their coaching skills and a path to advance into a management role. They wanted to help these new associates learn the ropes by sharing their experiences and expertise with them. However, they did not devote time to mentoring largely because of their current compensation structure. These sales associates were primarily paid on commission, which meant that they were not generating business when they spent time mentoring associates.

The second reason mentors did not devote time to mentoring was because of time constraints and work load. When they were not out in the field generating more leads and developing existing relationships, they were back in the office busy processing their sales. They could not see how they could fit mentoring into their day. Third, feedback indicated that the current program lacked structure, expectations, and guidelines. Management thought the program expectations were clear, but the feedback indicated that associates simply did not know what was expected of them and what to do once they were a mentor. Lastly, there was no measurement system in place to hold people accountable. If the team wanted to design a successful mentoring program, all of these underlying problems had to be addressed by the new redesign.

Key Factors for a Successful Mentoring Program

The second and third focus groups centered on asking both sales associates and sales managers to identify the key factors required for a successful mentoring program. This was done through open dialog. The ideas provided by participants were gathered, ranked in order of importance, and prioritized. The results from those sessions are summarized in Table 7-1 and formed a basic set of requirements for the redesign of the current mentoring program.

Table 7-1. Ranking and Prioritization of Critical Success Factors

Focus Group Feedback: Critical Success Factors of a Mentoring Program	
Mentee's Perspective	**Mentor's Perspective**
• The mentor is available to the mentee or protégé. • The mentor helps the mentee develop strong product and pricing knowledge. • The mentor helps the protégée develop business-sourcing skills. • The mentor helps the protégé learn how to effectively fulfill the sale.	• The mentor has enough time to mentor. • The mentor receives some type of compensation for her time. • The mentor's own performance does not suffer as a result of the mentoring. • The mentor would like to be in close physical proximity to her mentee.

Not surprisingly, new-hire associates indicated that mentor availability was the key requirement for a successful program. From a mentor's perspective, components of a successful mentoring program included some type of compensation or other incentive tied to the success of their mentees, having time for their mentees, ensuring that their own performance would not suffer as a result of the mentoring, and being physically located within close proximity to their mentees. The newly designed program would have to address these requirements in order to be adopted and effective.

New Structured Processes

The management team used the focus group feedback as a guideline for building out the new program. The new program incorporated several new processes for managing the program and ensuring it operated smoothly. For example, the new mentoring program included a mechanism to ensure that new associates were enrolled in the program by the recruiters before they officially started. When recruiters made an offer to a new hire, they enrolled the associate into the Partnering for Success program if he or she had less than one year of sales experience. The hiring sales manager was notified that their new hire was enrolled in the program and needed a mentor assigned to them. The sales manager then assigned the mentor and communicated this to both the recruiter and mentor. The recruiter informed the new hire of the mentor assignment and set the expectation that the mentor would contact them within 48 hours.

There was also a new process for sales managers to select mentors for their offices. The program design team provided sales managers with a competency model and evaluation criteria they should use when making selections. Once sales managers identified their mentors; a master list of mentors (and their mentees) was maintained and updated frequently by regional coordinators. The project team then reached out to prospective mentors and extended a formal invitation to the program. Once the mentors accepted, they were asked to sign a commitment letter detailing the expectations of the role, and the signed copy was placed in a file.

Clear Expectations, Training, and Tools

The team knew from feedback that expectations for the previous program were not clear and associates did not know what was expected of them as a mentor. Training was developed, expectations were outlined, and support tools were provided to mentors. Among these expectations was the requirement for mentors to contact their mentee within 48 hours of her start date. Mentors were also required to meet weekly, spending a minimum of two to four hours with their mentees each time. A series of inspection points, including sales-manager follow-up and surveys to associates, were established to ensure that mentors and mentees were adhering to the program guidelines.

Mentors attended training, where they received a new-hire competency model, mentoring checklists, and best practices. Mentors were provided with an outline of topics to cover with their new hires and were encouraged to conduct joint sales calls together. This was done so that the new hires could learn through observation, but also so that mentors could work mentoring into their existing daily routines. A proficiency checklist was also provided to mentors so they could assess new-hire proficiency with a specific topic. Coaching and sales best practices were developed for use in mentor-mentee coaching sessions. The mentor and mentee partnership lasted for eight months. After the eight months, the new hire had officially graduated from the mentoring program and the mentor received a certificate validating that they were a certified or qualified mentor.

Compensation for Mentors

The most unique change to the mentoring program was a new compensation component that rewarded mentors for their mentees' sales success. For every unit the mentees solid during their first eight months on the job, their mentors received a small cash incentive. The management team felt that the incentive, although nominal, was the key to getting mentors over the time-commitment barrier. It also created a sense of partnership between the mentor and mentee, because they were now aligned to achieve a common goal.

Conversely, the new incentive required tighter oversight and controls to ensure that the program was not abused, but this would be an added expense that required careful evaluation before the program could be deployed more widely. The test pilot evaluated the program to determine if any gains in sales production would be enough to offset the compensation expenditure. This cost-benefit analysis was conducted and presented to management when asking for permission to expand the program.

EVALUATION METHODOLOGY AND RESULTS

Partnering for Success was one of several Six Sigma improvement projects that were designed to improve the onboarding and hiring process. By structuring the project using Six Sigma methodology, the data collection and evaluation methodologies were aligned with both Donald Kirkpatrick's four levels of evaluation model and Jack Phillips's process for measuring the return-on-investment (ROI) of training programs.

Kirkpatrick's book, *Evaluating Training Programs: The Four Levels*, discusses evaluation concepts, principles, and guidelines for understanding and implementing the four-level approach to evaluating training programs (Kirkpatrick and Kirkpatrick, 2006). Data in this project was collected for each stage of the evaluation process. This chapter will discuss how the pilot was constructed and evaluated within the context of Kirkpatrick's four levels. Phillips's book, *How to Measure Training Results: A Practical Guide to Tracking the Six Key Indicators*, is geared toward learning practitioners who want to determine the return-on-investment (ROI) of their training programs. Phillips uses Kirkpatrick's four-level model as a foundation but then adds a fifth level called ROI. This project conducted a cost-benefit analysis to determine the ROI of the compensation component provided to mentors.

The Pilot and Control Group Methodology

The evaluation methodology for this project used pilot and control groups that were geographically distributed across the United States. This approach allowed the project team to isolate the impacts of Partnering for Success and compare adoption rates and new-hire sales production of the pilot and control groups. One pilot group was established for the mentoring program and compared against two control groups; one for the adoption evaluation and another for the productivity evaluation. The pilot and control groups were analyzed to ensure they had the same statistical sales production and attrition rates prior to the pilot. Although attrition was not the key metric in this project, the management team wanted to make sure that any changes or programs introduced into the sales environment would not place undue burden on associates or increase associate attrition.

In developing the pilot and control groups, the sales production and attrition rates of all the regions across the United States were analyzed. Sales data pulled from the reporting systems included the average number of sales units per associate per month, the sales office, region, month, and sales associate name. This data was collected for a period of six months. The data was then imported into a statistical analysis tool called Minitab. An ANOVA or Analysis of Variance test was run on the data to determine the average funded units per associate by region. An ANOVA is a statistical test that determines if the means of several groups are equal. Regions with like production were identified. Second, attrition rates for each region were analyzed to ensure that like regions were selected. This was done by collecting turnover data by region for the past 12 months. The data was analyzed, and regions with similar sales production and attrition rates were identified and carved out from the rest of the population to comprise both the pilot and control groups.

The pilot group consisted of three regions: the Mid-Atlantic, Southeast Carolinas, and the Pacific Southwest regions. These three regions covered both the east and west coasts. Twenty-nine new hires were enrolled in the pilot program. The control group for measuring program adoption included Northwest California, Los Angeles, and Texas/New Mexico regions. The control groups for the productivity evaluation included Northwest coast, central region, Southeast Georgia, upstate New York, and New England. With the pilot and control groups established, new hires in the pilot group would be enrolled in the Partnering for Success program, while new hires in both control groups would proceed as normal without the formal assignment of a mentor. The test would run for a period of eight months.

Level 1 Evaluation: Measuring Reaction to the Program

A Level 1 evaluation as defined by Kirkpatrick was not entirely applicable to the Partnering for Success pilot, because the program lasted longer than a traditional training program. While not considered a traditional end-of-program learner assessment, the Partnering for Success pilot conducted three separate surveys and one focus group during the eight-month pilot. The surveys gauged associate satisfaction with the mentoring program and program adoption. The focus group held at the end of the pilot collected additional robust qualitative feedback on the program. It gave the management team a chance to further explore the feedback provided in the earlier surveys and seek ways to improve the program. As a result of this feedback, the team was able to adjust the structure and address some concerns prior to a full-scale deployment.

Three surveys were sent to pilot participants in April, November, and December. They assessed overall satisfaction with the mentoring program using a five-point Likert scale. The survey findings indicated that satisfaction rates for both the mentor and mentee population increased as the mentoring program progressed over time. The team attributed the increase in mentor satisfaction to the time when they started to earn incentives on their mentee's progress. Initial lower satisfaction rates at the beginning of the program were attributed to personality conflicts between mentors and mentees. When this occurred, sales managers reassigned more compatible mentors. Table 7-2 provides percentage comparison results of the two groups.

Table 7-2. Mentor and Mentee Satisfaction With the Partnering for Success Program

% of associates reporting that they are satisfied or very satisfied with the mentoring program	April Pilot Survey	November Pilot Survey	December Deployment Survey
Mentee Satisfaction	85%	63.3%	90%
Mentor Satisfaction	66%	89.6%	85.5%

Level 2 Evaluation: Measuring Learning

A traditional Level 2 evaluation was not conducted in this type of program because of the protracted duration of the learning intervention. The project team did not conduct an assessment of knowledge transfer; however, evaluation tools were provided to mentors so they could assess mentee proficiency with certain topics.

Level 3 Evaluation: Measuring Program Adoption

The project team concluded that if mentors and mentees reported that they were meeting at the specified frequency, program adoption could be surmised. The team measured the frequency in which mentoring occurred and did not observe the mentoring sessions. The working assumption was that if the participants were meeting as planned, then the mentoring was occurring and the new hires would use their new skills to increase their sales production.

As mentioned in the Level 1 evaluation, the pilot group was surveyed at three distinct points in time to assess adoption of the mentoring program. New hires in the control group were also surveyed to assess whether they had enrolled in the prior mentoring program and if they were meeting with their mentors. As a result, the surveys specifically asked both the mentor and the mentee about the duration and frequency of their coaching sessions. Answers from the new hires were compared and analyzed with the responses from their mentors. Were the answers on the survey consistent between the mentors and new hires, and did adoption of the new program increase when compared to the prior mentoring program?

The team answered the consistency question by conducting three different statistical tests. A Gage R&R (which stands for repeatability and reproducibility) is a statistical tool that measures the amount of variation in a measurement system arising from the measurement device and those taking the measurement. This test compared the responses between the mentors and mentees in the two surveys that were administered in April and in November. The team concluded from the Gage R&R that the answers provided by the new hires and their mentors were indeed consistent. In April, the 14 surveys from the mentors matched the 14 surveys from the new hires, which gave the team a 95 percent confidence rate in the accuracy of the self-reported data. In November, 13 out of 15 returned surveys matched, which gave the team an 87 percent confidence rate in the accuracy of the self-reported data. The team concluded that the self-reported data was accurate and reliable. Table 7-3 provides the percent satisfaction ratings.

Table 7-3. Adoption Rates for Partnering for Success		
% of associates reporting that they are satisfied or very satisfied with the mentoring program	April Pilot Survey	November Pilot Survey
Combined adoption rates	78%	95%
Inspected and matched	14/14	13/15
Confidence in results	95%	87%

The second statistical test performed was a two-sample t-test performed by Minitab. The t-test assesses whether the means of two groups are statistically different from each other. This test analyzed the adoption rates of both the pilot and control groups and concluded that the pilot group demonstrated greater adoption of the program than the control group ($p = .035$). A p-value (range from zero to one) represents the probability that a test statistic is significantly different from the null hypothesis. In other words, it shows how likely it is that a treatment group is significantly different from a control group. The closer the value is to zero, the more likely the data is significant and not different by chance. A p-value of < 0.05 is commonly used as a cut-off point for showing significance.

The sample size was rather small for the control group, which only had nine new hires. Therefore, the team conducted a third statistical test. The limited sample size is an example of real-life challenges with evaluation in a business environment. However, even with these limitations, programs can be successfully evaluated and decisions can be made with many data points that are collected.

A sample size calculation was conducted for both the pilot group and the control group. The sample size calculations indicated that with 23 pilot participant responses, the team was 91 percent confident that adoption was occurring with the pilot group. However, the control group had a small sample size of only nine new hires. The sample size calculation revealed a 51 percent confidence rate. While the data in this analysis would have been inconclusive, the business had exit interviews that indicated 50 percent of associates did have a mentor, and the workforce survey indicated that 70 percent of all associates did not have a mentor. Together they validate this analysis. The management team made the decision to accept the finding that adoption was not occurring because they were able to triangulate the findings to support the conclusion. The team concluded that the participants in the pilot group had statistically significant greater adoption of the mentoring program than the control group.

Level 4 Evaluation: Measuring the Business Impact

Level 4 evaluations reveal the business impact of the training program, and ROI cannot be conducted without it. The project conducted a Level 4 evaluation to determine if new hires with a mentor outperformed new hires without a mentor. The analysis used a common unit of measure between the pilot and control group (average funded units per seller per month) to normalize the differences in the pilot and control sample size. Monthly sales data for the pilot and control groups were collected for a period of eight months, pulled from the reporting systems, aggregated into Excel, and analyzed in Minitab. Data samples for each month were tested using an Anderson-Darling Test. The Anderson–Darling test is a statistical test of a given sample of data that is drawn from a given probability distribution (in this case, of the mean monthly sales production). Results from this test indicated that the mean sales data was not normally distributed (p-values of 0.000). As a result, the median monthly sales production for each associate was evaluated instead of the mean. A median is a mathematical result that separates the higher half of a group from the lower half, revealing the true midpoint.

A Mood's median test compares the medians of two or more samples. The median sales production per new hire in the pilot and control groups was compared for eight months. Eight tests were conducted that concluded that the pilot group statistically (p < .05) sold more units per person for five out of eight months, and more units overall in the eight months, than the control group. Figure 7-1 shows the ramp-up curve for the pilot and control groups with the corresponding p-values for each month. The team concluded that the mentoring program was successful in generating more sales for pilot participants. The pilot group sold 20 units over a period of eight months compared to 12 units sold by the control group, a 55 percent increase.

Figure 7-1. New-Hire Ramp-Up Over Eight Months
Analysis conducted by Robert Rawlings, 2006.

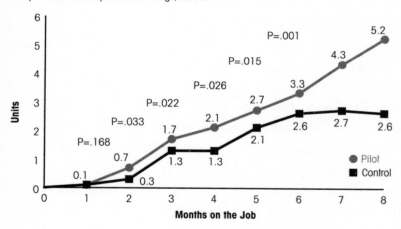

The project team wanted to make sure that the deployment of the mentoring program would not negatively impact associate retention. The monthly turnover rates for the pilot and control groups were also compared using a Moods Median test. The results from this test indicate that there was no statistical difference in the monthly retention rates for the pilot and control groups. The mentoring program had no significant impact (p = .20) on retention rates during the eight months.

Level 5 Evaluation: Measuring Cost-Benefit Analysis

The Partnering for Success mentoring program demonstrated a statistical increase in sales production for new hires. The finance team translated the increased sales production of units into a corresponding revenue number. For the pilot, the observed sales lift translated to a $211,000 sales increase compared to the $21,000 expense. The cost-benefit analysis indicated that the increase in revenue more than offset the additional incentive paid to the mentors. For every $1 dollar invested in the pilot, $10 dollars in revenue was earned. Given the pilot success, a three-year business case was developed for full program deployment. The sales lift was projected to result in $473,000 in revenue in year one, $2.3 million in year two, and $2.6 million in year three.

Table 7-4. Cost-Benefit Analysis for Partnering for Success

	Observed	Projected		
Summary	Pilot	Year 1	Year 2	Year 3
Productivity Lift	3.1	3.1	6	6
Turnover Rate	33%	33%	33%	33%
New Hires		460	660	1,325
Average # of Associates Eligible for Lift		230	330	663
# of Associates to Enter Program	41	92	231	265
Volume (units)	29,869	66,953		
Net Revenue	$211,000	$473,000	$2.3 M	$2.6 M
Comp to Mentors	($21,000)	($67,000)	($326,000)	($374,000)
One-Time Cost-Saving (program elimination)	$48,000	$0	$0	$0
Net Impact	$238,000	$406,000	$1.97 M	$2.26 M

Conclusion: For every $1 dollar invested in the Partnering for Success pilot, $10 dollars in revenue was earned.

Additionally, the program expenses (primarily associated with the mentor compensation) were calculated for the pilot through year three. Compensation expense was $21,000 in the pilot and expected to reach $67,000 in year one, $326,000 in year two, and $374,000 in year three. For every $1 dollar spent on the Partnering for Success program, it was projected that $7 dollars in revenue would be earned in year one through three. As a result, the management team decided to deploy the pilot nationally.

TM INITIATIVE MICRO SCORECARD

As illustrated in Table 7-5, the micro scorecard integrates all of the data that were collected in the evaluation process.

Table 7-5. TM Initiative Micro Scorecard				
Talent Management Initiative: Partnering for Success				
Target Audience: New-Hire Sales Associates				
Number of Attendees: 29 pilot participants; nine control group participants				
Duration: Eight months				
Business Objectives: Increase adoption of mentoring program; generate additional sales revenue.				
Results				
Reaction	Learning	Application	Tangible Benefits	Intangible Benefits
Level 1 Mentor Satisfaction: April = 66% Nov = 89% Dec = 85.5% Mentee Satisfaction: April = 85% Nov = 63% Dec = 90%	**Level 2** No data collected for this analysis.	**Level 3** The program had 100% associate adoption by December deployment.	**Level 4** $211,000 in net revenue during the eight-month pilot **BCR** 10:1 BCR	Associate Satisfaction Added to the value proposition for working at Bank of America
Technique to Isolate Effects of Program: Use of pilot- and control-group and variation analysis (ANOVA/Moods Median)				
Technique to Convert Data to Monetary Value: Standard value for unit of sales				
Fully-Loaded Program Costs: $21,000 (pilot)				
Barriers to Application of Skills: Lack of program controls, oversight, and structure				
Recommendations: Deploy nationally, after implementing improvements based upon associate feedback from the December focus groups				

CONCLUSIONS

- Although Partnering for Success was not a traditional training program, this case study demonstrated that even talent management initiatives such as a mentoring program can be measured using the pilot- and control-group methodology and statistical analysis.

- Within the typical business environment, ideal evaluation conditions may not exist. This case study shows that even with relatively small sample sizes, measurement was still effective and differences were detectable using a sample size calculation and statistical analysis. By using multiple data points, management can still make an accurate assumption about program effectiveness.

- The team reviewed the data and concluded that the incentives were significant enough to increase associate adoption from 30 percent to 100 percent for the pilot by the December deployment date.

- Based upon the results of the pilot-group and control-group units sold (20 vs. 12), it was concluded that the pilot would deploy nationally, after making some needed adjustments to further strengthen the design.

- Based upon the cost-benefit analysis conducted, the team concluded that the incremental cost associated with providing an incentive for mentors was offset by the gains in production for those new hires with mentors.

©2012 Bank of America Corporation

ABOUT THE AUTHOR

Michele Beane Ricchiuto is a senior vice president within the Global Learning Organization at Bank of America. She has a Six Sigma Black Belt and earned her MBA from Case Western Reserve University. She earned her master's and doctoral degrees in workplace learning and leadership development from the University of Pennsylvania, where she authored her dissertation on "Evaluating Training Outcomes: A Mixed-Method Case Study of a Sales Training Program."

REFERENCES

Kirkpatrick, D.L., and J.D. Kirkpatrick (2006). *Evaluating Training Programs: The Four Levels*, 3rd edition. San Francisco, CA: Berrett-Koehler.

Phillips, J.J. (2002). *How to Measure Training Results: A Practical Guide to Tracking the Six Key Indicators*. New York: McGraw-Hill.

Rawlings, R.B. (2006). ANOVA Statistical Analysis.

------. (2006). Two Sample T-Test Statistical Analysis.

8

CAREER DEVELOPMENT TO ENGAGE AND RETAIN HIGH-POTENTIAL LEADERS

Saundra Stroope

INTRODUCTION

This case study demonstrates how a career development program can engage and retain high-potential emerging leaders and be measured for impact. The program described in this study was strategically aligned with business needs and critical to driving culture transformation at a Fortune 500 company. It provides an example of how the needs assessment, program design, and evaluation methods—including pre- and post-program surveys and follow-up coaching conversations—can be utilized to measure behavior change on the job.

BACKGROUND

ATK is a global Fortune 500 aerospace and defense company with more than 60 facilities, approximately 15,000 employees, operating in 21 states and offshore. The company is divided into three business groups: ATK Aerospace Group, ATK Defense Group, and ATK Sporting Group. Change has been a continual part of the business over the past few years at ATK Aerospace Systems Group headquartered in Utah. The workforce was faced with continuous uncertainty as the president of the United States redefined the technology required by the Department of Defense. Moreover, the economic downturn in 2008, business organizational realignments, reductions-in-force, and new senior leadership all played a role in the changing business environment.

Talent management and leadership development is critical to driving culture transformation and desired business outcomes. Leaders and high-potential employees shape work activities, lead teams and critical work initiatives, and influence employee attitudes. There was critical need to build the leadership capabilities required to create an agile, empowered, and accountable workforce and to engage and retain our high-potential emerging leader population. This was especially important to an organization where the majority of sales stemmed from 30-year contracts that were expiring.

To tackle this challenge, we focused on the development of leaders in our early- to mid-career high-potential talent population. ATK Aerospace Systems partnered with Executive Development Associates (EDA) to design a customized career-development workshop targeted to individuals identified as high-potential emerging leaders. EDA was selected after an internal review of best practices in career development and a comparison to current ATK practice, and consideration of the services offered by several potential providers. Training grant money from the state of Utah was used to assist in covering the costs of the assessments and initial program design.

TALENT MANAGEMENT INITIATIVE

The goal for this talent management initiative was to provide a framework for career coaching and development and a process that created interactions between high-potential employees and leaders that would promote career development. The focus was on three key business objectives:

- Improve leadership pipeline readiness.

- Retain and engage early- to mid-career high-potential employees, with a focus on emerging leadership talent.

- Increase self-reliance and the ability of high-potential employees to consider career options within ATK, make career decisions, manage career change, and generate career development plans.

In support of these business objectives, the ATK Aerospace Systems human resources department led the initiative and partnered with EDA to design a program. The design was based on feedback gathered from interviews and a survey with company leaders and high-potential emerging leader employees, with the ultimate goal of creating an agile, empowered, and accountable workforce.

Needs Assessment

Information about career development services, resources, and best practices was gathered by talking with external training and development vendors, contacting professional associations, studying well-known books and articles on the topic, and researching the practices of competing companies in the Aerospace and Defense industry. Potential approaches to career development, such as the design of a career development model, metrics, career assessments, external career coaches, certification of internal career coaches, training workshops, online career portals, on-site career center libraries, career road maps, mentoring programs, and leadership training, were identified.

Members of the human resources team participated in a review of how ATK practices compared to best practices. A current-state scorecard was developed in which ATK was rated as having 1) the practice or resource in place, 2) limited practices or resources in place, or 3) no resources in place. This scorecard was presented to executive leadership along with the business objectives, proposed approach to career development at ATK, project plan, and investment required.

The talent management and leadership development team worked with EDA to complete a needs assessment that included a review of the talent management and leadership development strategy, interviews with key leaders, a short survey of a random sample of leaders and high-potential emerging leaders, and a one-day design session during which an outline of the program was established.

Thirty-minute interviews were conducted with key leaders and high-potential emerging leaders that revealed some of the strengths and the top career-related challenges within ATK Aerospace Systems. The assessment interviews revealed significant strengths, revealing a very hard-working, highly-skilled, and loyal workforce.

Leaders and high-potential emerging leaders were asked to respond to open-ended questions such as:

- What business challenges and changes will have an impact on our workforce in the next three to five years?

- What are the strengths of our organization?

- What are our weaknesses?

- What leadership capabilities do we need to develop within the next three to five years?

- Please describe the career development opportunities currently available within the organization.

- If we were to offer a career development program, what would you want to see included?

Challenges identified during the assessment interviews included:

- diverse views towards career development, especially between the incoming generation and the current leadership

- a changing business environment that requires more innovative and entrepreneurially-minded leaders

- changes in organizational leadership, structure, and focus on becoming a more integrated, collaborative team across the organization

- the need for organizational simplicity.

A short survey was also conducted that consisted of six questions intended to identify the most desirable career development-related services and delivery options that would add value in the organization. Results of the survey revealed a strong preference for personal assessments, coaching, and skill-building workshops.

Table 8-1. Career Development Feedback Survey

The Talent Management and Leadership Development team is researching best practice and potential future training and development offerings related to career coaching and development. It is our sincere desire to provide the highest-quality leadership and professional development experiences. We take our responsibility to help you perform better seriously. Please take a few moments to complete this survey. We appreciate your honest feedback.

Leadership Development:	Strongly Agree	Agree	Neutral	Disagree	Strongly Disagree
I would attend additional skill-building training or development sessions related to career coaching. Potential topics include helping others identify interests, giving development feedback, communicating about future direction, and assisting others with action plans.	5	4	3	2	1
I would be interested in completing assessments and receiving coaching related to career development. Possible assessment types include those related to personality, interests, abilities, and feedback.	5	4	3	2	1
I would utilize books and publications related to career development and planning if they were available.	5	4	3	2	1
As a leader, I would utilize an online or virtual career center if it was available.	5	4	3	2	1
Professional Development:					
I would recommend skill-building training related to career development and career planning for employees. Potential topics include self-assessment of interests, feedback of others, identifying options, and developing a plan.	5	4	3	2	1
I would recommend the use of assessments and coaching sessions for employees. Possible assessment types include those related to personality, interests, abilities, and feedback.	5	4	3	2	1
I would recommend offering books and publications related to career development and planning for employees.	5	4	3	2	1
I would recommend an online or virtual career center for employees.	5	4	3	2	1

What career coaching and development services would add value? (Comments)
Please share your comments and suggestions. (Comments)
THANK YOU for your feedback. We appreciate your comments!

The Career Development Program for High-Potential Emerging Leaders

The foundational program was designed to align directly with the CEO's strategic agenda. The design included pre-workshop assessments followed by an eight-hour career development workshop that teaches individuals to take ownership for career decisions, align personal interests with the needs of the organization, draft an ideal job description, consider alternative roles and responsibilities, utilize resources and tools within the organization, have a conversation with a leader or mentor, and set realistic goals. The training included four essential steps to "AIM your career at ATK":

- A—Understand ATK.
- I—Assess your personal interests.
- M—Develop multiple career options.
- Create an action plan.

The beginning of the workshop focused on the "A" in AIM—understanding ATK's business environment, the business case for the program, and how the changing environment affected the company's strategies and needs. Discussion focused on how the workplace culture influences the individual career, and how generational differences within the company may play out in office interactions. These higher-level discussions provided a context for the next portion of the workshop, which centers on personal interest—the most important indicator of job satisfaction and success.

Figure 8-1. AIM Your Career Model

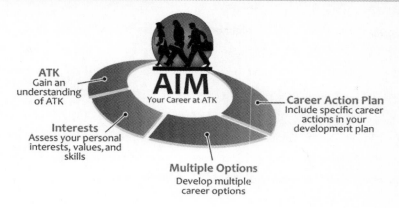

The next and longest section of the workshop focused on the "I" in the AIM model. It offered participants a chance to assess their personal interests, personality style, values, skills, experiences, and competencies. This information helped individuals pinpoint the specific kind of work they want to do on a day-to-day basis, the environment that is most preferable to them, and specific competencies to leverage or learn; as well as learn how to write an ideal job description.

The personal assessments could be completed as prework or during the program and helped participants accomplish one or more of the following:

- Choose a career path or specific job.

- Identify satisfying work environments.

- Enrich their current work.

- Generate ideas for volunteer or leisure activities outside of work that help achieve greater work-life balance and satisfaction at work.

The workshop took participants through a broad discussion of occupational themes within ATK, and then specific jobs associated with each theme. In fulfillment of the "M" in AIM—develop multiple career options—they were given information regarding career motivators and job tasks for careers that most highly align with their interests, and counseled to focus not on job titles, but on the actual work they might enjoy. They also discuss career path options including advancement, relocation, and lateral or downward moves across the business. In the last section of the workshop, participants write short-term and long-term career goals in addition to a 90-day career action plan.

The program includes eight hours of training, the Strong Interest Inventory, the CPP Work-Life Values Assessment, a personality assessment (Social Styles or Myers Briggs), a competency sorting assessment, post-training group learning review sessions, and individual coaching sessions.

Executive Sponsorship

Prior to the pilot workshop, the CEO of ATK Aerospace Systems wrote a personal statement about the importance of career development at ATK that was included in the program materials. Members of the executive leadership team also were invited to kick off each career development workshop with a brief 10 to 15-minute introduction. They were prompted with talking points and ideas for personalizing the message through the following questions:

- Why is career development critical to ATK's success?

- What does it mean to take ownership of your career and development plan?

- How can a meaningful career development plan contribute to personal effectiveness, job satisfaction, engagement, and performance?

- What situations have you experienced where understanding your own career interests and communicating them with a leader or mentor helped your success?

- What personal story can you share about your own career and the actions you have taken to grow and develop?

Inviting senior leaders to share their expertise and bring real-life experiences to the program helped increase participant engagement, communicate important messages, and link the program to business strategy and vision.

Leadership Training—Career Coaching

A second four-hour workshop for leaders was designed to focus on supporting and guiding others in generating career and development plans. Leaders are introduced to the business case for career development, the AIM process, a process for conducting coaching conversations, potential career-derailing behaviors, and a process for handling challenging career coaching situations.

The Career Development Self-Paced Guide

In an effort to reach a broader audience and offer a cost-effective, non-training alternative, the ATK Aerospace Systems talent management and leadership development team designed a brochure and self-paced guide called the "Quick Shot," covering all of the essential steps in creating a career plan. This guide contained information about tools and resources available to take charge of one's career. It was published on the company's internal website and incorporated into orientation materials. It could be used as a self-paced guide for any employee or as a coaching reference for leaders.

EVALUATION METHODOLOGY AND RESULTS

The Career Development program was first delivered in January 2008 at ATK Aerospace Systems. The workshop was delivered to more than 95 high-potential emerging leaders participating in a structured mentoring program. Evaluations were conducted during and after the program to assess participant reaction, learning, and behavior change using the Kirkpatrick model (2009) for training evaluation Levels 1 through 3.

Level 1: Reaction and Satisfaction Evaluation

The average evaluation rating was 4.35 on a scale of one to five. Participant comments indicated that the assessments used during the program helped provide insight and narrow down the decision-making process for choosing a career path. Others commented that it "opened my eyes to different ways of learning what I want from a career," and that "I need to develop a plan and communicate with my manager." The career coaching workshop was delivered to 26 leaders and mentors participating in a structured mentoring program. Participants commented that the content was "thought-provoking and relevant to management and employees," and "It made me think about all the things I typically don't have time or make time for."

The evaluation feedback was gathered at the end of the workshop and included questions to assess course content, the instructor, and overall value. Participants rated the following items on a scale of one to five, where 1 = strongly disagree and 5 = strongly agree:

- *Information and concepts were presented in a logical sequence.*
- *Learning activities supported and reinforced the content.*
- *I understood the concepts.*
- *There was effective participation, involvement, and interaction.*
- *The time spent on each topic allowed for clear understanding.*
- *The instructor was supportive and helpful.*
- *The instructor was organized and prepared.*
- *The instructor was knowledgeable on the topic.*
- *Participant questions and concerns were addressed.*
- *The instructor got the point across with understandable examples, stories, illustrations, or analogies.*
- *Overall, the course will contribute to better job performance.*
- *I am able to use what I learned on the job.*
- *I will recommend this program to my co-workers.*

Level 2: Learning Assessment, Survey, and Review Session

During the program, as part of the course design, learning activities such as quizzes and role plays were completed by participants to assess their knowledge and understanding of the content. Additionally, a pre- and post-assessment were completed to assess learning after attending the program. Two weeks prior to the workshop and 90 days after completing the program, participants completed a survey answering the following questions on a scale of one to five, where 1 = strongly disagree and 5 = strongly agree.

- *I am able to describe ATK's career development process.* Prior to attending, the average rating was 2.27; after attending the program, the average rating was 4.30.

- *I am able to describe the role of the employee, leader, and a mentor.* Prior to attending, the average rating was 2.73; after attending the program, the average rating was 4.30.

- *I am able to assess my interests, values, skills, experiences, and competencies and align them with my career choices.* Prior to attending, the average rating was 2.4; after attending the program, the average rating was 4.4.

- *I am familiar with ATK development resources and tools.* Prior to attending, the average rating was 2.0; after attending the program, the average rating was 4.7.

- *I know how to define clear career goals and specific development actions.* Prior to attending, the average rating was 2.67; after attending the program, the average rating was 4.07.

Three months after completion of the formal workshop, the participants received an invitation to a one-hour group learning review session. The one-hour sessions were conducted during a lunch time and participants were instructed to bring the program workbook and their completed action plan for discussion. The content of the session included a brief review of key concepts taught in the program along with interactive quizzes and discussion questions to assess learning.

Level 3: Survey and Learning Review to Assess Application

Participants reported increases in their ability to take ownership and a more proactive approach to managing their careers. The most common actions taken after attending the program included building a network, utilizing internal tools and resources, defining career goals, discussing career goals and associated action plans with others (leader, peers, and mentors), and gaining new development experiences at work. Information was gathered during follow-up coaching sessions with participants 90 days after the program to discuss career development action plans and to report on successes, challenges, and actions taken on the job.

Questions to assess the status of their career action plans and the impact of the program were also incorporated into the group learning review sessions and the post-program assessment survey. The post-assessment survey questions asked participants to identify actions they had taken on the job after completing the program, including:

- *Defined my career goals.* After attending the program, 50 percent of the participants had taken this action.

- *Discussed my career goals with a leader, mentor, or peer.* After attending the program, 60 percent of the participants had taken this action.

- *Made new contacts to build my career network.* After attending the program, 90 percent of the participants had taken this action.

- *Developed new skills or competencies.* After attending the program, 56 percent of the participants had taken this action.

- *Gained new experiences at work.* After attending the program, 61 percent of the participants had taken this action.

- *Gained new experiences through volunteer or leisure activities.* After attending the program, 39 percent of the participants had taken this action.

- *Explored career options.* After attending the program, 60 percent of the participants had taken this action.

- *Explored educational options.* After attending the program, 44 percent of the participants had taken this action.

- *Utilized ATK career resources and tools.* After attending the program, 80 percent of the participants had taken this action.

- *Achieved greater balance between work and leisure activities.* After attending the program, 20 percent of the participants had taken this action.

- *Made progress on my career action plan.* After attending the program, 56 percent of the participants had taken this action.

- *Other. (Please identify specific actions taken.)*

- *None of the above. (Please identify barriers to taking action.)* Some of the reasons for not taking action included other work priorities taking precedence over career action plans and late-career individuals close to retirement.

It also asked participants to identify changes they had made to their career, including:

- *Added projects or activities to develop myself within my current role.* After attending the program, 61 percent of the participants had taken this action.

- *Moved to another position: accepted a promotion, moved to another role laterally, accepted a new position with less responsibility, relocated to another geographic area, or rotated to a new assignment.* After attending the program, 20 percent of the participants had taken some action to move to another position.

- *Other. (Please identify specific actions taken.)*

- *None of the above.*

Participants were asked to also write in other comments and any additional examples of how they applied what they learned in the career development program. Group learning review sessions were conducted 90 days after the program to reinforce key concepts from the workshop, assess learning, and measure progress toward implementation of action plans. Participants discussed success stories and challenges in completing their career action plans and applying the content on the job. They also responded to questions anonymously using interactive polling equipment:

- Have you applied the knowledge or skills gained during the program?

- Was the workshop content relevant to your role in the business?

- Have you met with your leader to discuss how you will apply the course content?

- Did you complete the 90-day action plan you wrote at the end of the workshop?

As a result of the group learning review session, most participants committed to meet with their leader or a trusted mentor or peer to discuss their action plans, complete action plans if they had not yet done so, and to continue to apply the skills learned on the job. Leader coaching sessions gave participants an opportunity to practice skills taught in the program (such as conducting career conversations) and to ensure career plans were aligned with the business, and were realistic and achievable.

The talent management and leadership development team was encouraged to see individuals talking with leaders and mentors about how to develop skills and expand their capability and potential. An overwhelming majority of the participants reported defining career goals, utilizing career development resources, taking on new work assignments and gaining new skills or experiences to more fully contribute at work after attending the program. According to research (Grossman, 2011) more than 25 percent of high-potential employees plan to change jobs within the next 12 months. A comparison of the attrition rate for high-potential employees who attended the program versus those who did not attend is a potential additional measure of return-on-investment.

TM INITIATIVE MICRO SCORECARD

The micro talent management scorecard in Table 8-2 summarizes how the career development program was aligned with business objectives and measured for impact. The program was delivered to over 95 early- to mid-career emerging high-potential leaders. The participants' leaders or mentors were also invited to attend to encourage healthy career conversations between the participants and leadership. The objectives were to improve leadership pipeline readiness; retain and engage early- to mid-career high-potential employees, with a focus on emerging leadership talent; and to increase high-potential employees' self-reliance, their likelihood of considering career options within ATK, and their ability to manage their careers and generate development plans. In addition to participant satisfaction, the results showed increased learning in the participants' ability to describe the career development process, take ownership, assess career choices, use existing resources, and define career goals. The participants applied the knowledge 90 days after

Table 8-2. TM Initiative Micro Scorecard

Program Title: Career Development

Target Audience: Early- to Mid-Career High-Potential Emerging Leaders/Leaders/Mentors

Number of Attendees: 95+ (TBD)

Duration: 8-hour training with follow-up coaching sessions

Business Objectives:

- Improve leadership pipeline readiness.
- Retain and engage early- to mid-career high-potential employees, with a focus on emerging leadership talent.
- Increase self-reliance and the ability of high-potential employees to consider career options within ATK, make career decisions, manage career change, and generate career development plans.

Results				
Satisfaction	Learning	Application	Tangible Benefits	Intangible Benefits
Level 1	**Level 2**	**Level 3**	**Levels 4 & 5**	
Evaluation average rating of 4.35 on a scale of 1-5	Learning review sessions and pre- and post-assessment results comparison on a scale of 1-5 • ability to describe the career development process and roles Pre: 2.27 Post: 4.30	Survey results, follow-up learning review sessions, coaching, and application of the skills. Actions taken 90 days after the program including: • Defined my career goals: 50% • Discussed my career goals and action plan with others (leader, mentor, peers): 60% • Made new contacts to build my network: 90% • Developed new skills or competencies: 56% • Gained new experiences at work: 61% • Gained new experiences through volunteer or leisure activities: 39%	N/A Potential measures could include projected turnover/retention rate for high-potential emerging leaders who attended the program versus those who did not attend.	Morale Satisfaction Engagement

133

• ability to take ownership for career Pre: 2.73 Post: 4.30 • ability to assess self and align career choices Pre: 2.4 Post: 4.4 • familiarity with career resources Pre: 2.0 Post: 4.7 • ability to define career goals Pre: 2.67 Post: 4.07	• Explored career options: 60% • Explored educational options: 44% • Utilized career resources and tools: 80% • Achieved greater balance between work and leisure activities: 20% • Made progress on my career plan: 56% • Added projects activities to develop myself within my current role: 61% • Moved to another position within the organization (such as a lateral move, step down, relocation, rotation): 20%

Technique to Isolate Effects of Program: Participant perception

Technique to Convert Data to Monetary Value: N/A

Barriers to Application of Skills: Time constraints for employees and leaders, changing organizational culture and structure

Recommendations: Continuation of program

the program by taking various actions that included building a better career network, utilizing career resources, discussing career goals with others, and adding developmental projects to a current role. The program described in the micro talent management scorecard was strategically aligned with business needs and critical to driving culture transformation at a Fortune 500 company.

CONCLUSIONS

Career development was a critical element to the success of the ATK Aerospace Systems business. It was imperative to provide employees with an opportunity to grow and contribute in new ways, to challenge them, increase job satisfaction, and generate excitement about future opportunities. As employees developed careers that closely aligned with their personalities, competencies, interests, and values, they positioned themselves to contribute more meaningfully to the company and gain greater fulfillment from their work. Consequently, ATK Aerospace Systems was well-positioned to retain talent and maximize the intelligence and creativity of its workforce. Based on this experience at ATK, the career development program should be continued with the intention of measuring the impact on the attrition rates of the high-potential emerging leader population.

ABOUT THE AUTHOR

Saundra Stroope led the talent management and training department for the Aerospace Structures business division at ATK. She has 20 years of experience in human resources with an emphasis in talent, leadership, and organizational development. Her background includes creating development solutions that align with business strategy and achieve results in multiple industries (aerospace, defense, mining, energy, telecommunications, healthcare). She has worked with global and Fortune 500 companies recognized for leading practices by *CLO* and *Training* magazine's Top 125 Awards. She holds a master's degree in human resources management, a bachelor's in psychology, and several professional certifications.

REFERENCES

Kirkpatrick, J., and W.K. Kirkpatrick. (2009). "The Kirkpatrick Four Levels™: A Fresh Look After 50 Years, 1959-2009." Kirkpatrick Partners, LLC. Accessed at www.kirkpatrickpartners.com/Portals/0/Resources/Kirkpatrick%20Four%20Levels%20white%20paper.pdf.

Grossman, R. (2011). "The Care and Feeding of High-Potential Employees," *HR Magazine*, August 1, 2011. Retrieved from www.shrm.org/Publications/hrmagazine/Editorial-Content/2011/0811/Pages/0811grossman.aspx

9

PRE-LEADERSHIP DEVELOPMENT: FEEDING THE PIPELINE WITH EMERGING LEADERS

Lisa Ann Edwards, Cari Williams, and Melanie Brittle

INTRODUCTION

This case study describes a talent management solution designed to build the capability of emerging leaders and prepare them for future leadership roles. The program includes a two-and-a-half-day retreat and two coaching sessions for 12 participants in five regions. Utilizing the ROI Methodology™, the program was evaluated for reaction/satisfaction (Level 1), learning (Level 2) and behavior/application (Level 3) (Phillips, 2003). The program far exceeded its goals in all three levels of evaluation. Participants in the program gained insight on leadership behaviors they needed to improve and then applied at least five of these new behaviors.

BACKGROUND

DPR Construction (DPR) is a unique technical builder with a passion for results. Ranked in the top 50 general contractors in the nation since 1997 (just seven years after founding), DPR is a forward-thinking company specializing in technically challenging and sustainable projects for collaborative owners in the advanced technology, healthcare, life sciences, corporate office, and higher education markets. With 16 offices in the U.S., DPR is a fast-growing organization and in 2012 was ranked 13th on *Fortune* magazine's "Great Places to

Work" list. Recognized as a leader in the industry, the organization works hard to maintain its position in the market through the capabilities of its people.

TALENT MANAGEMENT INITIATIVE

Program Purpose

The purpose of the Professional Development (PD) program is to prepare emerging leaders, who are not yet ready for the leadership development program, for future leadership roles. DPR's growth demands that the organization continue to develop and build capability in its existing leaders, and its current leadership development program is a necessary component to its talent management strategy. However, due to the fast growth of the organization, DPR needs to prepare emerging leaders for future leadership roles, in addition to building the capability of its existing leaders. The leadership program for current leaders is positively regarded within the organization, and DPR wanted to create a way to "give back" to its emerging leaders and demonstrate their support of them by investing in a "leadership-lite" version of the leadership program. The key to success for this program is to invest just enough to enable improvements in specific leadership behaviors.

Program Objectives

The PD program has four objectives:

1. The primary objective of the program is to help emerging leaders gain new insights and awareness of the leadership behaviors necessary to become an effective leader at DPR. These make up the learning objectives of the program.

2. Secondly, emerging leaders were expected to apply some of these new behaviors in the workplace. These are the performance or behavioral objectives of the program.

3. Thirdly, the program is designed to provide emerging leaders, one level below the leadership level, with an engaging, inspiring program that demonstrated that organization was committed to their personal growth and development.

4. And finally, the purpose of evaluating the program was to capture baseline data on the program's effectiveness at Levels 1 through 3 so that improvements could be made, and so that the program could be run in future sessions at the ROI level.

Participant Selection

Participants were selected using DPR's "leadership characteristics sieve." The leadership characteristics sieve was created to identify current and future leaders and is comprised of four filters:

1. **"The right who's."** This filter identifies individuals who have the following characteristics: energy, enjoyable/fun, excellence, hard work, initiative, integrity, loyalty, passion, and striving to grow.

2. **Highly-skilled professionals.** This filter identifies individuals who have the following characteristics: accountability, exceptional execution, experience, focus and discipline, knowledge, and problem-solving ability.

3. **Leaders.** In this filter, individuals are rated for the following characteristics: aligns with business goals and strategies, approachable, balanced, committed, excellent communicator, manages conflict, empowers, and is flexible.

4. **Regional managers.** Finally, in this filter, individuals are rated for the following characteristics: authentic and genuine, courageous and tireless, creates and builds camaraderie, drives to improve, influencer, puts others above self, and is a strategic thought leader.

The first step in determining the list of candidates to participate in the PD program is for the business-unit leaders to assess their teams. Following their assessment through the sieve, the business-unit leaders discuss the readiness and availability of their candidates during a management meeting held to make the final selections of the participants.

Program Format

The PD program was offered in five regions in the U.S. at various times throughout the year. There are three components to the program, including:

- a modified version of a company-specific 360-degree feedback tool, and the Myers-Brigg Type Indicator (MBTI)

- one three-day offsite training session with an outside facilitator
- two private coaching sessions with the outside facilitator.

Assessments

The company believes that an individual cannot be a truly successful leader without a certain level of self-awareness. Therefore, feedback was gathered on each participant's behaviors and opportunities for growth using DPR's own personalized 360-degree feedback tool. The 360 tool was specially adapted for this program by aligning the questions around the characteristics and behaviors desired in leaders, with a focus on DPR culture. The goal was to keep it simple so that participants could complete the 360 in 30 to 60 minutes, therefore resulting in a high response rate. The 360-degree feedback tool was paired with the MBTI instrument so participants would gain even more insight into their individual leadership styles and personalities.

The MBTI instrument is the personality-inventory tool of choice for DPR because it creates a common language and understanding among the participants. The MBTI helps the participants gain self-awareness of how they perceive their surroundings and how they make decisions. It also provides a context for betters understanding others and thinking about how they engage with the teams they lead. As a result of combining the MBTI with the customized 360-degree feedback tool, the participants experienced tremendous growth and achieved new levels of self-awareness.

Retreat

The retreat was held over two-and-a-half days and was designed to increase participants' self-awareness and help them connect the dots between the 360 feedback, the MBTI, and their group dynamics. The retreat begins with an off-site hike or bike ride to clear the participants' minds so they can focus on their self-exploration. The retreat includes individual and group work, including self-portrait work, balanced life work, growth-goal reviews, and giving and

receiving feedback. All of the activities are creative, designed to help the participants reflect and gain the self-awareness needed to be an effective leader at DPR.

Coaching

All participants participated in two coaching sessions. The first coaching
session was held at the retreat and the second one was held 30 days following
the retreat. The facilitator of the retreat conducted both coaching sessions. The
purpose of the first session was to discuss what the participant had learned
about himself and what he planned to do as a result of the program. Challenges
of implementing their action plans were also discussed; the coach facilitated
the participant's problem-solving process for addressing those challenges. The
purpose of the second coaching session was to discuss the application of new
behaviors and actions. The coach and the participant discussed what worked
well, the challenges, how they overcame them, what they learned from the
process, and what they will do differently going forward.

EVALUATION METHODOLOGY AND RESULTS

Purpose of Evaluation

The purpose of the evaluation was twofold:

- Discover how the PD program was currently meeting success measures
  and what could be improved.

- Prepare the organization for a future ROI study of the PD program in
  another location.

Though the program is offered in five regions, at this time, data was only
collected for one region to benchmark the program.

General Description of Approach

The Phillips' ROI Methodology™ was used to determine three levels of value,
including participant reaction, learning, and on-the-job application of skills
and behavior. Evaluation data was collected from the participants for Level 1

(reaction) and from participants, managers, peers, and direct reports for Levels 2 (learning) and 3 (application) (Phillips, 2003). The company elected not to measure business impact or ROI at this time as it was determined that it was better to capture baseline data at Levels 1 through 3. Using this information, it was planned to evaluate the program at Levels 1 through 5 in a future session.

Needs Assessment

Planning the evaluation of the existing PD program required a thorough needs assessment with stakeholders to gain clarity and alignment about the purpose of the program and what measures could be expected to have improved. Stakeholders included representatives from executive leadership, participants, human resources, and the facilitator of the program. The result of the needs assessment clarified that the overall needs of the business were to:

- Ensure the PD program is relevant and important to successful job performance.

- Improve participants' understanding of the results of the 360-degree assessment.

- Implement at least five out of the nine behaviors on the 360 assessment.

- Business impact and ROI were not captured at this time, but will be captured in the next session.

Data Collection

The results of the needs assessment were used to create the data collection strategy. The strategy included acquiring credible, relevant evaluation data that would prove that the objectives outlined in the needs assessment were met.

- Level 1—Reaction/Satisfaction: Items measured at this level were related to the topics listed below. An objective of having an average of 3.6, or 88-percent, agree on a scale of 1 (strongly disagree) to 5 (strongly agree) was set. Below are the topics:
    - » relevance
    - » importance to success
    - » value-add

- » facilitator/coach effectiveness
- » likelihood of recommending program to others.

- Level 2—Learning: Learning items were related to gaining self-awareness on the most important topics from the 360. An objective of having an average of 3.6, or 88-percent, agree on a scale of 1 (strongly disagree) to 5 (strongly agree) was set. Below are the topics:
  - » approachable; listens well
  - » manages personal frustrations
  - » gives credit to others
  - » provides honest feedback
  - » gives people responsibility
  - » demonstrates the core value of "ever forward"
  - » has confidence and presence
  - » handles crucial conversations well.

- Level 3—Application/Implementation: These items were related to applying at least five new behaviors on the most important topics from the 360. An objective of having an average of 3.6, or 88-percent, agree on a scale of 1 (strongly disagree) to 5 (strongly agree) was set. Below are the topics:
  - » approachable; listens well
  - » manages personal frustrations
  - » gives credit to others
  - » provides honest feedback
  - » gives people responsibility
  - » demonstrates the core value of "ever forward"
  - » has confidence and presence
  - » handles crucial conversations.

- Level 4, Business Impact, was not captured.

- Level 5, ROI, was not captured.

Data for Levels 1 through 3 were collected 60 days after the conclusion of the program, using an online questionnaire. Survey completion was tracked so that individuals who had not completed the survey could be identified; however, it was not possible to track responses by survey participant.

Data was collected at 60 days because it was believed the types of behavior changes participants were expected to make were not simple task-related behavior changes, but rather fundamental shifts in self-awareness and behavior. While it was expected that short-term changes in behavior might be made immediately following the retreat and coaching session, there was greater interest in understanding changes that were sustained 60 days after the intervention; the kind of lasting changes that were desired by the organization. While it was possible to collect data both at the conclusion of the intervention and after 60 days, it was believed that this would cause too much disruption to the individuals surveyed and would decrease participation in the 60-day survey.

ROI Analysis Strategy

No ROI analysis was conducted for this session. However, ROI analysis is planned for a future session.

Level 1: Reaction Results

The Level 1 results met the program objectives for each item. They are summarized in Table 9-1.

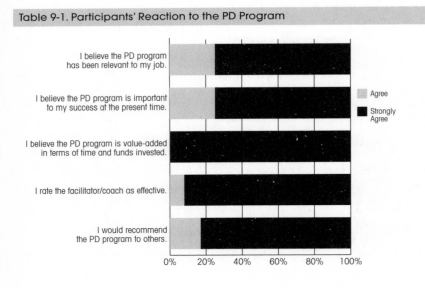

Table 9-1. Participants' Reaction to the PD Program

Level 2: Learning Results

Participants received their 360-degree feedback during the first day of the PD retreat and were required to select three areas of growth they wanted to work on during the retreat. Sixty days after the conclusion of the PD program, data were collected by a questionnaire from participants about the extent to which they believed that they gained self-awareness regarding each topic on the 360. The objective was for all participants to gain self-awareness on all nine items from the 360. The target performance was an average rating of 3.6 for all items, or an average 88-percent agree for all items. Participants self-reported learning on each item. Managers, peers, and direct reports reported their observations of the participants' gains in self-awareness for each item. Observations of learning are typically reflective of conversations about self-learning with the participant. In some cases, an individual may be gaining self-awareness but not yet applying their learning. Level 2 data was collected by the observer groups to see if this was true for participants. In other words, in comparing learning to behavior change, did observers see the participants gaining self-awareness but not yet applying their learning? This would inform any changes or improvements to the program to ensure better transfer of learning to behavior. These goals were met and are reflected in Table 9-2.

Table 9-2. Participants' Rating on Self-Awareness

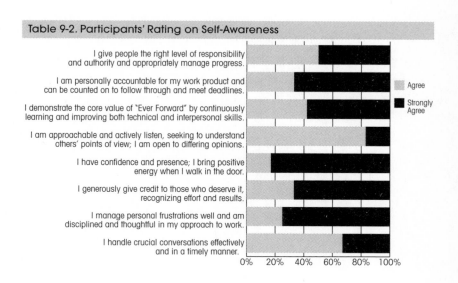

Data were collected from managers about the extent to which they believe they observed participants gain self-awareness for each topic on the 360. The target performance was an average rating of 3.6 for all items; or an average 88-percent agree for all items. These goals were met and are reflected in Table 9-3.

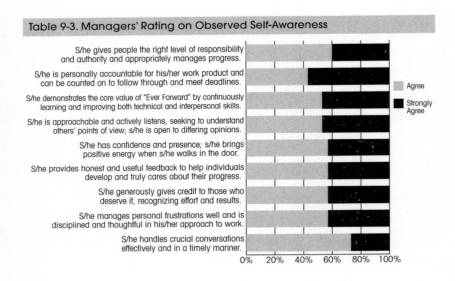

Table 9-3. Managers' Rating on Observed Self-Awareness

Data were collected from peers about the extent to which they believe they observed participants gain self-awareness for each topic on the 360. The target performance was an average rating of 3.6 for all items; or an average 88-percent agree for all items. These goals were met and are reflected in Table 9-4.

Table 9-4. Peers' Rating on Observed Self-Awareness

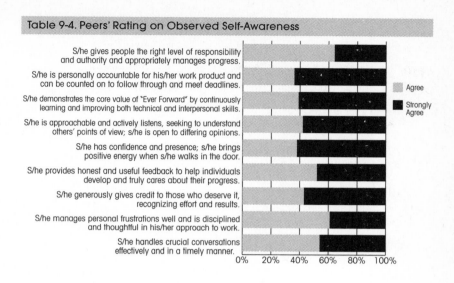

Data were collected from direct reports about the extent to which they believe they observed participants gain self-awareness for each topic on the 360. The target performance was an average rating of 3.6 for all items; or an average 88-percent agree for all items. These goals were met and are reflected in Table 9-5.

Table 9-5. Direct Reports' Rating on Observed Self-Awareness

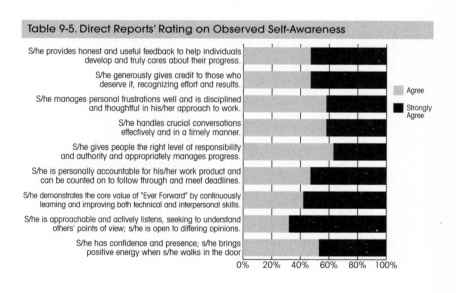

In comparing data across participants, managers, peers, and direct reports, it was discovered that overall, participants gave themselves the highest ratings while managers gave participants the lowest ratings. Significant gaps existed between participants and managers on the following items:

- *I am approachable and I actively listen, seeking to understand other's points of view; I am open to differing opinions (.80).*

- *I have confidence and presence; I bring positive energy when I walk in the door (.70).*

- *I manage personal frustrations well and I am disciplined and thoughtful in my approach to work (.65).*

Level 3: Application Results

The 12 participants from the Sacramento region completed questionnaires on the same learning items 60 days after completion of the PD program; however, items were rephrased, asking the participant to check all of the items where they implemented at least one new approach. Evaluation targets were set for a minimum of five new behaviors of the nine 360 items, or at least an average of 55-percent agree across all items. All items met the objectives and are summarized in Table 9-6.

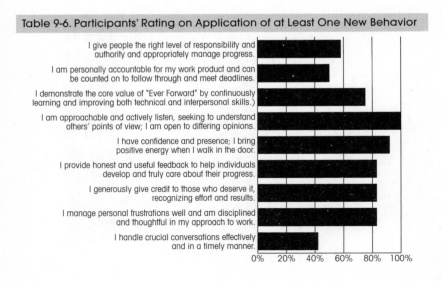

Table 9-6. Participants' Rating on Application of at Least One New Behavior

Data were collected from managers about the extent to which they believe they observed participants apply one new behavior for each topic on the 360. The target performance was a minimum of five new behaviors of the nine on the 360, or an average 55-percent agree across all items. These goals were met and are reflected in Table 9-7.

Table 9-7. Managers' Rating on Observation of at Least One New Behavior Applied on Each Topic

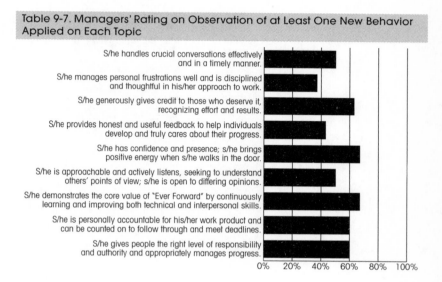

Data were collected from peers about the extent to which they believe they observed participants apply one new behavior for each topic on the 360. The target performance was a minimum of five new behaviors of the nine on the 360, or an average 55-percent agree across all items. These goals were met and are reflected in Table 9-8.

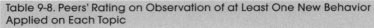

Table 9-8. Peers' Rating on Observation of at Least One New Behavior Applied on Each Topic

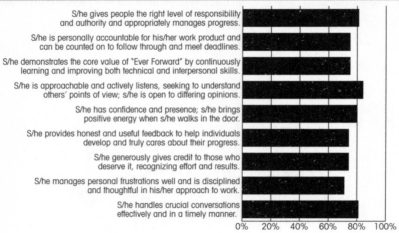

Data were collected from direct reports about the extent to which they believe they observed participants apply one new behavior for each topic on the 360. The target performance was a minimum of five new behaviors of the nine on the 360, or an average 55-percent agree across all items. These goals were met and are reflected in Table 9-9.

Table 9-9. Direct Report's Rating on Observation of at Least One New Behavior Applied on Each Topic

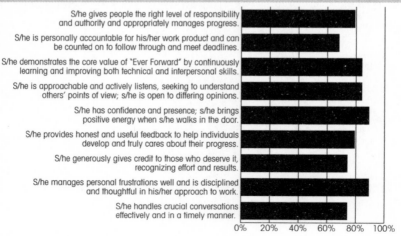

In comparing data across participants, managers, peers, and direct reports, it was discovered that overall, participants gave themselves the highest ratings, while managers gave the participants the lowest ratings. Significant gaps existed between participants and managers on the following items:

- *I am approachable and I actively listen, seeking to understand other's points of view; I am open to differing opinions* (.50).

- *I have confidence and presence; I bring positive energy when I walk in the door* (.25).

- *I provide honest and useful feedback to help individuals develop and truly care about their progress* (.43).

- *I manage personal frustrations well and I am disciplined and thoughtful in my approach to work* (.37).

TM INITIATIVE MICRO SCORECARD

Overall, this program met the talent management goals established at this time, as shown in Table 9-10. It was discovered that participants are very satisfied with the program. Additionally, participants and their observers agreed that they gained awareness of leadership behaviors related to the 360-degree feedback tool. Participants and their observers also agreed that they applied at least five new leadership behaviors related to the 360.

This program will be implemented in other offices in 2013, and at that time, the program will be evaluated for business impact and ROI.

CONCLUSIONS

Overall, this program was viewed as a success. It was discovered that participants are very satisfied with the program. Additionally, participants and their observers agreed that they gained awareness regarding leadership behaviors related to the 360-degree assessment. Participants and their observers also agreed that they applied at least five new leadership behaviors related to the 360.

Table 9-10. TM Initiative Micro Scorecard

Talent Management Initiative: Professional Development (PD) Program

Target Audience: 12 emerging leaders (pre-leaders)

Duration: 2.5-day retreat plus two coaching sessions

Business Objectives: To ensure there are enough future leaders to fill the pipeline as the business continues to grow.

Results		
Reaction	**Learning**	**Application**
Level 1	**Level 2**	**Level 3**
Positive reaction to and satisfaction with the program.	Gained self-awareness of nine behaviors as identified on the 360.	Application of at least five new behaviors out of nine behaviors identified on the 360.
Goal: Average of 88% agree on the following topics: • Relevance • Important to success • Value-add • Effective facilitator • Recommend to others	**Goal:** Average of 88% agree that participants had gained self-awareness on the following 360 topics: • Giving responsibility and authority • Personal accountability • Demonstration of "Ever Forward" • Approachability • Confidence and presence • Honest and useful feedback • Generous credit to others • Managing frustrations • Crucial conversations	**Goal:** Average of 55% agree that participants applied at least five new behaviors on the following 360 topics: • Giving responsibility and authority • Personal accountability • Demonstration of "Ever Forward" • Approachability • Confidence and presence • Honest and useful feedback • Generous credit to others • Managing frustrations • Crucial conversations
Result: Participants: 100% agree Managers: N/A Peers: N/A Directs: N/A	**Result:** Participants: 95% agree Managers: 90% agree Peers: 95% agree Directs: 98% agree	**Result:** Participants: 74% agree Managers: 55% agree Peers: 73% agree Directs: 80% agree

Technique to Isolate Effects of Program: Not applicable.

Technique to Convert Data to Monetary Value: Not applicable.

Fully-Loaded Program Costs: Not applicable.

Barriers to Application of Skills: Organizational readiness.

Recommendations: Evaluate the program at ROI in the next implementation.

Moreover, this work served to lay the foundation for evaluating the program for business impact and ROI. In the future, the program will be evaluated against the following:

- Are participants working to improve their leadership behaviors, as specified in their individual development plans?

- Does the program pay off in terms of monetary impact?

- Are more emerging leaders ready for future leadership roles as a result of the program?

ABOUT THE AUTHORS

Lisa Ann Edwards, MS, is a partner of Bloom Coaching Institute, an organization that advances coaching effectiveness through research, tools, training, and consultation on the ROI of coaching. Lisa's work has demonstrated as much as a 251 percent ROI and has increased employee engagement by 20 percent. As head of talent management for Corbis, a Bill Gates'-owned global media company, Lisa implemented talent development solutions such as leadership development and coaching. Lisa has authored or contributed to several books, including *Measuring the Success of Coaching* (2012); *ASTD Handbook for Measuring and Evaluating Training* (2010); *Managing Talent Retention: An ROI Approach* (2009); and *ROI in Action Casebook* (2008). She can be reached at Lisa@BloomCoachingInstitute.com.

Cari Williams has led the learning and development group at DPR Construction for six years. Prior to her transition into learning, Cari worked with DPR as a project manager and a project executive for 12 years, where she actively managed the budget, schedule, and quality of major construction projects. Cari creates and delivers the content for DPR's professional development, leadership development, and management training programs. When DPR Construction was ranked fourth in ASTD's BEST awards in 2009, Cari spoke at the awards conference about DPR's leadership development program.

Melanie Brittle has been with DPR Construction's learning and development team since 2005. Her areas of expertise include course facilitation, instructional design, training needs assessment, course evaluation, project management, learning-center management administration, career development, and recruiting. In 2008, Melanie was recognized by *Training* magazine as one of the year's Top Young Trainers. She is a certified MBTI practitioner and holds a professional certificate in training and HR from the University of California at Berkeley Extension. As a result of becoming more involved in DPR Construction's professional development process, Melanie will be completing an ICF-accredited coach training program in the next year. She is passionate about her role and the opportunity to contribute to the growth and development of those who make DPR Construction a truly great place to work.

REFERENCES

Phillips, J.J. (2003). *Return on Investment in Training and Performance Improvement Programs*, 2nd edition. San Francisco, CA: Butterworth-Heinemann.

10

ACHIEVING BREAKTHROUGH SALES PERFORMANCE THROUGH GLOBAL SALES LEADERSHIP PRACTICE

Cynthia Dibble and Barbra Sher

INTRODUCTION

This case study demonstrates how Hewlett-Packard, a Fortune 500 company, achieved increased revenue growth, improved customer satisfaction, and improved trusted partner status by implementing a successful talent management transformation. Through strong business and human resources (HR) partnerships and committed executive sponsorship, learning and development (L&D) was able to deliver industry-leading programs that contributed directly to Hewlett-Packard's dynamic growth.

BACKGROUND

The Hewlett-Packard Company (HP) is a $127.4 billion multinational information technology company with 349,000 employees worldwide. Headquartered in Palo Alto, California, HP provides products, technologies, software solutions and services to consumers, small- and medium-sized businesses, and large enterprises, including customers in government, health, manufacturing, financial services, and other industry sectors.

Through a series of customer roundtables, HP received feedback that rapid growth in the capabilities of global information technology could rapidly transform their business. Customers no longer looked to technology vendors to sell them products, but instead wanted to partner with vendors who understood their business and could apply complex technology solutions to solve their business problems.

Customers now expected technology partners to:

- Have deep industry expertise.

- Collaborate and engage with their most senior executives.

- Understand the operations of their business.

- Demonstrate how technology solutions can change their business and show a greater return on their technology investment.

In order to remain competitive in the enterprise computing industry, HP's previously successful sellers of product technology had to make vital changes. The company needed to hire or develop a new breed of account manager—one who blended technology knowledge with deep industry knowledge, business and financial acumen, executive presence, consultative selling skills, and general management capabilities. HP needed a robust performance improvement program to select and prepare HP's sales leaders to meet these evolving customer needs.

HP's response to customers' feedback was to transform its salesforce by creating a strategic customer-facing role: the Global Account General Manager (AGM). Established as an executive-level role, the AGMs were expected to act as trusted advisors to their customers and represent HP to the largest and most strategic Fortune 500 companies. AGMs had to develop a deep understanding of the customers' business issues and rationalize HPs' large and complex portfolio of offerings to develop solutions that would accelerate their customers' success. HP's customers typically represented global, multinational companies with business divisions whose functions ranged from building jet engines to producing small appliances within a single company.

At the same time, HP set expectations for AGMs to play an equally challenging role inside the company. AGMs were expected to assemble and lead large, integrated global teams that could meet the needs of their complex customer accounts. AGMs needed exemplary global leadership skills and had to be conversant in cross-business and cross-cultural norms.

There were several critical success factors that contributed to the success of HP's sales transformation: First, HP established a global program office to deliver the infrastructure and operational support for the AGMs. Second, HP provided sponsorship from the highest-level sales and business unit executives. Third and lastly, HP gave HR and L&D the strategic role of leading this robust performance improvement program. HR and L&D together drove a comprehensive talent management process compromised of several initiatives to select, hire, assess, and develop the required talent; and to ensure AGMs had the industry expertise and the necessary analytic, business, consultative selling, and executive engagement skills to meet their customers' needs. Key initiative components included:

- a well-defined job-role profile

- a baseline competency model

- a hiring and selection guide

- a development road map

- a sales leadership development program, called "License to Practice" (LTP)

- an executive assessment.

This case study reports on the business impact of one of the key initiatives, the LTP program, the longest-running sales development program at HP since 2004. The case also uses data from the executive assessment initiative to show further evidence of the tangible business impact of LTP.

TALENT MANAGEMENT INITIATIVE

This section describes two initiatives of the talent management (TM) process as shown in Figure 10-1. Although HP successfully implemented the entire process, the leadership development initiative (LTP) and the executive assessment initiative both played critical roles in ensuring HP had the talent in place to 1) drive strategic account revenue growth; and 2) increase customer satisfaction and customer loyalty. These two objectives were realized in part because they were built on a strong collaborative partnership between HR, L&D, and the Enterprise Sales function. Senior leaders took an active role in helping shape the LTP program and provided visible support during deployment.

A prerequisite key to success for both of these initiatives was the development of the job-role profile and a role-based competency model built specifically to drive business outcomes. The competencies were then threaded throughout the initiatives within the TM process. In particular, LTP and the executive assessment used the competencies as a benchmark to measure demonstrated performance.

Figure 10-1. Talent Management Process

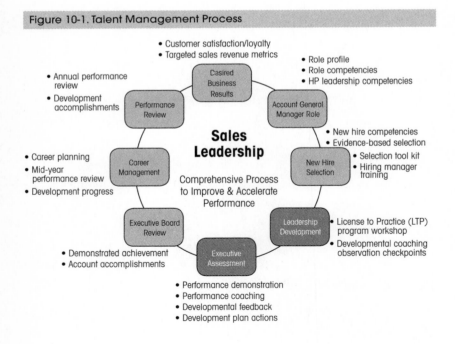

Leadership Development Initiative

The leadership development initiative is a suite of programs that includes the License to Practice (LTP) workshop and developmental coaching, as shown in Figure 10-2.

The program consists of integrated training and development activities which include executive coaching, on-the-job application, peer networking, best-practice sharing, and certification by a review board.

The performance objectives for LTP enable the following critical AGM sales competencies:

- executive engagement
- consultative selling
- business, financial, and industry acumen.

Recognized by the American Society for Training & Development (ASTD) as a best practice, the LTP program invested in internal and external industry thought-leaders who served as facilitators and executive coaches, a significant component that ensured successful on-the-job application of program concepts.

To complete LTP, participants must demonstrate achievement of the required performance through a formal certification process that is reviewed by a board of sales leaders. All participants are expected to show evidence of sustained on-the-job performance in these key areas:

- overall profitable account performance
- successful execution of their strategic account business plans
- demonstrated evidence of consultative selling, business management, account leadership, and successful executive engagement
- successful execution of their personal development plans.

LTP is completed over a two-year period. The program includes a five-day executive development workshop followed by four to six months of ongoing coaching with four formal coaching checkpoints. AGMs from across multiple geographies (Americas, EMEA, and APJ) are brought together for each workshop to learn best practices from industry thought-leaders and former executives. At the end of the workshop and after each follow-up coaching checkpoint, participants must demonstrate achievement of the required competencies (executive engagement, consultative selling, and business, industry, and financial acumen). Failure to complete the requirements results in having to participate in a remediation process that includes the AGM, her manager, the executive coach, and HR.

LTP presents a final certification of achievement between 18 and 24 months post-workshop. Participants prepare and present their portfolios of achievements to an executive review board. Citing customer references and evidence of actual improved sales metrics (such as quota attainment, increased revenue and share of wallet, customer satisfaction, and deal size), participants engage HP's senior leaders in an executive dialogue, demonstrating their capabilities while defending their portfolios. Those who pass are granted their LTP certificate.

Figure 10-2. The License to Practice Program

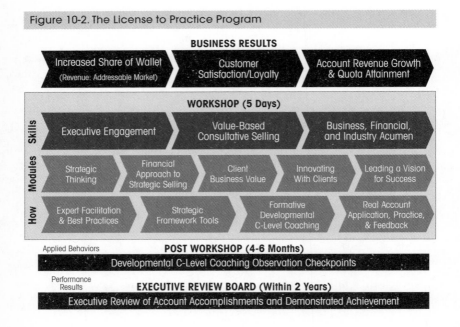

Since LTP was launched in 2004, more than 1,500 individuals have participated in the program. These 1,500 participants include global account leaders, account managers, and sales managers. To ensure relevance, each instance of the LTP program was highly customized. Participants were selected to attend with colleagues who supported similar vertical industry accounts (such as auto, high-tech, retail, and financial services). The LTP program team customized program content for each group of participants, including the industry content, AGM best practices, and specific financial and benchmark information about the customers represented in each session. Critical to the success of the program were HP industry thought-leaders, external former chief executive officers (CxOs), and sales managers, who facilitated the workshops, provided participant coaching, and helped model the behaviors that drive AGM performance. They helped focus the AGMs on delivering financially-based business results rather than simply delivering technology solutions.

Program content undergoes continual quality improvement and content updates to stay on top of industry and economic trends and to reflect the company's current strategy. During the early stage of the program's rollout, participant feedback indicated that the executive coaching and best-practice sharing during the workshops played a critical role in driving behavior change. However, feedback showed that once back on the job, participants had difficulty sustaining the application of their new skills. Program successes convinced HP's executives to make additional investments. A significant enhancement was made in 2008. L&D was able to engage the CxO and HP industry coaches to provide follow-up coaching for four to six months, and a formal checkpoint process was added to the program. HP saw immediate business results from the program with these enhancements. Through documented evaluation of immediate and sustained business impact (see the Evaluation Methodology section), the LTP program demonstrates the application of a systematic approach to achieve performance excellence and improvement. Sustainable results include:

- enterprise-wide consistency across a population of the technology industry's most senior account leaders

- business results sustained over a six-year period during dramatic changes in the technology industry

- continued commitment of participants and their managers to continually contribute new best practices

- acceleration of sales executives' transformation from technology-solution providers to trusted advisors who internalize the business results client executives need to deliver

- permanent behavior change sustained over time

- top-down alignment within the company from senior executives to sales managers, account managers, and extended account team members on expected performance.

The overall outcome was a significant positive change in customers' perception of HP and a parallel growth in account profitability.

Executive Assessment Initiative

The second program discussed in this case study is the Executive Assessment Initiative, which complements and evaluates the sustained effectiveness of the LTP program.

In 2009, new HP sales executives, who were leading the accelerated sales transformation, looked to HR and L&D for a talent inventory that would identify competencies for rapidly improving sales performance for an expanded set of 250 account general managers. The Executive Assessment enabled HP to examine the long-term sustainability and application of what was taught in the LTP program, and to continue the transformation of HP's salesforce. The Executive Assessment Initiative was an 18.5-hour commitment of time over a 12-week period. It was a highly customized, comprehensive approach to identify existing talent capability and close critical competency gaps, building on the LTP program. As in all of the TM initiatives, the assessment was created to accelerate account performance, as measured through account revenue growth, increased wallet share, and improved customer loyalty. The AGM job-role profile and the competencies were used to develop the Executive Assessment.

AGMs were selected to participate in the Executive Assessment Initiative after they had been in their jobs for one year and had completed the LTP workshop and coaching checkpoint reviews. The initiative assessed participants' capabilities against the competency model and resulted in a customized executive development plan.

Participant Assessment

The following describes the assessment process, prework, and assessment center activities. Participants completed the following prework before attending the assessment:

- 360-degree competency survey on 17 competencies

- Hogan Personality Inventory (Hogan HPI, 1995)

- pre-assessment meeting conducted by expert coaches.

Upon completion of the prework, participants attended the assessment center for an intense one-day program that involved the following activities:

- business case simulation with four role plays conducted with professional expert coaches

- formative performance coaching and feedback on each role play

- structured behavioral interviews and review of 360-degree reports.

Participant Development

After the assessment center activities, participants met with their assigned coaches and their managers for:

- verbal feedback on each business-simulation role play

- comprehensive written narrative feedback report using 360 surveys, HPI reports, coaches' narratives, and two scorecards: an individual development scorecard and an AGM account performance measures scorecard

- manager scorecard (stack ranking and talent gaps)

- verbal feedback from AGMs' managers

- development planning actions agreement with AGMs' managers and coaches.

EVALUATION METHODOLOGY AND RESULTS

The evaluation methodology and its results are shown in two phases. The first phase focuses on the evaluation of the program as it was delivered, referred to as Levels 1 through 3 (Kirkpatrick, 1998). The second phase focuses on post-deployment as well as a longitudinal look back at the effectiveness of LTP (Levels 1 through 3) and most importantly, the impact on actual business results (Level 4) (Phillips and Schmidt, 2004; Kirkpatrick, 1998). Both phases address multiple levels of evaluation, as shown in Figure 10-3.

Figure 10-3. Evaluation Methodology Phases 1 & 2

Phase 1: Deployment Evaluation During Program

Summary of techniques used: survey, CxO coach observation, demonstrated account achievement (executive review board)

LTP Workshop	Post-Workshop 6-Month Coaching	Board Review
L1 (Reaction): daily feedback survey L2 (Learning): skill and behavioral demonstration of performance objectives	L3 (Application): CxO coach observation checkpoints	L3 (Application): executive board account; performance and results

Phase 2: Post-Deployment Evaluation

Summary of techniques used: longitudinal interviews, self-reporting, expert coach assessment, sales performance data analysis

LTP Workshop	LTP Workshop	Executive Assessment	Performance Data Analysis
L1 (Reaction): longitudinal interviews content relevance quality of learning experience	L3 (Application): longitudinal interviews self-report	L3 (Application): demonstration with expert coach assessment and analysis	L4 (Business Impact): individual account performance and executive assessment of top-performer account performance

Phase 1: Evaluation During LTP Program Deployment

Phase 1 evaluation data was collected throughout the deployment life cycle of the LTP program: during the LTP workshop, at the completion of post-workshop coaching checkpoints, and after the executive board review. Data from this phase reflects Kirkpatrick's Levels 1, 2, and 3.

Level 1: Reaction and Results

Level 1 reaction data for LTP was collected using daily workshop feedback surveys to ensure the content of each module aligned with the objectives; the presenters were articulate, engaging, and effective; and finally, that the coaches were able to help participants interpret and apply the examples to their own jobs. The CxO coaches used in this workshop were also rated for their ability to help participants "formulate new ideas and expand their thinking" in a way that enhanced the value the participants would bring to their customers.

The surveys were gathered over 44 sessions conducted from 2004 through 2011. Each session received a final "overall" session rating on a five-point scale: strongly disagree (1), disagree (2), neutral (3), agree (4), or strongly agree (5). The participants were also asked open-ended questions after each module and at the conclusion of the workshop, such as: "My most valuable takeaway from [today] or [the LTP workshop overall was]…" and "What content or exercise changes would you recommend [today] or [to the LTP workshop]?"

The Level 1 results showed that 95 percent of the overall ratings averaged between 4.5 and 5.0 consistently throughout the 44 sessions. Feedback was rigorously reviewed, and presenters and coaches who did not receive at least a 4.0 were replaced in future sessions. The daily feedback survey was the primary driver of formative evaluation for the workshop. Table 10-1 shows a sample of the questions asked each day for each module. The final daily ratings were used to obtain an overall session rating. The results reported on the evaluation scorecard show the cumulative session rating for all 44 sessions.

Table 10-1. Sample Workshop Daily Survey

LTP Workshop: Day 1 Modules	
Scale: 1=Strongly Disagree; 2=Disagree; 3=Neutral; 4=Agree; 5=Strongly Agree	
Industry Case Study	
1. This session provided insight on how I can actively engage at the CxO level with my customer.	4.44
2. The session provided insight on how I can more effectively present value to my customers.	4.63
3. The coaches provided helpful feedback.	4.11
Strategic Thinking	
4. Best-practice presentation #1 gave me ideas on how to apply what I learned in LTP to further the strategic direction of my account.	4.22
5. Best practice presentation #2 gave me ideas on how to apply what I learned in LTP to further the strategic direction of my account.	4.90
Financial Approach – Part 1	
6. This session helped me understand what executives care about, and the financial and business language most relevant to them.	4.61
7. This session enabled me to understand how key financial ratios are utilized by clients as part of their business-case evaluation of HP solutions.	4.71
8. This session gave further insight on how solutions can positively impact financial ratios and metrics.	4.79
9. The exercises were effective in demonstrating how to have a financially-focused discussion with an executive to position a business opportunity.	4.80
10. The coach's feedback was helpful in understanding how to have a C-level executive discussion.	4.69
11. The presenter was articulate and effective.	4.88
Overall	
12. The topics presented matched what I am expected to learn.	4.7
13. I gained new insights and takeaways that I can apply to my account.	4.56
Day 1 Summarized Rating	**4.62**

Level 2: Learning and Results

The LTP program required participants to validate accomplishment of learning objectives (Level 2) by demonstrating their skills during summative role plays which were rated by CxO coaches. Coaches evaluated each individual participant during exercises and in a capstone 10-minute customer-engagement role play. Prior to each session, the CxO coaches attended calibration meetings to benchmark ratings of structured performance criteria derived from competency descriptors.

Participants were rated on a five-point scale: outstanding (5), very strong (4), competent (3), underdeveloped (2), not developed (1). The coaches were also asked to make specific comments on areas for development.

Level 2 results found that 92 percent of the participants in the 44 workshops were rated "competent" or better in demonstrating the key competencies: executive engagement, consultative selling, and business, industry, and financial acumen. CxO coaches evaluated their competency based on AGM attainment of the following workshop learning objectives:

- creating and sustaining business relationships with C-level clients

- developing a deeper understanding of executive motivations, goals, and decision-making processes

- expanding fluency in the logic and language of business to collaborate with C-level executives on creating and executing strategies for mutual business benefit

- increasing ability to develop innovative ways to help clients improve their financial performance and align with their strategic objectives

- broadening ability to align HP's industry and horizontal solutions with client business needs

- applying industry, business, and financial acumen to developing, presenting, and defending compelling business cases.

Level 3: Application and Results

Post-workshop, the participants received four to six months of ongoing coaching. They were evaluated during four formal coaching checkpoints on their demonstrated progress in on-the-job application of the required competencies. The primary competency areas rated were the same as those for Level 2: industry, business, and financial acumen, consultative selling, and executive engagement. Coaches evaluated each participant using a five-point scale: outstanding (5), very strong (4), competent (3), underdeveloped (2), or not developed (1). At the end of the six-month process, CxO coaches provided an overall evaluation of each participant's progress and current state. Coach ratings were used as Level 3 evaluation data. The Level 3 results from 44 sessions showed that 97 percent of those who completed the checkpoint reviews received a rating of "competent" or better.

The executive review board provided additional Level 3 data. The board's evaluation criteria consisted of analyzing documented evidence of the participants' individual work in their accounts and demonstrated actual performance of their accounts. As a result, 90 percent of those who participated in the board review passed and received their certifications.

Phase 2: Evaluation Post-LTP Deployment

Phase 2 evaluation was conducted longitudinally at least three years post-LTP deployment. Two post-deployment evaluations were conducted; the LTP Business Impact Study, and a second analysis using the Executive Assessment data in an Executive Assessment Business Impact Analysis.

LTP Business Impact Study

Using a vendor-partner, HP conducted a Business Impact Study over a two-year post delivery period, one in 2009 and another in 2011. The study analyzed and collected data on Levels 1, 3, and 4 from participants who had taken LTP between 2004 and 2011. The study consisted of 80 subjects, 42 in 2009 and 38 in 2010. They were randomly selected from each two-year delivery period. Sampling factors were used to ensure representation from different vertical industries and geographies.

Level 1 of the LTP Business Impact Study collected data from "look-back" interviews regarding the workshop content relevance and the quality of the learning experience. Participants were asked to rate "the degree of relevance of the content to their work and work-related challenges" using a five-point scale: very relevant (5) to not relevant (1). The second question, "the degree of the quality of the learning experience," was also rated using a five-point scale: excellent learning experience (5) to poor learning experience (1).

Level 1 results of the Business Impact Study, in terms of content relevance, showed that 91 percent of the participants interviewed years later still rated the program as "very relevant." In terms of the quality of the learning experience, 89.5 percent rated the program an "excellent learning experience."

Sample participant comments included:

"The LTP training was probably the best training by far that I have had in my career at HP. Every single waking minute was spent on sharpening tools we had accumulated over the years."

"I rate it a six (on a five-point scale)! All 20 years of my training has been focused on products. LTP wasn't, which is why I thought this was exceptional and relevant to my work."

The Business Impact Study did not evaluate at Level 2. We did however conduct a Level 3 application of learning evaluation that consisted of a self-reported application of learned behaviors to job performance. The Business Impact Study asked participants, "Have you applied what you learned in the program back on your job?" The study captured participants' references to specific actions that indicated behavior change and application of learning. A total of 80 participants was interviewed for 30 to 45 minutes. Agreement with the following behavioral change statements is shown in Table 10-2.

Table 10-2. Business Impact Study, Level 3: Learning Transfer and Behavioral Changes
Specific Examples of Applying LTP Learning to Job
Established a longer-term, more strategic relationship with my client.
Utilized client industry knowledge to analyze client's strengths, weaknesses, opportunities, and threats relative to their competitors.
Formulated long-term strategies to maximize revenue/profit for HP and address client's KPIs.
Created and presented a compelling business case that addresses client's issues.
Confidently interacted with C-levels to address their business and technology challenges.
Influenced a CxO to request a proposal from HP.
Used the business framework to demonstrate value to clients.
Shifted to a financial acumen mindset.
Shared best practices from LTP.

Level 3 results used a five-point scale, strongly agree (5) to strongly disagree (1). The final results showed that 91 percent of participants "agree" or "strongly agree" (rating of 4 or greater) that they "have applied what they learned in LTP."

Level 4 evaluation consisted of extensive data collection and analysis of account performance from 80 AGMs. The data included analysis of sales revenue, sales pipeline of future revenue opportunities, and additional customer satisfaction metrics. It is this Level 4 analysis from which the quantitative business impact benefits noted on the talent management scorecard are summarized. Table 10-3 shows improved results in revenue, share of wallet, future sales opportunities, and customer loyalty indices attributed to the LTP program as compared to a control group. A separate set of financial proof cases cite examples of deals won and sales opportunities for 2009-2010. The overall tangible business impacts showed $640.1M in total deals closed and $1,085M in opportunity or anticipated revenue.

Executive Assessment Business Impact Analysis

The Executive Assessment was launched post-LTP deployment in 2009 and focused on Level 3 and Level 4 evaluations only. For the purposes of this case study, the Executive Assessment was used to validate the application of LTP competencies. In particular, the business-simulation role plays demonstrated Level 3 application in real business problem-solving situations. Individuals were rated on these demonstrations using scorecards.

Level 3 evaluation consisted of compiling the data from two of the reporting tools used during the Executive Assessment, the individual development scorecard and the account performance measures scorecard. The assessment, executed over several years post-LTP, demonstrated the sustainability of the learning acquired during the LTP program.

The individual development scorecard reported an overall assessment score for each participant. The score was derived from ratings of individual competencies demonstrated during the business simulation role-plays, as well as results of the 360-degree survey and the Hogan Personality Inventory. A separate development category rating was reported based on closing gaps in the competency ratings. Only the overall assessment score was used to compile group data on the Level 3 evaluation scorecard.

Table 10-3. Impact on Sales and Increased Sales Metrics	
Sales Metrics	Difference After LTP (LTP Participants vs. Non-Participants)
Customer Satisfaction	Improved by 0.5 points
Sales Performance	Greater quota attainment by 11.6 points
Share of Wallet	Share of wallet 3.5 points higher
Revenue Growth	Revenue growth 8.8 points higher

Financial Impact Directly Attributed to LTP by Participants				
Cases	2009 Deals Closed	2010 Deals Closed	2009 Opportunities in the Pipeline	2010 Opportunities in the Pipeline
Case 1		$10	$220.8M	$675M
Case 2	$59M	$8M		
Case 3	$100M	$150M	$5M	
Case 4	$13.8	$160		
Case 5		$70	$400M	
Case 6	$3M		$20M	
Case 7			$30M	
Case 8	$45M	$7.5M		$10M
Case 9	$2M	$11.8M		$400M
Total	$222.80	$417.3M	$675M	$410M
Grand Totals	$640.10M		$1,085M	

Analysis of the Level 3 results of the Executive Assessment selected 116 AGMs out of the possible 250 AGMs who completed the assessment.

As illustrated in Table 10-4, the assessment showed that 80 percent (93 participants) of those assessed had continued to demonstrate the LTP competencies at an effective level or above.

Table 10-4. Executive Assessment Competency Effectiveness Rating Results

Executive Assessment	AMS	APJ	EMEA	Total
Very Effective to Exceptional	0 (0%)	0 (0%)	0 (0%)	0 (0%)
Very Effective	4 (10%)	0 (0%)	10 (18%)	14 (12%)
Effective to Very Effective	8 (19%)	6 (32%)	21 (38%)	35 (30%)
Effective	19 (46%)	9 (47%)	16 (29%)	43 (37%)
Subtotals	31 (27%)	15 (13%)	47 (41%)	**93 (80%)**
Somewhat Effective to Effective	10 (24%)	3 (16%)	8 (14%)	22 (19%)
Somewhat Effective	0 (0%)	1 (5%)	1 (2%)	2 (2%)
Lower Than Somewhat Effective	0 (0%)	0 (0%)	0 (0%)	0 (0%)
Count (N)	41 (100%)	19 (100%)	56 (100%)	**116 (100%)**

Effectiveness Scale:

6= **Exceptionally Effective**—not a target for development

5= **Very Effective**—can benefit from minimal targeted development

4= **Effective**—will benefit from some targeted development

3= **Somewhat Effective**—moderate development needed

2= **Exceptionally Effective**—significant development needed

1= **Ineffective**—this is a critical development need

For Level 4 results, HP ran an analysis of the 116 AGMs who participated in the LTP and the Executive Assessment (the treatment group) compared to a control group of 150 AGMs. A deeper analysis was then conducted of those who completed LTP and the Assessment to determine the relationship to achieved business results.

The business-impact data analysis showed a 41 percent gap in total performance between those who completed LTP and the Assessment and those who did not complete either program. Total performance is defined as a combination of quantitative data, such as account measures, and qualitative data, such as having successfully completed LTP and post-workshop coaching.

The deeper secondary analysis of the treatment group showed a link to business results. AGMs with a higher total performance score (75-100) achieved 12 percent greater account revenue. These AGMs are differentiated by their performance on a set of key competencies developed through the LTP program.

AGMs scoring in the top range in the Executive Assessment were 12 percent more likely to have a higher total performance score of 75 to 100 (54.5 percent versus 42.6 percent). This difference is statistically significant ($p = .03$). Their assessment effectiveness ratings differentiated the top range from the baseline. Top performers on average produced 12 percent greater revenue, as shown in Table 10-5.

Table 10-5. Top-Range Performer Definition	
AGMs in Executive Assessment (Global N=108)	**Percentage**
Percentage of AGMs with a total performance score of 75-100 and who scored in the "effective or better" range on the Executive Assessment	54.5%
Percentage of AGMs with a total performance score of 75-100 (baseline)	42.6%
Difference	**+12%**

In summary, Table 10-6 depicts the full scope of evaluation techniques used in the initiatives described and the breadth of evaluation reporting across all levels.

Table 10-6. Summary of Methods by Evaluation Type

Level 1: Reaction	Level 2: Learning	Level 3: Application	Level 4: Business Impact	Intangible Benefits
LTP: feedback surveys BI: longitudinal interviews	LTP: skill and behavioral demonstration	LTP: CxO coach observation checkpoints LTP: executive review board BI: self report: longitudinal interviews EA: expert coach assessment	BI: individual account performance data: • sales impact data • sales metrics EA: sales measures top talent	• Participant comments • Manager comments • GPO productivity tools • Sales organization alignment on common sales practices and processes

Key: LTP: License to Practice, BI: Business Impact, EA: Executive Assessment

TM INITIATIVE MICRO SCORECARD

The goal of HP's talent management process was a fundamental shift in their approach to sales leadership. This was accomplished through selecting and preparing sales leaders to meet evolving customer needs. The TM scorecard, using the template suggested by Phillips and Schmidt (2004), brings together evidence that the systematic processes underlying the talent management initiatives, specifically the LTP program, drove the required behavioral changes that resulted in tangible business benefits.

The Level 1 reaction data focused on content relevancy and the daily classroom surveys, which captured at-the-moment reaction. In the Business Impact Study, a separate set of longitudinal Level 1 data also showed that LTP stood the test of time years after AGMs participated in the program. The data showed that both the application of LTP competencies in the field and the LTP content were relevant for the AGM job, and that it was a quality learning experience.

Table 10-7. TM Initiative Micro Scorecard

Talent Management Initiative: Leadership Development

Program Name: License to Practice (LTP)

Target Audience: Global Account General Managers (Directors and VPs)

Program Duration: Over 2-3 year period:
- LTP Workshop: 60 hours (includes post-workshop periodic checkpoints)
- Certification and Board Review: 4-6 hours
- Executive Assessment: 18.5 hours

Number of Attendees:
- 1500 since inception in 2004
- Sample of 116 participants who attended LTP between 2009-2011 participated in a longitudinal assessment (Executive Assessment), as a validation of sustained/improved competence

Business Objectives:
- Double account growth over 3-year period
  - » Increase Share of Wallet (SOW) (an account revenue to account $ opportunity ratio)
  - » Improve account performance (customer satisfaction, quota attainment, revenue growth, portfolio deal size)
- Significantly increase customer satisfaction measures

		Results		
Reaction	Learning	Application	Tangible Benefits	Intangible Benefits
Level 1	**Level 2**	**Level 3**	**Level 4**	**Participants and Managers of AGMs reported:**
Workshop: 95% rated daily sessions 4.6 or higher on 5 pt. scale	Workshop: 92% rated competent in demonstrating end-of-workshop	Post-Workshop: 97% rated competent on application of LTP competencies to account, a rating of 3 or above (scored by coach observation of behavior)	LTP Business Impact Study: Impact on Sales: • $640.1M deals closed directly attributed to skills attained during LTP.	• Improved retention of top performers.

Business Impact Study: (Longitudinal) Content Relevance: 91% rated LTP program "very relevant to their work and work-related challenges" a rating of 4 or better on a 5-point scale Quality of Learning Experience: 89.5% rated LTP program "excellent learning experience," a rating of 5 on a 5-point scale.	performance-based objectives, a rating of 3 or better on 5-point scale	Review Board: 90% of participants who applied for certification were passed by an executive review board. Business Impact: 91% reported strongly agree they "have applied what they learned from participating in the program to "back on the job" Executive Assessment: Executive Assessment validated achievement of LTP performance objectives with 93 of 116 participants (80%) providing ratings of effective or better in demonstrating application of job skills and competencies.	• $1,085M in pipeline opportunity (anticipated revenue) attributed to LTP Increased sales metrics (2009-2011): • Customer satisfaction improved by 0.5 points (on 10-point scale). • Sales performance (quota attainment) improved by 11.6 points. • Share of Wallet (ratio of revenue to total addressable market) improved by 4 points. • Revenue growth by 8.8 points. Executive Assessment Business Impact Analysis validated the impact of applying LTP competencies on Account Sales Revenue Performance: Top-Range Performers achieved a12% higher account revenue.	• Enhanced CxO and client relationships. • Improved customer satisfaction. • Enhanced sales performance and revenue. • Improved account team productivity. • Improved employee morale.

Technique to Isolate Effects of Program: Participant perception, expert observation (coaches), executive board review of actual strategic account growth. Demonstration before the board of consultative selling skills, executive engagement, business/financial acumen. The Business Impact Study used a control group to determine differences in account measures. In the Executive Assessment, the analysis used a control group and compared them against a treatment group (116 AGMs) to assess differences.

Technique to Convert Data to Monetary Value: Reported sales organization financial results per account.

Fully-Loaded Program Costs: N/A

Barriers to Application of Skills: • Management alignment of LTP tools, processes, and performance expectations
• Limited exposure across HP business units to LTP strategic tools and concepts   • Non-alignment of cross-business unit sales metrics
• Quarterly focus on product sales numbers rather than on long-term strategic engagements
• HP incentive system that incentivizes specialists to sell "point product"

Recommendations: Continue program as designed. Increase focus on developing sales management and extended account team members to support desired performance. Build sustaining competency and professional growth initiatives as a continuation of the program.

Level 2 evaluation demonstrated that LTP was successful in creating competent AGMs before they left the classroom. What could not get teased out of the Level 2 evaluation was the effectiveness of the instructional design strategy to create long-lasting mastery of new skills and knowledge. These data had to be gathered later. When participants left LTP, data showed they accomplished what was expected, which was "demonstrating behavioral changes that enabled AGMs to build value-based executive relationships." Sustaining and building on this to grow successful careers is the purpose of the TM process.

The real TM story begins to unfold at Level 3. Overall, there were four types of Level 3 evaluation built into the program: 1) post-workshop CxO coaching checkpoints; 2) an account review before an executive review board that the participant either passed or failed; 3) the Business Impact Study self-report interviews, and 4) the Executive Assessment center analysis of competency demonstration during a business simulation.

The use of during-deployment and post-deployment evaluation techniques (Phases 1 and 2), showed that skill and knowledge acquisition stood the test of time and AGMs continued to apply them to improve job competencies and account performance.

Lastly, Level 4 evaluation showed AGMs improved as a result of LTP, even after several years, as demonstrated using real account data and financial results. The ability to conduct a Level 4 evaluation was made possible by a strong partnership and collaboration between sales operations, HR, and L&D.

The evolution of evaluation techniques ensured that the leadership development program dynamically improved as participants continually applied what they had learned, resulting in positive business outcomes for HP.

CONCLUSIONS

The enterprise sales organization came to HR and L&D to help them transform the salesforce. HR and L&D built a comprehensive TM strategy based on HP's business goals and measures. The TM strategy ensured that HP had the talent with the requisite skills, knowledge, and behaviors to achieve the business goals. The success of the LTP leadership development initiative changed the practice of selling value to customers and significantly "changed the game" for HP. The end-to-end talent management process, with LTP as a cornerstone of the HP sales transformation, created a repeatable set of best practices that AGMs used to improve account performance. LTP established core competencies that, when applied, had a significant measurable business impact.

Qualitative results that were collected from the Business Impact Study included best practices such as AGMs creating new customer relationships at the highest level of decision makers, improved account team productivity, greater employee morale, and greater retention of top performers.

It is with this result that HP business leaders continue to invite HR and L&D to the table as an equal partner in shaping the future of the company.

ABOUT THE AUTHORS

Cynthia Dibble is an independent consultant and assists organizations through major transitions. She focuses on developing business strategy and then aligning it with talent management and leadership development initiatives to drive change and performance outcomes. In addition to long-time client Hewlett-Packard, she has worked for the U.S. Government Defense Contracts Management Agency, Raytheon, AT&T, and Fidelity Investments. She has an MBA from the Simmons School of Management, an EdD in instructional media and technologies from Boston University, and an MS in journalism. She is also a proud FAA-licensed private pilot.

Barbra Sher is a Global Program Manager at Hewlett Packard in the Corporate Learning & Development Strategy Group, where she focuses on career planning and talent development. Previously, she worked with the Global Sales function enabling the talent management initiatives supporting HP's sales transformation. Barbra started her career at Digital Equipment Corporation, leading large change initiative programs in the services business unit. Barbra has focused on management development, sales leadership, and change management, developing strong partnerships with business unit leaders, HR, and L&D.

Barbra has won numerous awards for her work over the years. In 2011, she and her team accepted an award from ASTD for the License to Practice program. She has an MS in curriculum design and a BS in biology. In her spare time, she serves on the board of a nonprofit and volunteers at a free medical clinic in her community.

REFERENCES

Hogan, R., and J. Hogan. (1995). *Hogan Personality Inventory Manual*. Tulsa, OK: Hogan Assessment Systems.

Kirkpatrick, D.L. (1998). *Evaluating Leadership Development Programs: The Four Levels*, 2nd edition. San Francisco, CA: Berrett-Koehler.

Phillips, J.J., and L. Schmidt. (2004). *The Leadership Scorecard*. Burlington, MA; Elsevier Butterworth-Heinemann.

11

MEASURING THE IMPACT OF LEADERS
TEACHING LEADERS

Ellie Gates

INTRODUCTION

This case study demonstrates the impact of placing seasoned leaders into formal teaching roles. By sharing challenges and best practices, leaders can improve the consistency of management operations and productivity and engagement levels of both managers and their direct teams.

BACKGROUND

Adobe Systems, Inc. is a 30-year-old high-tech company with more than 10,000 employees, headquartered in San Jose, California. Adobe is the global leader in digital marketing and digital media solutions. The company's tools and services enable customers to create groundbreaking digital content, deploy it across media and devices, measure and optimize it over time, and achieve greater business success. Adobe helps customers make, manage, measure, and monetize their digital content across every channel and screen.

Like most high-tech companies, innovation and employee engagement are business imperatives. Research on employee engagement throughout the last decade has proven that people managers have the greatest impact in creating an environment of innovation, where co-workers connect, exchange ideas, and are willing to try new ways of working. The willingness of leaders to connect with other leaders and share lessons learned is critical to increasing their teams' innovation and productivity.

Many companies are adopting a model that encourages senior leaders to share their experiences in the classroom, in lieu of or in addition to having human resources (HR) representatives lead the discussion. Connecting seasoned leaders with emerging leaders in a shared learning experience improves individual management skills and builds collaborative relationships across the business, impacting both productivity and innovation.

Adobe provides many opportunities for leaders to teach in signature learning programs. For instance, the Adobe Leader Experience (ALE) and Adobe Business Leader (ABL) programs involve some of the most senior leaders in the organization. These executives are paired with external professors and consultants to teach aspiring broad-based leaders how to improve their business acumen, critical thinking, global mindset, personal leadership, and customer focus.

TALENT MANAGEMENT INITIATIVE

The Management Essentials (ME) program targets broad-based front-line, mid-level, and senior managers globally. The program consists of four full days of training that is organized into two two-day sessions. Leaders-as-teachers is a core element of the program, requiring a commitment of over 40 hours to teaching and mentoring a small cohort of leaders through the entire program. These ME leaders share their best practices and real-world examples, and help small groups of six to eight participants find solutions to core management problems. The program is taught by an external professional facilitator and an HR partner with strong organizational development or business partnering experience. While the facilitators share the core models with the class, the ME leaders conduct nearly 50 percent of the discussion. Prework and an applied learning assignment are also key components of the program to reduce lecture time and increase application of skills learned. The design of the ME program is illustrated in Figure 11-1.

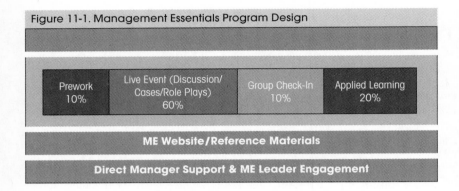

Figure 11-1. Management Essentials Program Design

Topics and areas for development are limited to a "critical few"; each day focuses on only three to four key concepts. Initial program content was pulled from Managing for Peak Performance (MPP), an internally developed management development course. The first modules in the pilot were built from the redesigned MPP content; however, learning effectiveness was increased by expanding both content and design. Additional topics were derived from the results of a needs assessment that occurred after the first pilot launched in July 2010. Figure 11-2 illustrates the full content covered in the program.

Needs Assessment Methodology and Results

In order to ensure adequate representation across the global management population, a proportionate worldwide sample group of managers were included in the survey. The sample group represented approximately 10 percent of the total management population and consisted of front-line managers, senior managers, directors, plus a small number of senior directors and vice presidents (VPs).

The needs assessment consisted of 18 questions to identify the remaining content areas for the ME program along with validation or suggested improvements on the design. Out of the 132 targeted participants, 67 percent (89) responded to the survey.

Figure 11-2. Management Essentials Program Content

	Management Essentials Overview: Two, Two-Day Sessions			
	Session 1		Session 2	
Module	Day 1 INTELLIGENT LEADERSHIP	Day 2 TALENT LEADERSHIP	Day 1 MANAGING EXCEPTIONAL RESULTS	Day 2 DEVELOPING SUCCESSFUL EMPLOYEES
Lead to Win Anchor	People & Personal Leadership	People & Results Leadership	Thought & Results Leadership	People Leadership
Topics Covered	• Leadership @ Adobe • Functions of Leadership • Leading with Emotional Intelligence • Managing Differences (SKI)	• Adobe's Talent Mindset • Creating a Great Interview Experience • Setting Your Employees Up for Success	• Making and Communicating Powerful Decisions • Using Delegation to Grow Talent and Get Results	• Effectively Giving and Receiving Feedback • The Power of Appreciation • Developing Yourself and Your Team
	PreWork, Discussion, Peer Connect, & Applied Learning			

Survey participants answered many questions about their learning needs and challenges as a people manager. Answers to two open-ended questions were top priority. These were:

- What are your primary challenges as a people manager?

- List your top three development needs as a people manager.

In order to capture the full spectrum of challenges and needs, respondents were not limited to a single response for each question, but were encouraged to list as many challenges and needs as applied. Table 11-1 illustrates the most prevalent topics which emerged from the open-ended questions.

Table 11-1. Identified Challenges and Development Needs

Primary Challenges	% Listed as Top Management Challenge	# Respondents Listed as Top Challenge n=62	Top Development Needs	% Listed as One of the Top 3 Development Needs	# of Respondents Listed in Top 3 n=98
Developing employees	29%	18	Feedback, coaching, and conflict management	32%	20
Motivating, inspiring, and rewarding employees	23%	14	Motivation, career, and employee development	31%	19
Delegation and decision making	16%	10	Execution, prioritization, expectation, goal setting, and time management	29%	18
Performance management	15%	9	Delegation, decision making	19%	12
Goal setting and prioritization	15%	9	Managing up	18%	11
Influence/ managing up	11%	7	Ownership/ accountability	16%	10
Feedback and coaching	11%	7	Trust and building relationships	13%	8
n=108 total responses *			n=135 total responses *		

Notes:

*Total responses varied due to open-ended questions and the *n* is listed for each above.

*All other responses represented less than 10% and weren't listed.

*n=62 respondents against open-ended questions. Variance for column on the right is they listed up to three needs in their response.

Questions on the survey targeted how the respondents preferred to learn in order to validate the learning design as well as determine methods to solicit the highest engagement from managers. Survey participants were asked to force-rank their most-preferred, preferred, and least-preferred learning methods. As a result, hands-on projects and experimentation were added to the design of Applied Learning Assignments to increase the synthesis and application of the participants' learning. Table 11-2 shows managers' top learning preferences.

Table 11-2. Managers' Learning Preferences

Rank	Preferred Learning Style	% Ranked Style as Preferred or Most Preferred	# of Respondents Ranked as Preferred or Most Preferred n=62*
1	Working on a hands-on project	53%	33
2	Experimentation (trying something new and learning from mistakes)	48%	30
3	Talking to others	32%	20
4	Reading materials	27%	17
5	Watching someone do it	23%	14

Note: *121 total responses (n=62 respondents with two ranked choices for preferred method)

Lastly, survey participants were asked to pick their top seven learning modalities preferences. A strong preference for coaching, case studies, and learning from others in discussion groups emerged as key components for the program. As a result, managers who participate in the program are asked to complete prework that involves reviewing real-world case studies and participating in coaching sessions with the ME Leader (MEL) and their small groups. Table 11-3 ranks the preferences on learning modalities across all survey respondents.

Rank	Preferred Learning Style	% Ranking Most Preferred in Top 7	# of Respondents Ranking in Top 7 n=62*
1	Coaching	50%	55
2	Case studies	48%	55
3	Leaders teaching leaders	40%	59
4	Discussion groups	40%	59
5	Trial and error	27%	60
6	Knowledge-sharing forums	27%	69
7	Books	27%	72

Table 11-3. Top Preferred Learning Modalities for ME Program

Note: *429 total responses (n=62 respondents with 7 ranked choices for learning style)

Design

The initial pilot consisted of six modules, which were consolidated to the current four modules in 2012 (illustrated previously in Figure 11-2). The current program runs for four months with six to eight weeks between sessions, allowing participants time to complete the applied learning assignment and receive coaching from their managers.

While ME effectively trains front-line, mid-level, and senior managers, another valuable benefit is the learning the senior leaders receive both from the core content as well as through the experience gained by serving as teachers in the program. Once an MEL has successfully led a local program, they have opportunities to expand their personal influence and global literacy by leading programs in other countries.

In addition to their personal preparation, the MELs attend a one-hour training prior to each session that is conducted by the program manager and facilitator(s). At this time they are assigned areas of focus. In the classroom, MELs guide participants through a discussion of the real-world application of each model and challenge assumptions about their own case studies. Two important management skills—coaching and storytelling—are culti- vated through this process. Storytelling also embeds core concepts, increases consistency in management practices, and shortens the learning curve for other leaders by using examples of what to do and what not to do to get results.

Another important element of leadership is vulnerability. MELs are asked to share openly, to the degree they are comfortable, their own challenges, areas of development, and lessons learned through trial and error. Building community requires trust and vulnerability. This modeling by MELs deepens the conversation, turning failure into a teaching tool. This sharing also promotes trying new things, being innovative, taking risks, and learning from mistakes.

The impact of leaders sharing their experiences is widespread. The real-life examples and open exchange allows participants to examine their own views and consciously continue with the same methods, or adopt new beliefs and methods that are more beneficial in solving their managerial challenges. This "vertical learning" is a benefit of leaders teaching other leaders, as they can directly challenge each other's opinions and practices in a more powerful way than an HR facilitator can. Additional benefits include increased managerial effectiveness, personal engagement, and satisfaction with the organization. Measurement clearly illustrates the value of this aspect of the program. Finally, through building community among leaders, a shared vernacular develops and common frameworks and approaches become more widespread, making teamwork, collaboration, and innovation more prevalent across the organization.

Since launching in 2010, 49 percent of all front-line, mid- and senior-level people managers worldwide at Adobe have attended the program, and more than 200 senior leaders have volunteered their time to serve as MELs. It is expected that up to 80 percent will have participated by the end of 2013. This level of participation has driven exceptional results across the business in several key areas. While the micro talent management scorecard clearly illustrates the quantifiable measures of the program, an additional benefit is that managers "pass it on" by teaching the content to their managers and their teams. In this way, leaders and employees who do not directly participate in the program are also benefiting.

EVALUATION METHODOLOGY AND RESULTS

The results of the ME program are measured in several ways. Jack Phillips (Phillips, 2003) identified several levels of evaluation for learning programs. The micro scorecard introduced by Phillips and Schmidt (Phillips and Schmidt, 2004) depicts all five levels for measurement as well as intangible benefits in one succinct format. All results for ME are summarized in this scorecard format in Table 10-6 at the end of the chapter.

Satisfaction (Level 1)

Adobe asked 10 core questions to assess the effectiveness of the ME program. This is in addition to nine questions that are common across all of the learning programs at the company. The survey is administered by a third-party vendor and captures both quantitative and qualitative data. It also captures direct feedback on the effectiveness of the facilitator and ME leader. This feedback is shared with the facilitators and ME Leaders for their own development.

On average, 45 percent of participants respond to the evaluations. Scores measuring content, learning modality, and facilitator effectiveness have been high, averaging 4.2 or higher out of 5.0 over the life of the program. In 2012, the program underwent a significant redesign aimed at simplifying content and materials, and scores ticked up slightly +.2 as a result. The three modules pulled from the program will be redesigned into a higher-level learning experience for directors and above. Additionally, a new module, based on the internally developed Hiring Essentials (HE) program and focused on expanding capabilities in Talent Leadership, was added to the ME program. Overall, the top results based on participant evaluations are:

- This learning experience was a worthwhile investment in my career development (4.6/5.0).

- I would recommend this session to a co-worker (4.6/5.0).

- I will apply the knowledge and skills I learned to my job (4.6/5.0).

The strength of these results reinforce the relevancy of the content, the modalities of the learning experience, and the impact of leaders teaching leaders. Figure 11-3 illustrates the results of all 10 core questions and each module by geographic venue.

Figure 11-3. 2012 Management Essentials Program Metrics

Overall Program Evaluation Scores Across All modules & Regions

Top 3 Questions (4.6/5.0): Worthwhile Career Investment, High Net Promoter; Applicable Skills

Overall Effectiveness	2012
1. This learning experience was a worthwhile investment in my career development.	4.6
2. This learning experience increased my effectiveness as a manager.	4.3
3. I would recommend this session to a co-worker.	4.6

Skill Impact	2012
4. I will apply the knowledge and skills I learned to my job.	4.6
5. I learned new knowledge and skills from this program.	4.4

Leaders Teaching Leaders	2012
6. The contributions from Adobe Leaders increased my learning.	4.4
7. The ME Leaders provided valuable, practical, insights.	4.2
8. The ME Leaders created a safe environment for discussion and questioning.	4.4

Community	2012
9. My colleagues helped me learn more than I could on my own.	4.5
10. I have built a stronger network/community as a result of this program.	4.2

Average across each Cohort		BEIJING	EAST COAST	EMEA	INDIA	OREM	SAN JOSE	SEATTLE	SYDNEY	TOKYO	Overall
2012	Module 1	4.40	4.24	4.30	4.32	4.63	4.44	4.15	4.21	4.47	4.35
2012	Module 2	4.42	4.54	4.24	4.39	4.68	4.48	N/A*	4.14	4.36	4.41
2012	Module 3	4.63	4.40	4.28	4.71	4.63	4.56	4.60	4.11	4.53	4.55
2012	Module 4	4.70	4.40	4.39	4.26	4.68	4.52	4.45	4.11	4.56	4.49

*Insufficient n to score

Qualitative feedback about the effectiveness of the ME Leaders reinforced the impact of sharing real-world examples and being vulnerable enough to admit when they don't know everything.

Learning (Level 2)

Each module of the ME program presents participants with two options to apply their learning back on the job. Participants are asked to select an applied learning assignment and execute it prior to their group check-in six to eight weeks after each session concludes. Many of these assignments are woven into the class activities so that the participants can apply key learning when they return to their jobs. In the pilot version of the ME program, accountability for completing learning assignments was not measured. However, in the 2012 redesign, the group check-in component was added to deepen community connections and increase accountability.

Application (Level 3)

Participants and their direct managers are also asked to complete a pre-assessment evaluating their current proficiency levels against key skills and behaviors taught in the program. These competency areas are measured to identify growth resulting from participation in the program. Results of the pre-assessment are provided to the participants to help them focus their learning at the beginning of the program and to identify areas where they may wish to get greater clarification from their managers.

Participants and managers also complete a post-assessment within 60 days of the last session. It's important to note that this element of the program has been very difficult to administer, resulting in a more limited data set.

Managers and participants who complete the pre- and post-surveys report significant improvement in the skills and behaviors taught in the ME Program. Participants report a 40 percent increase in skills, while direct managers report a slightly greater improvement at 44 percent. These improvements are much higher than the standard 10 percent retention of learning following an instructor-led program.

Participants who were newer to the role of managing people showed the greatest increases. Their pre-assessment scores were also generally lower to begin with as they rated themselves mostly at a two or three out of five (one being the lowest; five the highest). However, an interesting trend emerged of more tenured managers downgrading their competency scores on the post-assessment survey. Most of these seasoned managers who were participants in the program scored themselves lower, taking their scores down from fives to fours to threes across different areas. More research is needed to confirm exactly why that is the case. However, a reasonable hypothesis is that after completing the program the managers became more aware of their need for continued development. Self-awareness as a leader is one of the key concepts taught in ME. What is also fascinating to note is that in nearly 90 percent of cases in which the participants downgraded themselves, their direct managers' evaluation of their proficiencies was higher from pre- to post-skills surveys.

Case in Point (Level 4)

An example of a tangible result from the ME program is a breakthrough product innovation which was sparked from a discussion between a participant and his MEL, with a little inspiration from Shantanu Narayen, the company's CEO, who dropped in on the class and spoke about the importance of placing focus on creating the future.

Luc L., an engineering manager on the Acrobat® and Reader® Engineering team, had just worked with the Three Functions of Leadership model, adapted from the work of Stafford Beer. This model states that all functions of leadership can be broken into three core areas of focus: "Managing the Present," "Nurturing Identity," and "Creating the Future." The challenge is that most managers are consumed by managing the present and spend very little time creating the future, let alone nurturing the talents and capabilities of their teams. As Luc and his colleagues wrestled through the activity with their MEL and discussed how to shift behaviors to focus more on "Nurturing Identity" and "Creating the Future," the MEL shared a simple application she had learned as an alum of the program. She shared how she began color-coding her calendar by the three designations, picking one color for each and then reviewing how she had spent her time each week.

Luc latched onto this idea and began implementing it immediately, choosing blue for managing the present. The first week, he realized his calendar was nearly all blue. He decided to make "Creating the Future" a priority and added two-hour blocks of "Create the Future" time on the calendar to move forward on a special project on "PDF Actions in the Cloud."

He also delegated nearly one-third of his workload to two of the top performers on his team. A few short months later, Luc and his team delivered one of the important new features of Acrobat XI. The ME program can be credited with influencing the business through this example.

Direct Employee Feedback and Engagement Results
Obtaining direct feedback from teams is the best way to measure management effectiveness. Adobe conducts an anonymous company-wide engagement survey to do just that. In October 2012, the results of ME participants and MELs were measured against non-ME managers to isolate the effect of the program on leadership effectiveness.

The engagement survey measures an employee's engagement or satisfaction with the company and her confidence in her manager's abilities. Research on employee engagement has revealed that engaged employees are more willing to go the extra mile in their roles, are more productive, and show greater commitment to the organization.

Table 11-4 illustrates the increased satisfaction and confidence levels across all dimensions measured in the survey.

Table 11-4. Management Essentials Participants Engagement Survey Results

	Adobe OVERALL	Non-ME Managers BASELINE Variance From Company Results	ME Participant Variance From Company Results	ME Leader Variance From Company Results	Alum ME Leaders Variance From Company Results
Participation		-	+2	+4	+4
Engagement		-2	+3	+6	+11
Management Effectiveness		-2	+3	+1	+6
Expectations		-3	+5	+10	+15
Feedback		-1	+4	+4	+15
Growth and Development		-3	+5	+4	+12
Manager Capabilities		-4	+3	-2	+5
Strategy		-	+2	+8	+9
Culture		-	+1	+4	+8

Both ME participants and MELs showed great increases when compared to non-participants in several areas. Of particular note are the "Manager Effectiveness" and "Manager Capabilities" areas, which are designed to measure a manager's effectiveness in leading her team. When combined with the "Feedback," "Expectations," and "Growth and Development" dimensions, a full picture of managerial effectiveness emerges.

Both ME participants and ME Leaders had higher personal engagement scores in nearly every area. However, the greatest surprise in these results was the dramatic increase in personal engagement across all dimensions from the ME Leaders who were also previous alums of the program. While participants experienced an increase in personal engagement of +3, ME leaders were double at +6, and ME Leaders who were previously alums nearly doubled other ME leaders at +11. Additionally, the alum ME Leaders scored two to three times higher than other participants in the key areas of "Feedback," "Expectations," and "Growth and Development" (+15, +15, and +12 respectively).

While the personal engagement of the ME participants is high, the impact their participation in the program is having on the engagement scores of their direct reports is more important. Table 11-5 illustrates the results by geography of ME participants' direct reports' engagement scores.

Table 11-5. Management Essentials Participants' Direct Reports' Engagement Results

	BASELINE Non-ME Participant Managers' Direct Reports Scores	Overall ME Participant Variance	JPAC ME Participant Variance	EMEA ME Participant Variance	INDIA ME Participant Variance
Engagement		+3	+4	-1	+1
Management Effectiveness		+2	+8	+2	+6
Manager Capabilities		+3	+10	+5	+8
Expectations		+1	+6	-1	+5
Feedback		+4	+7	+5	+10
Growth and Development		+4	+8	+7	+7
Strategy		+4	+5	+2	+3
Culture		-	+1	-	+3

With the exception of the European region (EMEA), the company's engagement survey results showed that direct reports of ME participants were statistically higher in nearly every category over those who did not have managers who participated in the ME program. The variance in EMEA may be attributed to a more conservative culture that tends to rate lower on surveys overall. However, in other regions such as JPAC, which includes Japan, India, and Greater China, the results showed a significant increase over non-participant's scores, especially in the areas of Management Capabilities and Manager Effectiveness (+10 and +8 respectively). These results clearly illustrate that managers who invest in ME are becoming more effective people managers.

Intangible Benefits

The ME program has also resulted in some unexpected benefits. Loyalty to Adobe is higher among participants—nearly 40 percent of managers who have completed the program intend to remain with Adobe for five or more years, which is almost 3 percent more than those who have not attended the program.

Additionally, the ME program has become a movement within the company. Not only are managers teaching content to their leaders and other teams outside the program, they are excited about the results and knocking down the door to get more involved. They've asked to continue meeting, and as a result, Adobe will be building a new alumni community called the Adobe Leadership X-Change (ALX), knitting together alumni from all three signature learning programs—ALE, ABL, and ME—in order to continue their development outside the classroom. Also, participants are asking how they can come back and serve as MELs, even picking up international travel expenses in their business unit for this opportunity.

The program also has great brand value, internally and externally. Bersin & Associates recognized the program with a featured case study focused on transforming learning (May 2011) and the organizational development and learning team won recognition as the "Best Learning Team 2011" from Brandon Hall.

In addition to hard numbers, leaders investing in leaders builds managerial effectiveness across the broader teams. One MEL's passion and support for the program has resulted in some of the highest engagement scores across his entire business unit, with over half of his managers scoring 90 percent or higher on Manager Effectiveness.

As mentioned earlier, Adobe's business is split into two main areas, digital media and digital marketing. A core function across both organizations is the media and digital marketing team led by Mikel C. He leads a team of more than 100 marketers and is responsible for running Adobe.com; turning leads for Adobe products into sales opportunities for the sales teams; and creating media campaigns to promote products such as Adobe Marketing Cloud™ and Adobe Creative Cloud™.

Mikel is an avid student of leadership development and became an early stakeholder in ME as one of the first ME Leaders to launch the pilot program in 2010. After participating as a ME leader, Mikel required all of his people managers to complete the program. Additionally, he introduced activities such as book clubs, skip levels, and management off-sites, all focused on deepening understanding and application of core management concepts.

Two years later, his team has one of the highest engagement scores across the entire marketing division, at +13 above the company overall and a Management Effectiveness score of +7 above the company results. What may be even more impressive is that seven of his managers are ranked in the top 10 percent of all managers in the business unit (74 overall) across all management dimensions.

TM INITIATIVE MICRO SCORECARD

Measuring the impact of leaders teaching leaders can be challenging. The micro talent management scorecard, as illustrated in Table 11-6, captures the true value of the program in a succinct format, displaying results for all four levels of evaluation.

Determining how to represent business impact is an important decision. The ME program focuses on how leaders teaching leaders increases consistency in practice, management effectiveness, and engagement both for managers themselves and for their teams. This results directly in increased productivity of both managers and employees. Increased productivity has been a proven outcome among those with higher engagement scores. ME has positively affected both the engagement scores of ME participants, MELs, and the direct reports or employees of ME participants. This increased productivity translated to $17.3 million worth of benefit to the organization based on the following assumptions:

Table 11-6. TM Initiative Micro Scorecard

Project Title: Management Essentials Program

Target Audience: Front-line, Mid-level, and Senior Managers

Number of Attendees: 867

Duration: 4 days

Business Objectives: Increase management capability, increase employee enagement and discretionary contributions, retention

Satisfactions	Learning	Application	Results		Intangible Benefits
			Tangible Benefits		
Level 1	**Level 2**	**Level 3**	**Level 4**		Increased intent to stay with the ogranization for five or more years (39.25% ME participants vs. 36.7% non ME participants)
89% average overall rating globally	Applied learning assignments were given and ME Leaders held check-ins to evaluate learning but no formal metrics were gathered from these check-ins. *Measured in 2012 only	Participants of the ME program reported increased effectiveness across 39.5% of all managerial skills taught in the ME program. Direct managers of participants reported a higher increase in effectiveness across 44% of all managerial skills taught in the ME program.	• Increase in participant and direct report's engagement resulting in increased contribution and productivity • Managers: two hours more productive a week ($6.5M) • Direct reports of participants: one hour more productive a week ($10.8M)		
			Level 5		ME had become a movement resulting in leaders teaching content to others outside the program and their willingness to pick up international travel expenses to serve in the program.
			• Sum: Benefits ($17.3M)– Program Costs ($3M) / Program costs($3M) * 100=476%		
					Increased brand value for the program and Adobe internally and externally through recognition by key industry analysts such as Bersin & Brandon Hall.

Technique to Isolate Effects of Program:

Participant, manager, and direct report reported observations. Also comparing ME participants vs. non-participant control groups across core measurements.

Technique to Convert Data to Monetary Impact:

% of an average salary against increased productivity measures of both managers and employees. This is based on employee engagement research on the increased contributions and productivity of more highly engaged employees.

Fully-Loaded Program Costs:

~$3M program to date (cost of program build, facilitation, venues, travel, salaries of participants, cost of evaluation, overhead of L&D staff)

Barriers to Application of Skills:

Time demands on managers

Recommendations:

Program to continue to be delivered as designed with a greater emphasis on globally leveraging alumni as leaders, both for development experience for the leaders and increased impact on personal engagement

- Managers' increased engagement increases productivity a minimum of two hours or more a week. This could easily be higher as illustrated by Luc L.'s case study. This extra productivity is gained through effective delegation and fuller utilization of managers' teams. Calculating this extra two hours a week results in an added $6.5 million in revenue.

- ME participants have been proven to impact the engagement scores of their employees as evidenced by the 2012 engagement survey. Assuming that these employees are also more productive by just one hour more per week, this results in an added $10.8 million in revenue.

- Fully-loaded program costs include the cost to design and develop the program; all materials provided to each participant; cost for the instructor and facilitator, including preparation as well as delivery time; cost for the venue and facilities where the program is taught; average salaries for participants and leaders for duration of the program; administrative and overhead costs of the leadership development function; and cost of the program evaluation. Fully-loaded costs to date are approximately $3,000,000.

  » ROI (%) = Sum (Program Benefits - Program Costs) / Program Costs x 100
  » ROI (%) = Sum (17,300,000 - 3,000,000) / 3,000,000 x 100 = 476%

CONCLUSIONS

The ME program has a substantial impact on participants, their direct reports, and those teaching as ME Leaders. Measuring the full impact is critical to ensuring continued investment and sponsorship in the company. It is important to anchor leaders' participation in the program to tangible measurements, such as employee engagement and management effectiveness. In addition, it's critical to identify and build mechanisms to capture both qualitative and quantitative measures of success in order to showcase the full impact of these development initiatives.

The micro scorecard template is a tool that allows leaders to measure all aspects of the program's impact, from initial participant satisfaction to business impact. Here are a few suggestions on how to effectively implement a methodology to measure the impact of learning initiatives:

- Determine the desired business impact and participant needs through completing an in-depth needs assessment.

- Measure and optimize all learning modalities to drive greatest adoption and application of content. This includes blending content and applied activities with leader engagement.

- Measure smaller aspects of key programs. Use analytic tools to measure downloads of prework, sharing of articles, and so forth, in order to identify which content is resonating and the impact of the materials outside the classroom.

- Measure all levels of learning using the micro learning scorecard in order to succinctly tell the full story.

- Use a control group to illustrate differences between those who participate in the programs and those who do not.

ABOUT THE AUTHOR

Ellie Gates is the director of managerial effectiveness at Adobe. She has a great passion for inspiring, coaching, and developing others to achieve break-through leadership. Ellie has more than 20 years of experience working in leadership positions across HR consulting, organizational development, and talent management with small business and Fortune 500 companies, including Microsoft, T-Mobile, Pitney Bowes Management Services, and MCI Telecommunications. She is a lifelong learner and has earned master's degrees in organizational leadership and business administration. She loves being creative through music, art, and photography. Ellie resides in Salt Lake City, Utah, with her husband and three children.

REFERENCES

Phillips, J.J. (2003). *Return on Investment in Training and Performance*. Burlington, MA: Elsevier Butterworth-Heinemann.

Phillips, J.J., and L. Schmidt. (2004). *The Leadership Scorecard*. Burlington, MA: Elsevier Butterworth-Heinemann.

12

ACCELERATING GLOBAL MILLENNIALS TOWARD FUTURE LEADERSHIP

Glem Dias
Eileen Springer

INTRODUCTION

This case study demonstrates how a CEO-sponsored, global high-potential leadership development program with a robust 18-month roadmap can be measured for impact. It outlines components of the road map that include the social media platform, engagement of C-suite executives, and tangible benefits in terms of retention, accelerated development, and business outcomes.

BACKGROUND

Pitney Bowes (PB) is a leading provider of customer communication technologies. It is a $5.3 billion company with 29,000 employees in 32 countries, who serve both large and small-to-medium businesses in more than 100 countries. PB software, equipment, and services help businesses communicate more effectively, so they can build long-term customer relationships and drive profitable growth. PB is leading the revolution in customer communications by leveraging physical, digital, and hybrid channels.

PB employees come from different disciplines that include software development, engineering, marketing, sales, customer service, finance, human resources, information technology, and operations. It is an organizational priority to attract, retain, and develop early-in-career (EiC) talent, particularly for the digital and growth businesses. Murray Martin, Chairman, President and CEO, has been passionate about investing in the development of global EiC talent who have the capability but not the experience. From Murray Martin's personal experience, as well as what he has learned from other top executives, 90 percent of them had senior management roles by their mid-30s, which accelerated them toward C-suite executive roles later in their careers.

Martin comments, "While you are building for the future, you have to focus on early-in-career talent and accelerate their development to ensure there are no gaps. As senior leaders, we have a responsibility to develop the next generation of global leaders to ensure the long-term success of the company."

The leadership review process (LRP) at PB ensures that the company has the leaders required to sustain and grow the business. LRP is a structured review process for succession management planning. LRP enables the company to objectively assess the leadership talent base, assess bench strength in critical positions, identify talent gaps, and drive leadership development planning.

At the LRP meeting in September 2011, Martin and his leadership team made a commitment to launch and sustain a high-potential leadership development program targeted at global early-in-career talent. This particular talent pool was lacking in the high-potential leadership pipeline. The talent management team at Pitney Bowes had two months to develop and launch the program.

TALENT MANAGEMENT INITIATIVE

The global EiC program targets early-in-career talent with fewer than 10 years of total industry experience. Those eligible for the program also need to be high performers with significant accomplishments and demonstrated capability for growth. The participant pool is a mix of individual contributors and managers. The EiC candidates were nominated by their respective C-suite executives, and were selected as part of the LRP process.

The program runs for 18 months. At the time of publication, one year of the roadmap is already complete. There are activities in progress and some that will be implemented in 2013. In its first year, the program has already made an impact on the global organization. The potential tangible benefits of the program include improved retention, accelerated mobility, and qualitative contributions to business outcomes. PB has moved the needle as it relates to engaging the millennial generation. The approach, design, and delivery model is outlined in this section.

Aligning Organizational and EiC Talent-Pool Needs

To start, the organizational and EiC talent-pool needs were analyzed and prioritized in order to develop the right approach and design for the program. Table 12-1 outlines the organizational and EiC talent-pool needs that guided the design of the program.

Table 12-1. Organizational and EiC Talent-Pool Needs

Organizational Needs	EiC Talent-Pool Needs
Address gap in the leadership pipeline to ensure long-term success of the company.	Develop broad and strategic perspective.
Attract, retain, and develop Millennials.	Align EiCs with vision and direction of the company.
Engage senior leaders to develop the next generation of leaders.	Accelerate their leadership development.
Create a global community of Millennials that can contribute to innovative initiatives and strategic task forces.	Create opportunities to improve their visibility in the organization.

Design Principles

Based on the organizational and EiC talent-pool needs, the program design had to incorporate how this generation of talent engages, learns, and grows. The program needed to be both conceptual and action-oriented to enhance development. Activities such as a strategic thinking course, action-learning projects, and sessions with C-suite executives would be critical to align EiCs with the company vision and develop their strategic perspectives. Other components, such as personal development planning, 360 feedback, and mentoring, would accelerate their leadership development.

Senior leadership also needed to be engaged, to share their career stories, lessons learned, and other guidance. Finally, given that there were 49 participants from North America, Europe, and Asia Pacific, the program delivery and ongoing communication required flexibility. Table 12-2 lists the design principles and the actions that shaped the program.

Table 12-2. Addressing the Design Principles

Design Principles	Actions
The program is not an event; instead it integrates developmental actions over a time period.	The talent management team created an 18-month road map for sustained development.
Engage leaders to build leaders.	The company's chairman and CEO is the global sponsor for the program; local senior leaders were tapped as sponsors in Europe and Asia Pacific. The talent management team designed a mentoring program and matched senior leaders as mentors to EiCs. The team planned structured networking sessions with C-suite executives and other senior leaders.
Integrate action learning to broaden EiCs' business and strategic perspectives.	Each participant leads or co-leads a stretch project that is aligned to a key strategy, innovation, customer experience, or operations.
Program must be global and dynamic.	The program has remained flexible to respond to changing business requirements. Examples include participation on a global task force, branding focus groups, strategic projects, or holding networking events with senior leaders during their global travels.
Leverage social media to create an online global community.	The talent management team created a global Yammer community for the EiCs.

EiC Program Road Map

One of the key design principles was to ensure that the program is not a one-time event, but sustained over 18 months by integrated developmental actions. The components of the roadmap that have been completed include EiC launch, personal development plans (PDP), the emerging strategic thinkers course, structured networking with CEO and C-suite, the action learning projects, Yammer online community, and 360-degree feedback. The mentoring program is in progress and components such as the preparing for leadership workshop, PB ambassador program, and graduation will be implemented in 2013. Figure 12-1 outlines the 18-month EiC program roadmap.

Figure 12-1. EiC Program Roadmap

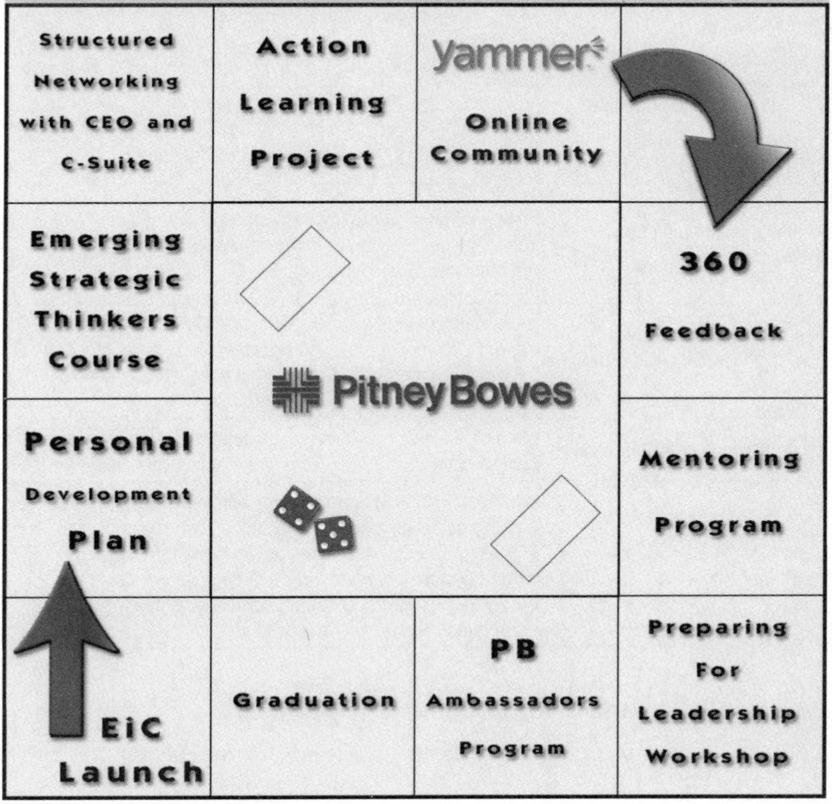

EiC Launch

Murray Martin kicked off the two-day program in North America in December 2011. The two-day program launches in Europe and Asia Pacific were kicked off by the president of communications solutions, the largest line of business within PB. The 49 participants representing all business units and functions globally are from the United States, Canada, the United Kingdom, Germany, France, Poland, Japan, South Africa, and India. The Global EiC program includes regional launches and events as well as global initiatives that include task forces, webinars, and focus groups. Table 12-3 provides the components of the North American Program Launch.

Table 12-3. Program Launch Agenda

Program Components	Description
Keynote by Murray Martin Chairman, President and CEO	Murray Martin is the global program sponsor.
Development Planning Workshop	Participants walk away with a practical framework and tools for creating and implementing their personal development plans.
Strategic Leadership Conference	A strategic planning event that brings together senior leaders from the company. EiC participants attend part of this event. They gain exposure to the strategic direction and priorities of the company.
Networking With Senior Leaders	Senior leaders share their career stories and leadership perspectives over networking dinner and panel discussions.
Launch of the 18-Month Program Roadmap	Components include personal development plan, emerging strategic thinkers course, structured networking with the CEO and C-suite executives, action learning project, Yammer online community, 360-degree feedback, mentoring program, preparing for leadership workshop, PB ambassador program, and graduation.

Personal Development Plan (PDP)

PDP represents one of the most effective methods for developing employees and leaders. It requires reflecting on personal career goals, analyzing feedback, and ensuring ongoing dialogue with others in the organization to assess their developmental goals and progress. In summary, it provides a targeted action plan for accelerated development of high-potential employees.

Participants walk away from the program launch with a draft PDP. They finalize their PDPs after seeking input from their direct managers and their HR business partners. The PDP focuses on opportunities to round out the participant's experience and develop capabilities that will make a difference in his career development.

Emerging Strategic Thinkers Course

Participants attend a two-day Emerging Strategic Thinkers course, delivered by the PB enterprise learning and development team in partnership with the American Management Association. This workshop offers key insights into strategic thinking as well as actionable steps. It enables participants to assess strategic possibilities and influence key stakeholders. They also benefit from a strategic frame of reference that they can apply to their action learning projects.

Structured Networking With CEO and C-Suite

Leaders building leaders has been an integral part of the program, with senior leaders actively engaged in shaping the company's next generation of leaders. This also contributes to a "talent culture" within the company. Chairman and CEO Murray Martin has been the chief talent champion and has personally engaged with the participants in small groups over 10 different meetings, in which he listens to their ideas and suggestions for the company.

Senior leaders at the highest levels have also actively engaged with the participants in 15 structured networking sessions, either in person or virtually. During these sessions the EiCs hear about the company vision, business-unit strategies, and personal leadership stories; and they have an opportunity to ask questions. In addition, participants meet with their business-unit president to get input and sponsorship for their PDPs on a one-on-one basis.

Action Learning Project

Each EiC leads or co-leads an action learning project in addition to their daily responsibilities. Some EiCs are part of a project team or a global task force. In 2012, EiCs were advised to identify an action learning project that serves a critical business need and provides opportunities to raise their visibility.

Action learning projects focused on the following broad categories:

- Creating customer value.

- A broader initiative labeled "drink our own champagne" which encourages the use of PB products, solutions, and services internally. Projects that were identified under this initiative are known as "champagne challenges."

- Go-to-market strategies for new products and solutions, innovation, marketing, and operational initiatives.

There were some 35 EiC action learning projects in all. Examples of action learning projects include creating go-to-market strategies for new products or solutions, creating a social media marketing program, handling migration to a new campaign management platform, and implementing a customer retention initiative. Through these projects, EiCs were exposed to leadership teams through broadening their experiences and networks outside their functional areas.

EiCs get buy-in and input from their project sponsors and are responsible for the outcomes of their action learning projects. Most of the EiCs had an opportunity to present their project updates and get feedback from Murray Martin. These projects create value for the company and are on track to deliver tangible business outcomes.

Yammer Online Community

Yammer is a social media platform from Microsoft that PB employees use as an internal global communication tool. An invitation-only Yammer group was created just for the global EiC community. This group platform is designed to be a secure place to share information. All global EiCs can also share stories or ask questions, post interesting articles and pictures, and simply collaborate online.

360-Degree Feedback

EiCs invite their managers, peers, team members, and internal or external customers to participate in a 360-feedback survey. The 360-survey tool, OPTM360 by the Talent Strategy Group, is customized to incorporate the seven

PB core competencies that collectively include 22 behaviors. The 360-feedback report lists three priority areas for development with practical suggestions from the respondents. Participants are expected to incorporate the feedback into their PDPs.

Mentoring Program

As EiCs prepare to formally graduate from the program, it is important to maintain support for their ongoing development. Mentors are recommended by the senior management team as well as EiCs. Both mentees and mentors complete a brief profile and participate in an interview which makes the best possible matches. The mentoring partnerships run for a year and are supported through the talent management team.

Preparing for Leadership Workshop

This workshop is designed to prepare EiCs for leadership. EiCs will come together for two days to:

- Review lessons learned from 2012; revisit PDPs and address any specific challenges.

- Provide suggestions for developmental themes that have emerged from the 360-feedback of the group.

- Participate in networking events and panel discussions with senior leaders.

- Connect with the new 2013 EiC cohort.

- Attend a one-day workshop on leadership presence and high-impact presentations.

PB Ambassador Program

The company's annual engagement survey results indicate that there is a need to communicate the new vision and strategy of the company in a way that better connects with employees globally. This seemed like a good opportunity to involve the EiCs because they are uniquely positioned to understand the challenges and benefits of more thoughtful engagement.

The project is comprised of a global task force of five EiCs who are currently working with internal communications to create the PB ambassador program. This project will be launched to all EiCs in the first quarter of 2013. The goal of this project is to provide training and a toolkit for EiCs to operate as global ambassadors across the company.

They will partner with their local senior leaders, plan town-hall meetings, conduct focus groups, and communicate the company vision to employees on the front lines. The corporate marketing group held three focus groups with the global EiCs in November 2012. The purpose of these focus groups was to seek their feedback and input as Millennials to develop the external and internal brand.

Graduation

EiCs will graduate from the program at the end of 18 months. Post-graduation, they will continue to work with their mentors and also as PB ambassadors. They will retain their membership to the global Yammer EiC community. They will also be paired with new EiC participants to "pay it forward" by sharing what they have gained and guiding the new EiCs in their journeys.

Career Advancement

Ultimately, in order to engage and retain EiCs, they need to see opportunities for career advancement. Both personal and organizational accountability for career advancement has been instituted. EiCs are expected to continue working on their PDPs, build their relationships with senior leaders and HR business partners, and take ownership for their career development. Business unit presidents are accountable for proposing developmental roles for EiCs as part of the LRP process.

EVALUATION METHODOLOGY AND RESULTS

It has been 12 months since the North American program was launched. So how does PB determine if this program has been successful? This section will address the following questions:

- What are the return-on-stakeholder expectations?

- Have organizational and talent-pool needs been addressed?

- What tangible and intangible talent and organizational outcomes have been tracked so far?

Return-on-Stakeholder Expectations

Based on the Kirkpatrick Return-on-Expectations Model, the qualitative and quantitative benefits realized from the program are reviewed from the perspective of stakeholder expectations. The stakeholders, the CEO, and C-suite executives who have championed the program, made a strong case for a structured program that accelerates the leadership development of early-in-career talent. They have expressed how pleased they have been with the engagement, retention, mobility, and overall feedback from the EiC program. The stakeholders have committed to continue investing in the global EiC program. Another global class of 45 participants will be added in 2013. The overall EiC program has approved funding of $145,000 in 2013.

Progress on Addressing Organizational and Talent-Pool Needs

The global EiC program has created a solution for addressing the gap in the leadership pipeline. This program is also serving as one of the means of attracting, retaining, and developing Millennials. Four of the EiCs have been profiled on the PB LinkedIn page to share their experiences working at the company. This program is also part of the employee value proposition for campus and other recruitment initiatives. The EiC program and the commitment to diversity and inclusion are also shaping the PB employer brand in emerging markets like India. Pitney Bowes India has been rated as the eighth Best Software Employer in India in 2012 by *Dataquest* magazine.

A total of 65 senior leaders have actively engaged in speaking at program events or mentoring EiCs through 2013. The global EiCs are now better aligned with the company vision and strategy through their active dialogue with the C-suite executives and other senior leaders. In addition, the emerging strategic thinking course, action learning projects, and participation in task forces or focus groups are helping EiCs develop a broad and strategic perspective. The networking opportunities have clearly raised the profile of EiCs with the C-suite executives and senior leaders within their respective business units. They have also gained leadership insights from the senior leaders, coursework, and the 360-feedback that they have received.

Tangible and Intangible Outcomes

The tangible and intangible organizational and talent outcomes are outlined in this section. Based on the Phillips' evaluation model, the evaluation data has been collected and analyzed through the program evaluation survey, feedback from regional conference calls, turnover analysis, promotions, talent mobility, and records of the business impact of action learning projects.

Level 1: Reaction

The EiCs were surveyed to understand whether the two-day program launch was effective. Based on the feedback, it was clear that the global launch of the program had generated excitement among the participants, and the momentum was building both with the participants and senior leaders. A multiple rating scale was used for the program evaluation survey with values ranging from one to five ("poor" to "excellent"), where five is the highest rating. Based on the program evaluation surveys of the three regional launches, the average rating was 4.6. Figure 12-2 provides a summary of the participant evaluations.

Figure 12-2. Program Launch—Participant Evaluations

Topic	North America	Europe	Asia Pacific
This workshop was effective for me.	4.6	4.2	4.5
Had the right amount of participant interaction.	4.7	4.4	4.8
I can see where/how I will take action.	4.5	4.5	4.3
Gave me insights/ideas to make a create and execute my development plan.	4.6	4.4	4.5
Conversations/networking with senior leaders	4.6	4.7	4.7
Keynote by Chairman & CEO	4.9	N/A	N/A
Keynote by President, Communications Solutions	N/A	4.4	4.7
Overall program kick-off experience	4.8	4.3	4.7
Subject matter expertise of the facilitator	4.8	4.7	4.8
The value of the knowledge/tools provided	4.8	4.3	4.5
Overall facilitator effectiveness	4.8	4.6	4.8
Overall Rating	**4.7**	**4.5**	**4.6**

Figure 12-3 provides the list of the descriptors that the participants used to describe their program launch experience.

Figure 12-3. Program Launch Experience—Descriptors

North America	Europe	APAC
Inspiration	**Insightful**	**Enlightened**
Self Reflection	Discovery	**Inspiring**
Revitalized	Reassuring	Retrospection
Eye-Opening	Encouraging	**Refreshing**
Exciting	Strategy	**Insightful**
Ownership	Assessment	**Focused**
Motivational	Delivery	Direction
Empowering	**Focus**	Action
Opportunity	**Opportunities**	Clarity
Enlightening	Successful	**Self-Realization**
Enriching	Collaborate	**Empowering**
Refocused	**Networking**	Practical
Collaborate	Initiative	
Timely	Investment	
Networked		

*Bold indicated repeated theme

Participants listed the following as key takeaways from the program launch:

- ability to build and implement development plans

- ability to take ownership for personal development

- tools to support team development

- excellent opportunity to network and learn from senior leaders

- clarity, direction, tools, insights, and support needed.

The experience of the program launch was also captured through the testimonials that were sent by the participants and their leaders, following the initial program launch. Here is a sample of the several testimonials that were received.

"As we move ahead in our careers, we will all remember the program as the organizer for a pivotal change in thinking."—*North American participant*

"The program was inspiring (for me, because of the senior leaders' commitment, participation, and advice); motivational (plenty of examples from senior leaders and stories that fostered a 'can do' attitude); a very good framework for creating a personal development plan (which can be rolled out to the team as well); a roadmap that included 360 feedback, training, mentoring, and other actions. Clearly demonstrated commitment to develop and therefore retain talent for the future!"—*European participant*

"We had a great session last week with all the participants. The program was very well structured and the feedback from participants was very encouraging. I thoroughly enjoyed the interaction and found it to be a very enriching experience. We have all agreed to stay in touch for the remainder of the year to continue this momentum."—*Local sponsor, Asia Pacific*

Level 2: Learning

At the end of the program launch, the EiCs created a draft of their PDPs by using the framework and tools that were covered. This was the main objective of the program launch. There was no other measurement for learning at the end of program launch.

Level 3: Application

The execution of the EiC road map, as described above, has engaged the participants and sustained their development. Overall EiCs have implemented 65 percent of the developmental actions in their PDPs through 2012. Many of the Level 3 measures will be available in 2013 as the action learning projects are completed. At this stage the Level 3 measures are qualitative and are described below.

A check-in call with each participant was scheduled 30 days after the program launch to sustain the momentum and drive accountability for implementing her PDP. EiCs were required to share what actions they had taken and what progress they were making since the program launch. It was exciting to hear how EiCs were proactively working on their development. Here are some examples:

- EiCs shared development planning tools with their team members.
- Some EiCs were invited to share their program experience and learning at their local executive and town-hall meetings.
- One participant was spending 15 percent of her time in a different functional area to gain exposure and develop skills.
- One participant spent one day each week in a different function, resulting in a promotion to a managerial role in that new function.
- Participants met with their direct managers and had also reached out to several senior leaders to get input for their PDPs.

This forum was serving a purpose to reconnect participants and share learning. EiCs were also picking up ideas and practices from their peers that they could incorporate into their PDPs. This practice of conducting check-in calls was continued.

The 15 structured networking sessions with C-suite executives and other senior leaders has been the hallmark of the program. This huge commitment from senior leaders has inspired and engaged the participants through the year.

Other qualitative measures from the program include:

- Through the branding focus groups, EiCs have provided valuable insights and feedback that will shape PB external and internal brand.

- One EiC participant is creating a partnership with a university and PB as part of his action learning project, to create an institute of business analytics.

- A global task force of five EiCs is creating the PB ambassador program by partnering with internal communications.

The participants had rich opportunities to apply their learning through action learning projects, task forces, and focus groups. As some participants have taken on expanded roles or earned promotions, others have approached their current roles with more innovation and have operated outside their comfort zones. Below is an example of feedback from one of the managers.

"Over the past year, [an EiC participant] has taken on responsibility for key initiatives outside the scope of his current role. He has done this both under my direction and with his own independent initiative, which I value very much. Given all the initiatives that he has led over the year, it is clear that he is ready to lead a team. He is a critically important member of my team and will continue to move our organization to new levels of success."—*Director*

Level 4: Tangible Benefits—Business Impact

The EiC program was designed to create medium- to long-term impact, and all indicators are that it is on track to achieving that. So what are these indicators? One of the senior leaders said it best: "What's important for me as I assess impact of the program are three things—upward or lateral moves, retention, and evidence that we are engaging the EiCs in initiatives that are part of our strategic direction." Here is an update on these three indicators.

Through 2012, 41 percent of the participants have been either promoted or have taken on expanded roles. These include three director-level appointments, six manager-level appointments, two other promotions, and nine expanded roles or lateral movements. Turnover for this group is 8 percent, well below the average 20 percent turnover of EiC high-potentials before this program. The action learning projects, PB ambassador program, and the branding focus groups are enabling the EiCs to connect with the strategic direction of the company. This first pilot group has an impressive list of 35 action learning projects. The program provided high-quality resources for these critical business projects. These resources would be the equivalent of five full-time employees (FTEs). Table 12-4 outlines a sample list of action learning projects with their potential outcomes.

Table 12-4. Sample List of Action Learning Projects

Action Learning Project	Potential Outcomes
Built a best-practice social media marketing program across all verticals.	Branding and business development.
Created an account-based marketing strategy for a global telecom company.	Produced an opportunity for the sales team. Other business units are leveraging it.
Oversaw migration to new campaign management platform (the Champagne Challenge Initiative). Goes live December 31, 2012.	Replaced current marketing automation with PB solutions. Reduce campaign costs and increase revenue.
Implemented the Customer Retention Initiative – Europe.	Increase customer retention by 50%.
Implemented Order to Payment Project.	Will significantly affect billing, account support, customer satisfaction scores, and call volumes.
Developed a solution for the Employee Communication Market.	Business development.
Managed the new cloud-based solution launch in Japan.	Business development.

Level 4: Intangible Benefits

As described above there have been several intangible benefits from the EiC program. Some of these benefits include high levels of participant engagement, enhanced employee value proposition for campus and other entry-level hiring, a rewarding experience for senior leaders, and increased visibility of EiCs in the organization.

TM INITIATIVE MICRO SCORECARD

The scorecard is based on data one year into the 18-month program roadmap. The scorecard includes data for Levels 1, 2, 3, and 4. Level 5 data have not been determined and will be analyzed at the end of the 18-month roadmap. Table 12-5 is the talent management scorecard of the EiC program for 2012.

CONCLUSIONS

- It is critical that a high-potential program is aligned with business strategy and sustained by engaging senior leaders and participants beyond the program launch.

- The program has to be dynamic; to be integrated with real business opportunities and providing real-time and relevant learning.

- Senior leaders get a lot out of their interaction with the next generation of leaders and find the experience very rewarding. They express an interest in doing it again. Leaders building leaders has been an integral part of the program.

- Manager effectiveness in supporting EiC development is critical.

- An initiative to create bi-annual forum with managers of the participants will be launched in 2013. The goal is to create an ongoing dialogue between participants and their managers, clarify expectations, and provide tools to support PDPs and retention of participants.

- Investing in this program is about planning for the future and preparing the organization for long-term success.

Table 12-5. TM Initiative Micro Scorecard

Talent Management Initiative: Global Early-in-Career High-Potential Program

Target Audience: Early-in-Career (EiC) high-potential employees

Number of Participants: 49 from North America, Europe, and Asia Pacific

Duration: Data in scorecard was collected one year into the 18-month duration

Business Objectives: Improved retention, accelerated mobility, and qualitative contributions to business outcomes

Results				
Reaction	Learning	Application	Tangible Benefits	Intangible Benefits
Level 1	**Level 2**	**Level 3**	**Level 4**	
Program launch received an overall rating of 4.6 on a scale of 1-5 (5 being the highest). Positive feedback and testimonials were gathered from participants and managers.	EiCs were able to create Personal Development Plans (PDPs).	Overall EiCs have implemented 65% of their development actions from their PDPs.	41% of EiCs were promoted or have expanded roles. Turnover of EiC high-potentials was reduced from 20% in 2011 to 8% in 2012. EiCs are working on 35 action learning projects that are on track to deliver tangible benefits in 2013. **Level 5** To be determined in 2013.	Overall very high engagement levels of EiCs. Enhancing our employee value proposition to attract campus hires. Senior leaders are engaged in developing leaders. EiCs developing strong networks and developing their team members.

Technique to Isolate Effects of Program: Participant evaluations, stakeholder estimates, organizational data on turnover and promotions.

Technique to Convert Data to Monetary Value: To be determined in 2013.

Barriers to Application of Skills: Manager effectiveness with career development support.

Recommendations: Launching a bi-annual forum with the managers of participants. The goal is to clarify expectations and provide tools to support career development and retention.

ABOUT THE AUTHORS

Glem Dias is the director of integrated talent management at Pitney Bowes, Inc. He has global responsibility for succession management, high-potential leadership development, talent mobility, and mentoring. His diverse experience comes from industries such as investment banking, software, telecommunications, pharmaceuticals, and retail. He has worked in Canada, India, the U.S., Europe, and Latin America. He is the recipient of the Pitney Bowes Impact Award, the Talent Management Award by the HRPA, and the Top 25 Canadian Immigrants Award. His prior roles include leading talent management at Wal-Mart Canada and serving as an HR leader for Morgan Stanley India.

He regularly speaks at leading talent management conferences and serves on multiple industry advisory committees on talent management.

Eileen Springer is the vice president of integrated talent management at Pitney Bowes, Inc. Her current responsibilities include overseeing the recruitment and development of executive-level staff, succession planning, performance management, talent assessment for new businesses and acquisitions, organizational architecture, executive services, and high-potential development programs. Additionally, Eileen oversees the global enterprise learning and development organization. Eileen has been with Pitney Bowes for 13 years and has held several global HR leadership roles in the company, including leadership of the HR function for the core mailing solutions management businesses and global financial services. Prior to Pitney Bowes, Eileen spent 10 years at Citigroup, where she was a vice president of human resources.

REFERENCES

Jack J. Phillips. (2011). *Handbook of Training Evaluation and Measurement Methods*, 3rd edition. New York: Routledge.

Kirkpatrick, J., and W.K. Kirkpatrick. (2009). *The Kirkpatrick Four Levels: A Fresh Look After 50 Years 1959-2009*. Kirkpatrick Partners, LLC.

13

EVALUATING LEADERSHIP IMPROVEMENT: USING EXECUTIVE COACHING TO DRIVE CHANGE

Kristen P. Claudy, Anthony I. Lamera, and Brian O. Underhill, PhD

INTRODUCTION

This case study explains how the California Public Employees Retirement System (CalPERS) has effectively developed its leaders through a 360-degree feedback and coaching program over a 15-year period. Levels 1 and 3 (Kirkpatrick, 2006) metrics demonstrated positive participant reaction and improvement in leadership effectiveness.

BACKGROUND

The California Public Employees Retirement System (CalPERS) manages the pension and healthcare benefits of approximately 1.6 million California state employees. CalPERS oversees an investment portfolio of $238.4 billion (per corporate website), making it the largest public pension organization in the world, well-respected both in the government and for-profit investment communities. The organization employs over 2,700 people, most of who are based in Sacramento, California. Of these, almost 500 are in leadership roles; the remaining employees are represented (unionized) staff.

Beginning in the late 1990s, one of CalPERS' key initiatives was to become a "destination employer." The "war for talent" (McKinsey, 1997) was certainly underway, and CalPERS would have difficulty attracting and retaining talent (particularly high-salaried investment staff). To address this challenge, the CEO at the time initiated the "All-Staff Training Project" (which later became a formalized unit known as All-Staff Training and Development) as one of the key priorities for the organization. Additionally, California's state training center, run by the Department of Personnel Administration, was scheduled to close, further driving CalPERS to create in-house training.

One of the key outcomes, which continues to this day, is the CalPERS 360° Leadership Feedback Program. Now about to begin its fifth round, four previous rounds of the program have been provided for nearly every leadership employee enterprise-wide. Leaders undergo the CalPERS multi-rater 360° tool, a coaching component, and follow-up metrics. The 360° Leadership Feedback Program has become a standard part of every leader's career at CalPERS.

Following each round, satisfaction (Level 1) and impact analyses (Level 3) are performed. As this chapter will show, the 360° Leadership Feedback Program continues to earn high marks among participants, and the program has consistently demonstrated strong improvement in leadership effectiveness over time.

CalPERS' commitment to leadership development is among the best-sustained for both profit and governmental organizations. Other organizations have called upon CalPERS to benchmark their process, and a short vignette has even been written in an executive coaching "best practice" book (Underhill, McAnally, Koriath, 2007).

TALENT MANAGEMENT INITIATIVE

Initial Program Design

The All-Staff Training and Development initiative commenced in 1997. At that time, a full-scale training needs analysis was undertaken. Extensive interviews and focus groups were conducted with every leadership employee, as well as a cross-section of staff representatives. Key recommendations were presented to executive staff, and as a result, training initiatives were then designed and implemented. These included:

- a custom-designed leadership competency model

- a 360-degree feedback tool, based on the CalPERS leadership competency model

- a multi-day leadership offsite workshop (the Leadership Challenge workshop), which included 360-degree feedback, coaching, a Meyers-Briggs assessment, and various outdoor teambuilding activities

- other specialized organization-wide training initiatives on topics such as communication, customer service, teamwork, problem solving, decision making, project management, career development, personal development, wellness, recognition, organizational knowledge, and desktop education (Microsoft Office Suite)

- a follow-up "mini survey" to measure a leader's improvement six months after the workshop (as part of the 360° Leadership Feedback Program)

- appointment of the first ever "training manager" (a CalPERS version of a chief learning officer).

CalPERS executive-level staff were first to pilot the new offerings for the 360° Leadership Feedback Program. Not only did the pilot help to refine the program in preparation for eventual organization-wide roll out, it also provided an important message to all staff that 360-degree feedback and coaching were critical to leadership development and CalPERS success. The CEO and his executive staff went through the 360° Leadership Feedback process first to show its importance and their support of the program. It also demonstrated their commitment to developing CalPERS' leaders. Program adjustments were made following feedback from the test group.

Round one was officially underway and would take approximately two years to cascade throughout the organization. Follow-up results were collected, which demonstrated positive improvement in leadership effectiveness (a Level 3 analysis). Further details on the Level 3 metric for the most recent round are provided later in this chapter.

Coaching Over the Years

After that initial success, CalPERS committed to requiring every leader, from the frontline supervisor to the chief executive officer, to participate in the 360° Leadership Feedback process every two years. While that timing may have been a bit ambitious, CalPERS has now completed four rounds, which averages a round every three or so years. This is impressive considering the organization has had three different CEOs during this time, as well as four different human resources division chiefs. Round two took place from 2001 to 2002; round three from 2005 to 2006; and round four from 2009 to 2011.

In each round, due to participant feedback and the increasing demands on the workforce, modifications were made to the program, the most significant of which was shortening its timeline. Over the years, the offsite leadership workshop was reduced to a two-hour session and brought on site, and the coaching requirement was also reduced. Yet despite this, results are still continuing to demonstrate the value of the process.

During this time, CalPERS used the 360° Leadership Feedback Program to develop the Leadership Skills Assessment (LSA) process—its version of a talent management framework. Leaders would self-nominate and receive feedback on their preparedness for executive and senior management positions in the organization. They underwent an assessment process, which examined their education background, career history, performance and potential, strengths and weaknesses, as well as future opportunities. This information fed into the talent management pipeline, and candidates were given a variety of development opportunities based on the commonly accepted 70-20-10 principle of development (70 percent of a leader's development comes through actual experience; 20 percent in learning through others; and 10 percent through formalized teaching; Lombardo & Eichinger, 1996). Since 2005 (when the LSA process began), 50 leaders have participated.

Round Four

In the most recent iteration of the 360° Leadership Feedback Program, the 360° assessment tool was somewhat modified—a few items (behavioral statements) were added, a few deleted, and a few altered slightly, based on the changing needs of the organization. This was done in conjunction with the CalPERS human resources, the workforce management and leadership programs (WMLP) teams, and CoachSource. The adjusted 360-degree assessment tool was transmitted to the scoring vendor (Assessment Plus of Atlanta, GA) and turned into a new 360-degree tool.

Once again, every leader at CalPERS was encouraged to go through the process. Leaders were invited to participate in one of 23 groupings. Executive leaders went first, followed by senior managers, and then all other leaders. A total of 458 participants began the program, with 409 completing it (the difference due to retirements, attrition, or other reasons).

While the 360-degree program was not considered "mandatory," the workforce management and leadership programs team did a nice job of strongly encouraging leaders to participate; an estimated 85 percent or more engaged in the process. The program was presented as a positive development opportunity, rather than a "performance management" experience. CalPERS culture is generally considered open and conducive to feedback, and prides itself on developing its leaders (especially after several years of this program), so it was not difficult to get leaders to participate.

As noted, executive staff and senior leaders participated first, so that they also played a role in encouraging participation. The program kicked off with an executive sponsor, someone well-respected by the rest of the organization, who would then encourage others to participate. This individual would also share his or her insights and experiences, having been through the program several times.

Each group received a one-hour classroom orientation from CalPERS WMLP staff. Leaders were shown how the 360-degree process worked, how to select raters, rules on confidentiality, and so forth. While many organizations might normally skip this step, CalPERS felt the orientation was important for those leaders less acquainted with the 360-degree experience (many leaders to CalPERS come from other State of California departments and agencies, where 360-degree processes are less commonplace). During the orientation sessions, past participants would speak to new groups about how valuable the program was for them.

The 360-degree feedback scoring process then commenced, with introductory emails sent from the scoring vendor directly to each participant. Leaders nominated feedback-givers (their managers, direct reports, peers, and so forth) through the online system. Approximately three to four weeks later, feedback was compiled and reports shipped out to CalPERS.

Leaders then gathered for an "Encouraging Feedback" workshop with an external leadership consultant from CoachSource. The two-hour workshop highlighted details on how to read the reports, follow up with others, and make the most of coaching. The confidential reports were then provided to participants.

Each month for the next six months, there was some form of contact with the participants: telephone coaching, Development Engine reminders (an online reminder system; further details below) and support, and a follow-up "mini survey."

Most importantly, participants received four one-hour telephone coaching sessions: one immediately after the workshop to interpret the reports, and the remainders spaced over the next six months. Approximately two-thirds of participants took advantage of all four coaching sessions, and those who did not make use of the first two sessions were not given the opportunity to continue in the program, simply to save the organization unnecessary costs for those less committed to the coaching process.

The executive coaches were a pool of six practitioners who had each worked with CalPERS for many years (some were even part of round one). Coaches were oriented prior to the beginning of round four, and then participated in occasional conference calls with WMLP to share their observations of the leadership development themes at play within the organization.

The executive coaches were selected to work with CalPERS based on a number of criteria: Generally all possess an advanced degree in organizational behavior or a related field, specialize in leadership coaching, have been coaching for at least five years (and have been running their own businesses for at least two years), and have worked with CalPERS or other state agencies in the past. (Interestingly, California requires a certain percent of contracted work to be conducted by disabled veterans, whenever possible. Two of the coaches on this program were Navy veterans prior to establishing their own consulting businesses.)

The Development Engine tool (provided by Fort Hill Company) is an online action-planning and reminder system that was deployed to support this process. With the aid of their coaches, participants entered their development objectives into the system and crafted their action plans online. Participants were then able to update their progress periodically. In addition, participants used the Development Engine tool to solicit additional feedback from their key stakeholders. The tool also included a customized online resource guide, which gave participants tips and strategies regarding their particular development objectives.

Leaders were also able to "ping" their coaches through their Development Engine updates; thus coaches were kept informed on each leader's progress between sessions. The coach could also offer additional coaching tips to the participant via this tool. While not all leaders took full advantage of this online system (about 32 percent of Development Engine requests were responded to by participants, which is in line with norm for this tool), it still provided an additional "touch point" for participants over the six-month period.

After six months, each leader participated in a short online "mini survey" to give feedback on their improvement efforts (a Level 3 metric). Each survey was custom-designed for each respective leader, based on their individual development objectives. Those working around the leader also provided feedback on observed improvements (this could include peers, direct reports, and managers—usually the same individuals who completed the initial 360-degree assessment). Reports were compiled by the same scoring vendor, and distributed to the participants and their coaches. After the distribution of these reports, coaches conducted their final follow-up calls.

Mini-survey results were aggregated for the entire organization, and viewed by a number of different cuts on the data. Satisfaction surveys for the program (a Level 1 metric) were also conducted at this time. Further details on both metrics are provided below.

EVALUATION METHODOLOGY AND RESULTS

The 360° Leadership Feedback Program used both a Level 1 and Level 3 evaluation process to measure the satisfaction and effectiveness of the executive coaching program. Results are presented below.

Level 1 Evaluation

The 360° Leadership Feedback Program used a fairly standard Level 1 evaluation throughout most rounds. The most recent version, in round four, consisted of six questions rated on a five-point scale. The overarching question asked, "How satisfied were you with your coach in the following areas?"

1. Identifies clear priorities for my growth and development.
2. Genuinely listens to me.
3. Provides specific, actionable suggestions and advice.
4. Communicates in a direct and concise manner.
5. Helps me gain better insight into how my behavior impacts others.
6. Overall satisfaction with your coaching experience.

Four open-ended questions were also posed to participants, allowing for a rich collection of qualitative data as well. These questions were:

1. What worked well in your coaching experience?
2. What could be improved in your coaching experience?

3. Would you recommend your coach to others? Why or why not?

4. Please share your observations or suggestions about the entire CalPERS 360° Leadership Feedback Program.

Two hundred ninety two surveys were distributed (not all groups received a survey due to an administrative error), with 151 responses (a nearly 52 percent response rate). Surveys were collected electronically.

The average scores for each question are provided in Figure 13-1. All questions scored above a 4.65 (1.0 is "highly dissatisfied" and 5.0 is "highly satisfied"), with the highest-rated question being "Genuinely listens to me" (4.79).

Figure 13-1.

How satisfied were you with your coach in the following areas:

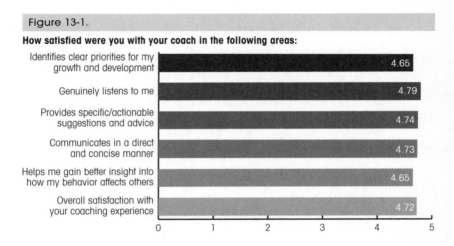

It was also possible to break down results both by participants' leadership levels and by coach. Results showed that all levels of leadership demonstrated roughly similar levels of satisfaction (4.71 to 4.74). Comparison scores of the six external executive coaches also revealed relatively similar levels of satisfaction (4.60 to 4.90).

Qualitative responses were also helpful, with various comments in multiple areas. Comments were analyzed to uncover common themes, which would assist in making recommendations for future rounds. Some positive comments the program elicited included:

"The CalPERS 360° Leadership Program was well worth my time and it helped me focus on my strengths as well as in areas that provided me with personal growth as a manager and leader."

"Each time I've experienced this process I always initially think, I don't have time for this right now. During and after, I realize why it is important."

"Individual coaches are an excellent part of this program. It's helpful to get a perspective from a third-party individual."

"I am blessed that CalPERS offers this mentorship program for its leaders. It demonstrates its commitment of building from within its walls."

"The process is very valuable and I'm grateful that the organization places a high value on leadership development."

"I encourage all managers to readily engage in the process, to promote growth in both personal and professional endeavors!"

"I think every manager would benefit from this experience."

"This program is the absolute best that I've encountered in my 29 years of state service."

Level 3 Evaluation

The 360° Leadership Feedback Program made use of short "mini surveys" to measure behavioral improvement over time. First created by Marshall Goldsmith in the 1990s, multisource mini surveys have been shown to be an effective way to measure leadership improvement back on the job. Such surveys have been used in every round of the 360° Leadership Feedback Program.

Each participant selects one to two areas for development through the coaching process. Often the development area stems from the original 360-degree assessment, or sometimes the participant and coach write an evaluative statement. These areas are noted in the participant's action plan, and are transmitted back to the original 360-degree scoring vendor. Some examples of such customized development questions include "Manages his time effectively,"

"Gives people specific direction when they need it," "Identifies a clear strategy for achieving the vision," or "Provides performance feedback in a timely manner."

Six months into the program, the scoring vendor creates a short online survey that is unique to each participant. The survey is then distributed to the participant's key stakeholders (the same feedback-givers who completed the original 360-degree evaluation of the participant). The survey includes both the specialized development objectives for the participant, as well as several generic questions common to all participants. The stakeholders complete the survey and results are summarized into a report, viewable to the participant and coach only.

Questions used on the CalPERS mini survey were:

1. Since the feedback session, has this person discussed with you what he learned from the feedback? (Answer: Yes or No)

2. Since the feedback session, how often has this person followed up with you concerning how he can improve? (Answer: None, Little, Some, Frequently, Constantly)

3. Do you feel this person has become more or less effective as a leader since the feedback session? (Answer: -3 "less effective" to +3 "more effective")

4. Customized question 1 (Answer: -3 "less effective" to +3 "more effective")

5. Customized question 2 (Answer: -3 "less effective" to +3 "more effective")

6. What has been done by this person in the past several months that you have found particularly effective? (Qualitative Question)

7. What can this person do to become more effective as a leader in the areas noted above? (Qualitative Question)

(The "feedback session" referenced refers to the initial coaching session that took place immediately after the 360-degree results were delivered. The customized questions are unique to each individual's development objectives.)

Aggregated results from question three ("Do you feel this person has become more or less effective as a leader since the feedback session?") are displayed in Figure 13-2. Total number of respondents is 2,966.

Figure 13-2.

Question: Do you feel this person has become more or less effective as a leader since the feedback session?

Answer: -3 "Less Effective" to +3 "More Effective." Conducted six months following original 360-degree assessment.

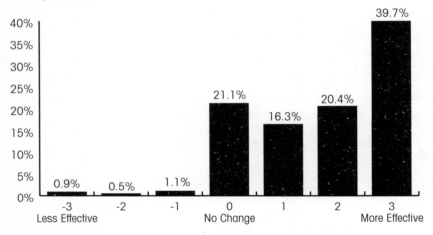

Those working with CalPERS leaders rated them as strongly improved. Just over 60% of raters noticed improvement at a +2 and +3 level; over 76% noted improvement at the +1, +2, +3 levels. The average improvement score was a +1.71, beating round three's average improvement of +1.60.

N=2,966

The scale asked stakeholders (again, direct reports, peers, and managers) for a rating from -3 (less effective) to + 3 (more effective), with 0 meaning "no change." As the figure portrays, those working with CalPERS leaders rated them as strongly improved; just over 60 percent of raters noticed improvement at a +2 and +3 level. More than 76 percent of raters noted improvement at the +1, +2, +3 levels. Of course, with the majority of raters observing leaders' improvement back on the job, this is considered a very positive result.

The average improvement score was a +1.71 (again, on the -3 to +3 scale). Generally, any score above +1.00 is considered an indication of improvement. Comparison among other companies using the same mini survey shows that +1.71 is above average for most clients. (Round four showed greater improvement than round three, where the average improvement score was a +1.61.)

As mentioned, participants also selected individual areas for development to work on with their coaches. These items were also rated by the same stakeholders. Figure 13-3 portrays the results. Improvement in these individual areas was more impressive than improvements in overall leadership effectiveness. In this case, nearly 70 percent of raters saw improvement at a +2 and +3 level. Nearly 83 percent saw improvement at a +1, +2, and +3 level.

Figure 13-3.

Question: Do you feel this person has become more or less effective in the following areas for development? (Show individual area(s) for development.)

Answer: -3 "less effective" to +3 "more effective." Conducted six months following original 360-degree assessment.

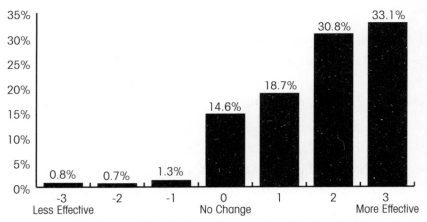

Improvement in individual area(s) for development was more impressive than for overall leadership effectiveness (depicted in Figure 13-1). Nearly 70% of raters saw improvement at a +2 and +3 level. Nearly 83% saw improvement at a +1, +2 and +3 level.

N=5,247 responses

Year-Over-Year 360° Leadership Feedback Program Comparison

After rounds one through three, a comparison of 360-degree scores was also conducted. Average 360-degree scores improved in each round. For example, in one particular group of leaders, their improvement was rated by "peers" at 4.3 in round one and 4.4 in round two. This same group received a 4.21 (round one) and a 4.32 (round two) from "direct reports." A separate analysis found an improvement of original 360-degree items for all groups from round two to round three. Though some minor changes were made to the 360° Leadership Feedback Program after each round, the surveys were generally similar enough to provide this comparison. Of course, it also must be noted that the participants—and their raters—may not necessarily be the same year-over-year.

Intangible Benefits

While undergoing this talent management initiative, a variety of additional intangible benefits was also realized. Firstly, the program allowed for aggregation and review of CalPERS' collective development opportunities, and additional interventions for addressing them. For example, following round two, aggregated 360-degree reports showed that "coaching and mentoring others" was a development opportunity for CalPERS leaders. In answer to this, a "leader-as-coach" training program was provided to all leaders. CalPERS leaders were taught how to better coach their direct reports, the benefits of which then cascaded through the organization.

Another important outcome of the 360-degree program has been the establishment of an organization-wide recognition program. At an all-staff town-hall in 1999, the CEO and COO at the time indicated their 360-degree assessments revealed that giving recognition and showing appreciation were low-scoring areas. From that point, a formal recognition program was designed and rolled out. The 360-degree scores were instrumental in demonstrating the need for this program, which is still solidly supported to this day.

Other initiatives that have emerged from this program include:

- The development of a strategic leadership framework that includes the Progressive Leadership Series (PLS), which is based upon CalPERS leadership competencies. It consists of three sequential learning programs that provide professional development for CalPERS leaders.

- A Leadership Skills Assessment (LSA) process that helps to anticipate future leadership positions and ensure CalPERS is prepared to fill expected vacancies (as described in this chapter).

- A workforce-planning workshop to prepare for future workforce needs, with consideration given to CalPERS' mission and strategic plan, budget, and knowledge and skills gaps.

- A Strategic Thinking and Results (STAR) process to shape leaders' strategic thinking, planning, and deployment skills.

TM INITIATIVE MICRO SCORECARD

The talent management micro scorecard is shown in Table 13-1. Four hundred and nine leaders participated in the program over a period of six months. Level 1 and Level 3 metrics were used to measure the effects of the program. The Level 1 evaluation consisted of a six-question quantitative survey (with additional qualitative questions). Results were very favorable, with answers to each question averaging at least 4.65 on a 5.00 scale and above. Level 3 evaluation surveyed those observing CalPERS participants, asking them whether they had seen improvement in overall leadership effectiveness over six months. The average improvement score was an excellent +1.71 on a -3.0 to +3.0 scale.

CONCLUSIONS

CalPERS' commitment to its 360-degree program over the past 15 years is quite impressive, especially in the midst of high turnover of its CEOs and human-resource division chiefs. Now the organization is gearing up to begin a fifth round of the program that will take place over the next two years.

This program has provided a variety of key benefits for the organization, including:

- One-on-one coaching with an external professional coach. The coaches provide unbiased feedback to the participants. The coaches' familiarity with CalPERS' culture and core values helps them to understand the expected behaviors and competencies necessary for leaders to be successful in their roles. They also share their industry expertise when working with the participants. The coaching component has been an integral part in positively shaping the leadership culture at CalPERS.

Table 13-1. TM Initiative Micro Scorecard

Talent Management Initiative: CalPERS 360° Leadership Feedback Program

Target Audience: All leaders, from executive staff to front-line supervisors (409 leaders in total)

Duration: 6 months per leader

Business Objectives: Establish a development culture; attract and retain the best and brightest; make CalPERS a destination employer.

Results			
Reaction	Learning	Application	Intangible Benefits
Level 1	**Level 2**	**Level 3**	
6-question quantitative survey (plus qualitative remarks) distributed for each leader; 5-point scale.	None conducted.	Question: "Do you feel this person has become more or less effective as a leader since the feedback session?"	Development themes identified and addressed; such as growing coaching skills and increasing employee recognition.
Questions (average rating):		-3: 0.9%	
• Identifies clear priorities for my growth and development. (4.65)		-2: 0.5% -1: 1.1%	Enhanced culture of feedback and development.
• Genuinely listens to me. (4.79)		0: 21.1.% 1: 16.3%	
• Provides specific, actionable suggestions/ advice. (4.74)		2: 20.4% 3: 39.7%	Development of additional processes, such as workforce planning, strategic thinking, and so on.
• Communicates in a direct and concise manner. (4.73)		Average improvement in leadership effectiveness: +1.71 on the -3 to +3 scale.	
• Helps me gain better insight into how my behavior affects others. (4.65)			
• Overall satisfaction with your coaching experience. (4.72)		Individual leadership behaviors were measured as well.	

Technique to Isolate Effects of Program: Survey measuring perceived improvement in leadership effectiveness since coaching began.

Technique to Convert Data to Monetary Value: None attempted, but being considered for next round.

Fully-Loaded Program Costs: Not available.

Barriers to Application of Skills: Participant time to institute new leadership behaviors; organization in the midst of large technology implementation.

Recommendations: Program to repeat in 2013-2014; will continue both Level 1 and Level 3 metrics to allow for year-over-year comparisons. Restructuring participant requirements to better align with individual workload demands.

- Using 360-degree feedback results, individuals better understand their weaknesses and are able to create short- and long-term plans for personal development. The leaders are responsible for their personal and career development. They take ownership of their development plans, which are customized to each leader's development needs.

- Staff observed their leaders responding favorably to the feedback. This demonstrates the importance of self-awareness and openness, qualities which are characteristic of the culture at CalPERS.

- The 360-degree feedback results revealed skills and knowledge gaps which are now being addressed.

- Creates an environment that promotes personal development and optimal career satisfaction through the cyclical application of 360-degree feedback.

One of CalPERS' main goals for this program was to become a "destination employer." While that specific business objective was not empirically tested, one leader's evaluation provided some anecdotal evidence of success in this area: "It is one of the main reasons I have not left CalPERS for employment with another state agency."

ABOUT THE AUTHORS

Kristen P. Claudy manages the CalPERS workforce management and leadership program. She is responsible for administering programs that provide development opportunities for nearly 500 leaders and oversees workforce management efforts, including the Strategic Leadership Framework (Succession Plan) which is essential for the continued growth and efficiency of CalPERS. Kristen has worked for Kaiser Permanente and Packard Bell NEC, and has been in the human resources field for 16 years. She holds a bachelor's degree in business administration. She lives with her husband in Sacramento and enjoys spending her free time traveling.

Anthony I. Lamera is the manager of education and training development. He has oversight of enterprise-wide training delivery, training administration (learning management system), and workforce management and leadership programs. He has been with CalPERS for more than 13 years and the State of California for 23 years. He holds a bachelor's degree in business administration with a focus on marketing and finance. He is a competitive youth soccer coach and has coached soccer at various age and skill levels for more than 25 years.

Brian O. Underhill is the co-author of *Executive Coaching for Results: The Definitive Guide to Developing Organizational Leaders* (Berrett Koehler, 2007). He is the founder and CEO of CoachSource, the world's largest executive coaching firm, with over 900 coaches in 43 countries. Brian previously spent 10 years managing executive coaching operations for Marshall Goldsmith. Some of his clients include Dell, Microsoft, and CalPERS. He holds a PhD in organizational behavior and is an internationally sought-after speaker. Brian lives in Silicon Valley where he is an avid soccer player and worship leader, as well as dad to active 9- and 12-year olds.

REFERENCES

CalPERS. http://www.calpers.ca.gov

McKinsey & Company. http://autoassembly.mckinsey.com/html/downloads/articles/War_For_Talent.pdf

Kirkpatrick, D.L., and J.D. Kirkpatrick. (2006). *Evaluating Training Programs*, 3rd ed. San Francisco, CA: Berrett-Koehler Publishers.

Lombardo, M.M., and R.W. Eichinger. (1996). *Career Architect Development Planner*, 1st ed. Minneapolis, MN: Lominger.

Underhill, B., K. McAnally, and J. Koriath. (2007). *Executive Coaching for Results: The Definitive Guide to Developing Organizational Leaders*. San Francisco, CA: Berrett-Koehler Publishers.

14

COACHING FOR IMPACT

Chris Pollino

INTRODUCTION

This case study describes a unique approach to measuring the business impact and return-on-investment (ROI) of executive coaching. The focus is on evaluating outcomes that business leaders can relate to, including promotions, performance levels, and retention of key talent. It demonstrates how to assign dollar values to these outcomes that have a significant positive impact on the bottom line of the business. The reader will also gain practical information for implementing an internal coaching practice.

BACKGROUND

Considered the founder of the biotechnology industry, Genentech has been delivering on the promise of biotechnology for more than 35 years, using human genetic information to discover, develop, manufacture, and commercialize medicines to treat patients with serious or life-threatening medical conditions. Today, Genentech is among the world's leading biotech companies, with multiple products on the market and a promising development pipeline.

In March 2009, Genentech became a member of the Roche Group. As part of their merger agreement, Roche and Genentech combined their pharmaceutical operations in the United States. Genentech's South San Francisco campus now serves as the headquarters for Roche pharmaceutical operations in the United States. Genentech research and early development department operates as an independent center within Roche.

Genentech employees consistently cite the opportunity to make a difference in the lives of patients as the primary reason they enjoy working at the company. The company places great value on its approximately 11,000 dedicated and mission-driven employees, and rewards them accordingly with a comprehensive and diverse set of benefits and services. The company is consistently recognized as a top employer by such publications as *Fortune, Science*, and *Working Mother*. In January 2012, *Fortune* named Genentech on its annual list of the "100 Best Companies to Work For" for the 14th consecutive year.

TALENT MANAGEMENT INITIATIVE

In 2006, the company's tremendous growth placed new challenges on its leaders and leadership development support. Many home-grown leaders were promoted into larger roles requiring new skill sets. Technical leaders transitioned into management roles with little or no formal leadership experience and training. The learning and development organization created new programs and processes to ensure a strong pipeline of talent would be available to meet business demand and goals.

Executive coaching was one solution formed to support the development of key talent. Executive coaches were becoming a popular resource in the company and were used for a variety of purposes. The executive talent development group believed the organization would benefit from a more formalized approach to executive coaching, to ensure it was used for accelerating the development of high potentials, and not for fixing performance issues or other issues that might be solved through mentoring or classroom training.

In the early stages of formalizing the executive coaching solution, the objectives were primarily process-related. They included:

- Articulating Genentech's perspective on where, when, and how executive coaching is best used.

- Providing Genentech leaders with guidance on how to enlist an executive coach's services.

- Establishing and maintaining a preferred network of qualified coaches who understand the current demands of the leaders.

- Clarifying the roles of the executive and coach, as well as others who are usually involved in the coaching work.

- Ensuring the coaching system provides consistent, high-quality coaching services that meet the needs of the executives across Genentech.

Between 2007 and 2009, the primary focus was building a preferred network of coaches and establishing a consistent coaching process. Approximately 25 executive coaches were assembled as the "go-to" pool when coaching services were needed. They were comprised of hand-picked coaches from a few talent management firms as well as independent coaches.

A structured process was established for vetting all prospective coaches. The first step for all coaches interested in joining the preferred network was to complete an application. An internal team with representatives from executive talent development group and human resources then conducted structured behavioral interviews for those that were considered strong candidates. Finally, a reference check was completed before extending an invitation to join the preferred network. All new coaches completed an orientation session with the executive talent development group to learn more about the company's business and culture, and gain an understanding of the coaching process and expectations of the preferred network coaches.

The executive talent development group put considerable effort into creating a coaching community where the coaches felt they were members of a larger coaching cadre that was adding real value to the business. "Coach community meetings" were initiated three times a year, and all coaches in the preferred network came together with the executive talent development group and other internal leaders. The agenda for these meetings included providing the coaches with business updates, peer learning on specific coaching topics, coach observations about the leaders and the business environment, and social networking. These coach community meetings continue to be an important element of Genentech's coaching program today.

There is mutual value to the company and coaches from this coaching community. The company benefits by having a highly-engaged, qualified pool of coaches who are committed to the success of its leaders and the coaching practice, and have a strong understanding of the business and culture. The coaches are getting value from networking with peers and gaining valuable company information to help them succeed with their clients. The coach community meetings also provide a venue to discuss the executive coaching process and identify what is working well and what improvements are required. For example, one issue that arose during a community meeting was that managers were not involved enough in the coaching process. The vice president of operations was invited as a guest speaker to a coach community meeting and shared his view on this topic, which resulted in an agreed standard of practice in the preferred network on how and when to involve the manager in the coaching engagement.

At this juncture in the development of the coaching solution, the process and preferred network of coaches was gaining momentum. One challenge was keeping track of the coaching. A system was instituted in which the coaches completed status sheets prior to the coach community meetings. The status sheets were a rudimentary tracking mechanism that provided information about who was being coached and what competencies the coaches were focusing on with leaders. Based on this information, as well as the obser-vations gleaned from the coaches in the coach community meetings, the executive talent development group developed a quarterly executive coaching scorecard. This scorecard was a good start for collecting executive coaching activity; however, it was woefully insufficient for responding to an unexpected request from the CEO.

A Defining Moment

In early 2010, the executive coaching program received an email from the vice president of human resources asking for the "ROI" on executive coaching. At a recent budget-review meeting, the executive committee discussed how much money was being spent on executive coaching. The CEO then requested the ROI on this spend. The executive talent development group was ill-prepared to answer this question. The only data available was from the scorecard, which contained activity data but not ROI data.

To respond to the CEO's request, anecdotal information was quickly collected from coaching participants about how they benefited from coaching. This painful experience forced the executive talent development group to realize that a better system was needed to measure the ROI of the executive coaching program. In 2007, there was an attempt to use Jack Phillips' ROI methodology (Phillips, 2007) to capture the ROI of executive coaching. The perception of the executives, however, was that too much time was spent on collecting data pertaining to ROI, when they wanted to be spending that time with the coaches. Hence, a new approach was required for collecting the data necessary to prove the return of executive coaching.

The executive talent development group created a survey to be completed by the leaders and their managers at the end of each coaching engagement. The survey asks questions in line with Kirkpatrick's four-level evaluation model (Kirkpatrick, 1994), and also collects information about the effectiveness of the coach. In addition to the survey, the executive talent development group collected information on the impact of coaching on talent management outcomes such as promotions and retention of key talent, and the ROI associated with these results. More detailed information about the business impact survey and ROI findings are described in the Evaluation Methodology and Results section of this case study.

In early 2011, the executive coaching program took another major step in its maturity. Since its inception, executive coaching was a stand-alone solution. A new business need was emerging for the development of cross-functional leadership programs for high-potentials. The director of executive talent development believed the executive coaching process needed stronger integration with these leadership programs, as well as the succession and talent management process.

To integrate executive coaching with the high-potential leadership programs, the managers of the executive coaching and leadership programs worked together to develop an approach for leaders to continue with coaching post-program if they desired. During the high-potential programs, leaders are provided with a list of development resources and key contacts available to them, including executive coaches, and asked to discuss the need for ongoing coaching with their managers. Enhancements were also made in the succession and talent management process by focusing more on individual development. Senior leaders are expected to come to talent reviews prepared to discuss the plans and actions in place regarding the development and retention of key talent. Executive coaching is an important solution for accelerating the development of key talent.

EVALUATION METHODOLOGY AND RESULTS

The evaluation methodology and reporting of results has evolved since the inception of the executive coaching process in 2006. As described earlier in this case study, the initial approach used for measuring executive coaching entailed collecting coaching activity and anecdotal stories from leaders. Triggered by the CEO's inquiry about the ROI of coaching, a business impact survey was instituted at the end of each coaching engagement to gather quantifiable business impact data. In addition to the business impact survey, the executive talent development group began looking at the impact of executive coaching on the performance, retention, and development of key talent and its associated ROI.

In this section, the methodology and results from the business impact survey and ROI measurement will be discussed. The coaching program manager categorizes the results from the surveys at the end of engagements as the "micro-analysis." The ROI measurement, based on changes to talent management outcomes, is called the "macro-analysis." The coaching program manager is aware that senior management is more interested in the macro-analysis than the micro-analysis. The micro-analysis, or business impact survey, is the price of entry. Management expects that some type of evaluation is conducted to show that the solution is effective. Results from the macro-analysis concern senior management more, as they relate to critical business issues such as their talent pipeline.

Coaching Micro-Analysis

In developing the business impact survey, several objectives were identified. The first objective was to quantify the bottom-line impact to the business as a result of the coaching. However, an efficient process was needed to collect this data, given the company's feedback about collecting detailed ROI information in prior attempts. A second objective was to collect data about the effectiveness of the coach and the coaching process, to monitor quality and make adjustments as needed. This survey is sent at the end of the coaching engagement to both the leaders and their managers.

The business impact survey contains four sections as shown in Figure 14-1. Sections one through three utilize a five-point agreement scale, while section four is for write-in comments.

Figure 14-1. Sections of Business Impact Survey

	Description	Completed By
1	Satisfaction with coaching experience and process	Leader and Manager, Coach
2	Learning acquisition, application, and impact	Leader and Manager, Coach
3	Effectiveness of the coach	Leader and Manager
4	Other suggestions and comments	Leader and Manager, Coach

Section one of the survey captures Level 1 information about overall satisfaction with the coaching. In addition, it contains questions about the coaching process. The responses to these questions are used as a diagnostic about potential areas of enhancement in the coaching process. Figure 14-2 provides a sample of questions in this section of the survey.

Figure 14-2. Sample Questions, Section 1 of Business Impact Survey					
	Strongly Disagree	Disagree	Neutral	Agree	Strongly Agree
Overall, the coaching was a valuable investment.	1	2	3	4	5
An accurate assessment (for example strengths, development needs, business demands, and career interests) was done at the beginning of the coaching process.	1	2	3	4	5
The coaching plan included target goals and actions to support this person's development.	1	2	3	4	5
Appropriate and effective mechanisms were in place for monitoring progress against the coaching plan.	1	2	3	4	5

Section two of the survey captures Level 2 through 4 information about learning acquisition, application, and business impact from the coaching. The aim is to have the leaders and their managers quantify the actual bottom-line impact of coaching on the business. Figure 14-3 provides a sample of questions in this section of the survey.

Figure 14-3. Sample Questions, Section 2 of Business Impact Survey

	Strongly Disagree	Disagree	Neutral	Agree	Strongly Agree	Don't Know
He is more knowledgeable in those areas in which they have received coaching.	1	2	3	4	5	6
He has applied the knowledge or skills gained from coaching back on the job.	1	2	3	4	5	6
Improvement in his new skills and behaviors have had a positive impact on business results.	1	2	3	4	5	6
Please estimate the bottom-line results achieved by the company due to coaching received by this person (for example, "New negotiation skills helped save $1M in a recent contract renewal" or "New skills in motivating others helped retain a key direct report, saving $250K of replacement costs").	Open Ended					

Section three of the survey captures information about the effectiveness of the coach. This information serves two critical purposes. First, it provides the coaching program manager with a monitoring mechanism to ensure that the coaches are providing high-quality services. Secondly, it provides the coaches with a feedback mechanism to hear how they are doing directly from their clients. At the end of the survey, the leaders and managers are asked for their approval in sharing their feedback with the coach. If approved, then the feedback is forwarded to each coach. This feedback loop has received a positive response from the coaches as they appreciate hearing direct feedback, both positive and constructive, from their clients. Figure 14-4 provides a sample of questions in this section of the survey.

Figure 14-4. Sample Questions, Section 3 of Business Impact Survey

	Strongly Disagree	Disagree	Neutral	Agree	Strongly Agree	Don't Know
The coach was knowledgeable about our business and culture.	1	2	3	4	5	6
The coach was well prepared for the coaching meetings I attended.	1	2	3	4	5	6
I would recommend this coach to others.	1	2	3	4	5	6

Section 4, the final section of the survey, contains open-ended questions. These questions ask for overall comments about the coaching engagement and suggestions for ways it could be improved.

Results from the business impact survey are tallied and analyzed quarterly. The results are shared with internal stakeholders and with coaches during the coach community meetings. The information collected from the business impact survey is extremely important in showing the value of coaching, especially the bottom-line impact as estimated by the leaders and their managers. It is very powerful to show internal stakeholders that the leaders see significant value to the business from the investment made in coaching. Also, showing the results to the coaches helps keep them highly engaged and committed to being part of the preferred coaching network and delivering high-quality services.

Coaching Macro-Analysis

With the business impact survey process in place, the coaching program manager decided to take the evaluation approach a step further, as there was curiosity about how coaching was affecting talent management. Termed "macro-analysis," an effort was undertaken to determine the impact of coaching on promotions, performance ratings, and retention of key talent.

The first step taken was to identify which coaching participants to include in the analysis. This resulted in examining 47 executive coaching engagements over a two-year span. The next step was to collect talent management information on each person. Employee data was collected from the human resources operations group, and augmented with succession and talent management information from the executive development group. The goal was to find changes in the defined areas during or after the coaching engagement took place.

The analysis uncovered positive results across a number of areas. Of the 47 executives analyzed:

- Sixteen, or 34 percent, were promoted during or after the coaching engagement.

- Nine, or 19 percent, had increases in performance ratings during or after the coaching engagement.

- One hundred percent of those identified as key talent (15 of the 47) remained with the company after coaching was completed.

These results caught the attention of key stakeholders more so than data from the business impact surveys. They spoke to leaders who understand the importance of having the right talent in place in order to meet their business plans and goals.

To determine the ROI of the coaching program, the coaching program manager chose to use the data from the macro-analysis instead of the Level 4 data collected from the business impact survey. The reason for this choice is that the Level 4 data indicates an extremely high ROI; similar to historical ROI studies done for coaching, such as the MetrixGlobal LLC study on a Fortune 500 telecommunication company that showed a 788 percent ROI (Anderson, 2001), and the Manchester Study which showed a coaching ROI of 5.7 times the investment (McGovern et al., 2001). The coaching program manager believed that a more credible and believable ROI could be derived from the data from the talent management outcomes.

The results from the macro-analysis are converted into monetary results so that an ROI of coaching can be calculated. In regards to promotions, the assumption is made that 25 percent of the 16 promotions could be filled with external candidates. Using an average annual salary for senior leadership positions, and a cost-to-hire figure of three times the annual salary (Personnel Decisions International, 2006), the estimated cost savings are calculated for promoting from within versus hiring externally.

Increases in performance ratings results in an improvement in productivity. To calculate the monetary value of this, the assumption is made that an increase in performance is worth a 15 percent increase in productivity. This 15 percent is multiplied by the average annual salary of a senior leader to estimate the worth of gain in productivity.

Retention of key talent also is translated into monetary worth. A first assumption is that coaching helps contribute to retention. Then, the number of key talent retained is multiplied by the company's voluntary turnover rates to identify the number of people who might have left but stayed. This number is then multiplied by the annual salary of a senior leader to estimate the cost savings from retaining key talent.

The final monetary worth associated with the macro analysis is related to increased engagement of key talent. The first assumption is that investing in the development of key talent through coaching leads to high levels of engagement. According to research from the Center for Creative Leadership, engaged employees put forth 57 percent more effort than less engaged employees (Corporate Leadership Council, 2009). Multiplying this 57 percent by the annual salary of a senior leader and the number of leaders who were coached results in significant value to the company, merely from having more highly-engaged engaged employees.

TM INITIATIVE MICRO SCORECARD

The micro- and macro-analyses described above result in significant value to the company. Evaluation from the business impact survey, or micro-analysis, shows positive results on Levels 1 through 4. On a five-point scale, scores for each level were 4.81, 4.52, 4.85, and 4.69 respectively. Leaders and managers also cited intangible benefits due to coaching that they could not quantify.

The main areas noted were increased productivity of the leader and team, and improved working relationships.

The analysis of the impact of coaching on talent management outcomes, or macro-analysis, also showed significant results. Promotions of those coached are estimated to save the company $2.7 million versus having to hire externally. Increases in performance ratings of those coached are estimated at a value of $.4 million; the increase in engagement levels of those coached is estimated to be worth $1.9 million; and retention of key talent is estimated to be worth $.7 million through avoiding costs associated with voluntary turnover. Collectively the estimated value of this analysis is $5.7 million. According to the ROI Institute, it is necessary to isolate the effects of the solution to calculate an accurate ROI. In other words, how much of the $5.7 million derived from the macro-analysis is directly attributable to coaching? Using a 70 percent isolation factor per the estimate of the coaching program manager, the adjusted benefits from coaching are approximately $4.0 million.

The costs of the coaching program are comprised of two key components. One is the actual cost of the coaching for the 47 coaches, included in the macro-analysis. The second cost is the internal costs of managing the coaching program. The total of these costs are estimated to be $1.2 million.

To calculate the ROI of the executive coaching program, the net program benefits are divided by the program costs and multiplied by 100. Using data from the macro-analysis, the ROI is calculated to be 233 percent ($2.8 million/$1.2 million x 100).

Table 14-1. TM Initiative Micro Scorecard

Title: Genentech Executive Coaching

Target Audience: High-Potential Leaders (primarily director-level and above); N=47 for this case study

Duration: Typically 6-month coaching engagements

Business Objectives: Increase performance, readiness, and retention of key talent

Results				
Reaction	Learning	Application	Tangible Benefits	Intangible Benefits
Level 1	**Level 2**	**Level 3**	**Level 4**	
Average rating of 4.81 (5-point agreement scale) to question: "Overall, I was satisfied with the coaching experience."	Average rating of 4.52 (5-point agreement scale) to question: "I am knowledgeable in those areas in which I've received coaching.	Average rating of 4.85 (5-point agreement scale) to question: "I have applied the knowledge or skills gained from my coaching back on the job."	Average rating of 4.69 (5-point agreement scale) to question: "Improvement in my skills and behaviors has had a positive impact on business results." Quantified examples from participants and their managers on the impact of coaching on the bottom line of the business.	Increased productivity of self, of team, and improved working relationships identified as top three benefits.
			Level 5 Conducted macro-analysis showing positive results in areas of promotions ($2.7M), increased performance ($.4M), increased engagement ($1.9M), and retention of key talent ($.7M). Using 70% isolation factor, estimated ROI on coaching spending is 233%.	

> **Technique to Isolate Effects of Program:** Coaching Program Manager estimation
>
> **Technique to Convert Data to Monetary Value:** Coaching Program Manager estimation of Macro-Analysis
>
> **Fully-Loaded Program Costs:** $1.2M
>
> **Barriers to Application of Skills:** Organizational change; heavy workload of leaders
>
> **Recommendations:** Continue investing in coaching of high-potential leaders
>
> **Note:** Not all questions from the business impact survey and their average ratings are listed in this scorecard.

CONCLUSIONS

Designing a coaching evaluation methodology and approach has been an iterative process. It started with tracking coaching activity and spending, progressing to a survey to collect business impact data, and augmenting this with a broader analysis of talent management outcomes and ROI. The key lessons learned from the work in this arena are:

- *Use an approach to which the business leaders will relate.* The experience from those involved in this case study suggests that key stakeholders are more likely to be impressed with data pertaining to talent management outcomes such as promotions, increases in performance, and retention of key talent, than estimations of business impact and ROI percentages.

- *Collecting the data is a challenge.* It is important to have a plan for collecting the data needed to generate an accurate analysis. Even something as simple as collecting the number of coaching engagements and associated spend can be difficult. Find key contacts in procurement, finance, and human resources to partner with to get the information and analysis needed.

- *Involve the coaches in designing an evaluation approach and share results with them.* The coaches have a vested interest in showing the value of the services they are providing, and will be more than willing to help design an evaluation approach. Sharing the results of the evaluation is a great way to keep them engaged and committed to providing high-quality services to the company's leaders.

ABOUT THE AUTHOR

Chris Pollino joined Genentech's executive talent development group in 2007. His responsibilities include managing the succession and talent management process, as well as executive assessment and coaching. Prior to joining Genentech, Chris was a vice president and general manager for Personnel Decisions International (PDI). At PDI, he was responsible for leading the San Francisco operating office and also consulted in various areas, including executive assessment, coaching, and 360 feedback. Prior to PDI, Chris held numerous positions in human resources, finance, and operations in organizations across many industries. Chris holds a bachelor's of science from Babson College, an MBA from Northeastern University, and an MA in counseling psychology from the University of San Francisco.

REFERENCES

Phillips, J. (2007). *Performance Improvement* 46(10).

Kirkpatrick, D.L., and J.D. Kirkpatrick. (1994). *Evaluating Training Programs: The Four Levels.* San Francisco, CA: Berrett-Koehler.

McGovern, L.M., M. Vergara, S. Murphy, L. Barker, and R. Warrenfeltz. (2001). "Maximizing the Impact of Executive Coaching: Behavioral Change, Organizational Outcomes, and Return -on-Investment." *Manchester Review* 6(1): 1-9. [This citation is most frequently known as the "Manchester Study."]

Anderson, M. *Executive Briefing: Case Study on the Return of Investment of Executive Coaching.* MetrixGlobal, LLC.

Personnel Decisions International. (2006). *Assessment Key Concepts.*

Corporate Leadership Council. (2009). *Top Drivers of Discretionary Effort.*

15

ASSESSING THE EFFECTIVENESS OF TALENT MOVEMENT WITHIN A SUCCESSION PLANNING PROCESS

Allan H. Church

INTRODUCTION

While most organizations have well-established succession planning processes directed at future leadership requirements, fewer have a comprehensive means for assessing the effectiveness of the talent-movement aspect of these systems. This case study will provide an overview of key outcomes and ways in which to measure them, drawing on experiences and practices used at PepsiCo.

BACKGROUND

PepsiCo is a growth-oriented consumer products company that generates annual revenue of $66 billion and operations in over 200 countries and territories around the world. With an employee base of more than 300,000, it is critical that the organization has highly effective and efficient human-resource processes that ensure a well-managed, engaged, and motivated workforce. The core business strategy is Performance with Purpose (PwP) which is defined as delivering sustainable growth by investing in a healthier future for people and our planet. This strategy breaks down further into three components: human sustainability, environmental sustainability, and talent sustainability. While all three areas are critically important for the future success of the organization, it is the third element of the PwP framework that is most relevant to the area of talent management and succession planning.

Talent sustainability has been defined by the organization as investing in our associates to help them succeed and develop the skills needed to drive the company's growth, while creating employment opportunities in the communities we serve. More specifically, and for the purpose of this discussion, this translates to having HR systems, practices, and processes that ensure the effective differentiation, movement, and development of leadership talent to drive the organization forward.

In general the organization has had highly effective performance management and talent development processes dating back to the 1980s. The approach to talent management can be broken down into three key components: talent acquisition, organizational learning, and talent development. It is the development aspect that is the focus of this discussion, and in particular the sub-process of moving talent across the organization in order to build future leadership capability.

TALENT MANAGEMENT INITIATIVE

Although its talent management processes are well established, given the changing nature of the workforce and increased need for strategic global thinking, innovation, and learning ability in future leaders, the organization has placed a greater emphasis on understanding the effectiveness of the succession planning and talent movement efforts. The increasing need to provide experiences across different parts of the business and ensure that planned moves are actually executed to deliver critical learning has become of paramount importance. As a result, while the philosophical underpinnings of the talent processes have not changed, the approach to assessing and measuring the impact of those efforts has been significantly enhanced. This has been driven by the need to reinforce new behaviors with respect to talent movement, and ensure there is accountability through a more formal scorecarding process. The focus here is on the talent movement component of the succession planning process, and how the organization has approached the measurement of critical outcomes with respect to their bench-building efforts.

A Framework for Assessment

In general the success of a talent management process can be defined in a number of different ways. While some practitioners would align their framework to a version of the standard HR employee life-cycle model (attract, select, onboard, perform, develop, and retire), others would argue for a more strategic focus on the needs of the business. Although many of the core applications might be the same regardless of the framework selected, their outcomes may vary depending on the conceptual approach taken. For example, a life-cycle model might yield targets such as 100 percent completion of performance reviews or an average of 10 hours of training annually per employee. A business-strategy planning approach, on the other hand, would likely be focused on the percentage of executive positions filled by internal candidates versus external hires, or the percent utilization of high-potentials in international assignments.

At PepsiCo a strategic business lens is applied. The process by which talent is classified, reviewed, and strategically planned for is called "People Planning." The purpose is to calibrate and align on the differentiation of talent into various category schemes and talent pools, discuss the individuals and their strengths and development opportunities, outline long-term strategic plans for their development, and create slates or lists of candidates for succession to current and future roles. Related to this effort is the game-planning process, which involves the more tactical aspects of planning specific short- and mid-term movement for individuals. Often referred to externally as "talent brokering," these meetings are held multiple times a year and involve a number of leaders and HR representatives to map out detailed movement plans.

Together, people planning and game planning form the framework that collectively represents talent management, succession planning, and talent movement. Aligning the framework with a set of metrics for this process is critical for ensuring the right results. So what constitutes successful talent movement in a succession planning process? What are the expected outcomes? In general there are five areas to consider, which range from immediate to long-term impact.

Talent Differentiation and Alignment

First, and arguably one of the most fundamental aspects of any succession planning and talent movement process, is the differentiation and alignment of talent into some classification or grouping of individuals. While much has been written about the challenges, issues, and models associated with identifying future potential (see Silzer & Church, 2009, 2010), the important point here is that a successful talent management process must deliver a limited and agreed-upon list of individuals on which the organization can focus its attention and plans to move into new roles going forward. This segmentation into pools of talent is critical because it provides a means for selectively applying greater amounts of developmental resources and attention to some groups and lesser amounts to others.

It is also significant because it drives the alignment and utilization of that classification process across different leadership teams. Alignment in this context means that all parties are operating with a common approach, language, set of standards, and selection criteria. This not only makes the discussion of talent more consistent in general, but it also makes actual movement more likely to occur because leaders in different businesses and functions have a shared mindset and criteria for assessing future potential. Finally, it supports the credibility and integrity in the process overall, particularly in the eyes of the end-users and recipients of the process. In fact, an argument can be made that leaders and managers should actually be held accountable for using an aligned talent model in the talent management process.

Plan Execution and Deployment

The second element of an effective succession planning and movement process is perhaps the most obvious; that is, the follow-through of the detailed plans that are made during the discussions. Given the considerable amount of time and effort required to gather data from employees, managers, and human resources via feedback and assessment tools (Church & Waclawski, 2010) it is no wonder that actually executing these plans is an important and expected outcome.

Not only does failure to execute talent plans result in wasted resources but it builds cynicism and negativity in all those involved, including the broader employee population. If real movement does not occur these meetings will quickly lose their perceived value and alternative means of developing talent will be established by line leaders. The way to avoid this splintering is to ensure that a robust process and set of metrics (and shared accountability) are established.

Development

Another important aspect of the execution of a talent movement plan is achieving the intended outcome of the plan itself—the enhanced development or growth of the individuals for whom the plans were created. After all, the planning process is not conducted for its own sake but with the expectation that the leaders being transitioned into new roles will develop additional skills and capabilities based on their experiences and capacity to learn. This in turn will result in stronger candidates for future leadership positions. Although this may seem synonymous with the basic plan execution, it is distinct and therefore worthy of additional measurement efforts for two reasons.

First, not all talent movement plans (even when executed as designed) will result in a leader learning what he is intended to from a given job role or experience. For example, just because someone spends some time in an international assignment does not guarantee that they will develop the "global mindset" that was the reason for placing them in that role. Similarly, putting a high-potential in a job that is intended to lead a merger will not deliver the full experience if the merger falls through.

Secondly, individuals can learn new skills and build capability in other ways beyond changing jobs in an organization. While many talent management practitioners would argue, as does PepsiCo, that experiential learning is perhaps the most robust approach leaders can build skills through means such as coaching and mentoring, formal training, action learning projects, leadership councils, special task forces, and external activities such as board memberships. In general these options represent the construct of developing in place. In fact, many organizations are exploring various job-enrichment methods given the increasing lack of mobility and changing nature of the employment contract.

Talent Availability and Bench Strength

One very important outcome of a successful talent management process is the availability of qualified talent to take on leadership roles at some point in the future. This is, without a doubt, the most relevant outcome to the business itself and to C-suite leaders and external stakeholders such as the board of directors. However robust the development tools and processes are for an organization, if they do not yield the right talent at the right time, they are fundamentally ineffective. When leadership positions open or are newly created, it is critical that the organization has a ready list of potential candidates slated to fill those roles.

While there are no fixed rules as to how many or at what level these candidates need to be, nor what is the right level of mix between internal versus external individuals on a slate, it is generally agreed that having the option of sourcing a leadership role from within is a good thing for most organizations. This is true because of the high level of failure rates reported for onboarding external hires to senior positions, and the increase in the time it takes for external candidates to make an impact when compared with those from inside the organization. As a result one of the key metrics that many organizations report externally to stakeholders is the degree of coverage for succession. In general this outcome is both time-dependent (not an immediate result of the movement process) as well as somewhat subjective in nature. Still it is commonly used in practice.

Employee Engagement and Employer Brand

The fifth aspect of a successful talent movement and succession planning process is the level of engagement and perceptions of employees regarding the broader talent management agenda. More specifically, how employees feel about the talent review, development, and movement efforts in the company can have a direct impact on their levels of engagement. For example, the extent to which employees feel that the talent planning processes are objective, fair, and transparent has been linked through research at PepsiCo to their overall satisfaction and commitment. Moreover, employee engagement has a direct link to business performance, so ensuring employees believe in the talent planning system is vitally important to overall business success.

Beyond the relationship between engagement and performance, however, is the longer-term impact of employee perceptions on the external talent marketplace. As individuals leave an organization they are likely to share their experiences and attitudes with others, which can influence general perceptions among prospective employees, headhunters, and students about the employer brand of an organization. While perhaps the most ethereal of the outcomes described here, it is nonetheless one that should be considered with respect to long-term impact.

In sum, these elements are important for understanding and measuring the success of any talent planning and movement process. The next section will review some important factors to consider when developing specific outcome measures at each level of evaluation.

EVALUATION METHODOLOGY AND RESULTS

Although succession planning and talent movement processes are not programmatic in nature, it is possible to apply the standard evaluation criteria

(Phillips, Phillips, Ray, 2012) of execution (Level 0), reaction (Level 1), learning (Level 2), application (Level 3), business impact (Level 4), and return-on-investment (Level 5) by utilizing various forms of internal data. These include data-driven tools such as the performance management system, 360-degree feedback, organizational surveys, and internally-developed metrics regarding talent movement and tracking. This is the approach taken at PepsiCo as part of its overall talent management strategy.

Level 0: Talent Movement and Deployment (Execution)

Perhaps the most straightforward measure of the effectiveness of a talent movement process is the extent to which the detailed movement plans are actually executed. Overall it is a relatively easy task to require leaders to commit to a set of moves within a given time period (six months or a year), and then track the successful completion of those moves. Table 15-1 provides an example of a scorecard tool that can be applied to measure such outcomes.

Table 15-1. Example of Talent Movement Tracking Tool

Level	Name	Talent Pool	Type of Move (Import/ Export)	New Title	Bench Consequence (for example, promoted hi-po, experiences being gained in new role, replaced blocker, and so on)
Total	xx Successful /Executed xx Planned Moves				

Level	Name	Talent Pool	Reason for Not Executing Planned Move	Next Steps
Total	xx Not Executed xx Planned Moves			

PepsiCo has developed a measure called the "Bench Quality Index" (BQI) which represents the successful execution of the movement plans that were defined in the prior year's people-planning and game-planning processes. The challenge in measurement here is the degree of complexity and number of variables that exist in executing the actual talent plans. While it is relatively easy to match individuals with various assignments to deliver needed learning and capabilities, other factors such as mobility, criticality of the incumbent to the business, presence of a ready backfill, career aspirations and motivation, and life-stage all play an important role in the successful execution of the talent plans.

This means that while one might expect a measure such as the BQI to yield 100 percent completion annually, depending on the number and complexity of the moves outlined, 50 to 75 percent of planned moves achieved might be a more realistic and achievable goal. Clearly judgment must be applied when creating talent movement plans and numeric goals to avoid only measuring "easy" plans versus those that, while perhaps more difficult to measure, would yield a better long-term benefit in terms of leadership bench strength.

Level 1: Attitudes and Engagement (Reaction)
Employee attitudes and perceptions about the talent planning and movement process can affect business performance. These can be measured through the

use of organizational surveys. Many companies have opinion surveys in place and use these to evaluate employee engagement in the workplace. Far fewer companies, however, strategically leverage their survey programs to also assess employee attitudes regarding the impact and effectiveness of their planning and movement processes. In doing so they would be able to use their survey as a talent management evaluation tool.

PepsiCo takes this strategic approach to their survey efforts. The organization has a long history of effectively using their Organizational Health Survey to measure a wide range of content areas, including the effectiveness of talent planning and development efforts. Questions are included that focus on employee attitudes towards talent management, the processes themselves, manager capabilities, and expected outcomes. Table 15-2 provides some sample survey items with respect to talent management processes.

Table 15-2. Sample Talent Management-Related Survey Items

Question (Rated 1=Strongly Disagree to 5=Strongly Agree)	Action Planning Target
Career advancement opportunities (vacancies, promotions, project teams, and so on) within the organization are clearly communicated to all employees.	Talent Planning Processes
How satisfied are you with your opportunity to get a better job at your company?	Talent Planning Processes
There is a high-quality backfill (high potential, outstanding performer) ready to take my role within six months if I were to move to another role.	Talent Planning Processes
I feel that this is a company where I can have a successful career.	Career Development and Pathing Tools
I am given a real opportunity to improve my skills in this company.	Talent Development Offerings
Managers are effective at building the talent for the future.	Manager Capability
My manager encourages and engages in candid discussion of my career opportunities at my company and other divisions.	Manager Capability
My manager ensures that I understand our people processes and tools, including our respective responsibilities. [Specific sub-item selection for talent planning]	Manager Capability and HR Communications

In terms of measurement in this area the organization utilizes a simple scoring template that is applied to all items. Using percentage favorables (the percentage of "strongly agree" and "agree" responses to a given question using a five-point scale) any item score at 75 percent or better is a clear strength, 74 to 55 percent is considered an area to watch, and fewer than 55 percent is a clear opportunity. In order for the talent management efforts to be considered effective, one would expect the survey items in this area to be at 75 percent favorable or better. While the data collected from this type of survey represent perceptions only, they provide an important set of insights and can be used to drive behavioral change by enabling the organization to survey different businesses, functions, or even individual managers with respect to the effectiveness of their talent management efforts.

If external perceptions of talent management effectiveness are important to an organization, surveys can also be used to measure attitudes from individuals outside the company, such as search partners, headhunters, recruiters, or even potential candidates themselves. While this type of data is even more removed from the day-to-day experience of actual employees, it does represent an important scorecard for the talent agenda, particularly if a company is hiring externally in sufficient numbers.

Level 2: Mapping of Critical Experiences to Roles (Learning)

At the learning level of evaluation, the outcome of interest is the extent to which the individual taking on a new position is gaining exposure to the learning experiences intended to further develop his or her skills as a leader. Building on the example provided earlier, if an individual is placed in a strategic role in support of a merger, it is important to be able to measure if she is gaining the requisite experiences, such as involvement in the due-diligence process, supply-chain harmonization, and staffing and resource rationalization. If the transition to a new role has occurred but the individual is not exposed to the needed experiences, then the desired outcome of the process does not occur.

Although longer-term impact of learning on the job will be measured through other means such as performance and behavior change, from a more intermediate perspective it is possible to assess whether the roles identified for the individual will deliver the experiences required. To do this, it is important to begin by listing developmental experiences that are important to an organization in building future leadership bench. At PepsiCo these are called "Critical Experiences," and there is a list of 15 that have been developed from prior succession planning efforts. Having a single consistent taxonomy for these across the organization ensures that leaders are using the same lens and planning criteria when engaging in talent discussions.

Next, the organization needs to identify a set of critical developmental jobs or roles that will be used for talent planning and movement purposes. While all jobs provide some level of learning for any incumbent, there are certain roles that are more developmental in nature because of unique aspects, such as their location in an emerging market. The critical experiences are then mapped to these key developmental roles so that it is clear what experiences an individual is expected to obtain from a given assignment. This level of clarity is critical for both the organization and the individual moving into the new role.

Finally, the learning evaluation is measured following the planned movement (anywhere from three to four months into the assignment) by the degree to which the individual is actually gaining exposure to the critical experiences. This learning outcome can be assessed using a simple checklist approach whereby the individual is given a 0 "no exposure," 1 "some exposure," or 2 "significant exposure" to each of the planned experiences on the job. Creating a checklist is not only useful in calibrating expected future performance and behavioral learning outcomes, but also in subsequent talent planning efforts.

Level 3: Performance and Behavior Change (Application)

The next level for measuring the effectiveness of a succession planning and talent movement process concerns the impact of learning on key performance outcomes over time. In general there are two ways to approach the application of this metric.

The first method is to measure the performance of the individual placed in the new role. While business performance itself is generally not the primary focus of a talent movement process, clearly organizations do not want to place their highest-potential talent in roles that do not deliver results. Since most mature organizations that have talent planning processes also have formal performance management systems in place, this assessment should be a relatively simple endeavor. The only caveat is to consider using more than just the first year's level of performance in developing this metric. In many cases it can take more than a single business cycle to make a significant impact in a role. Thus, an average of two or more years might yield more telling results. Research has shown, for example, that some high-potentials initially receive lower performance ratings than their more tenured peers, because the high-potentials change roles more frequently and are therefore always getting up to speed.

The second approach to measuring the behavioral impact of talent movement is more complex, but also more reflective of the objectives of the succession and bench-building process—that is, measuring whether the individual's skills, capabilities, and leadership behaviors have been enhanced as a result of the experiential learning from the new role. Although there are many ways to assess this outcome, standard OD data-based feedback tools are particularly useful here, such as 360-degree feedback and functional competency assessments. Since many organizations already have feedback tools in place it would be a relatively simple effort to incorporate a pre- and post-job assignment (movement) assessment tool to determine improvement in leadership or functional capability. PepsiCo has used this approach to measure increases in leadership capability over time following movement into more senior-level roles.

While direct comparisons in 360-degree feedback ratings across different roles (and between individuals) can introduce error into the measurement process, and probably should not be used as sole inputs for talent management decision-making (London 2001), an individual's patterns and trends are typically consistent over time, making career growth- and development-related interpretation possible at a macro level. If the analysis provides some indication that additional skills and capabilities have been mastered and enhanced leadership behaviors are demonstrated, this would be a meaningful measure of success for the talent movement process.

Level 4: Talent Availability and Bench Strength (Business Impact)

As a measure of success of the movement process, talent availability and bench strength are perhaps the most important outcomes for senior leaders and key internal and external stakeholders such as board members. For the most part organizations with robust succession planning processes use some form of talent availability, readiness, or bench-strength metric. These are typically derived by calculating the number of potential candidates for some subset of key or critical leadership roles as identified earlier in the process. This subset might consist of the top 10 most senior roles in the organization, including the CEO, or perhaps a unique collection of jobs that deliver a competitive advantage to the business. If a readiness indicator is also used in the calculation (such as ready now, ready in one to two years, ready in three to five years, and ready in five or more years) it affords the organization with an even greater degree of precision in planning, because it provides a timing horizon for when individuals will become ready for new leadership positions. Either way the concept is straightforward and measured by the number of qualified candidates who exist for each role, yielding a coverage index.

While there is no standard value for this index, in practice having at least two potential candidates qualified to fill each role (also known as "two-deep bench") is considered an acceptable result. Some organizations prefer a "three-deep bench" of candidates instead, given the logic that one individual will take the role, one will likely stay with the organization, and the third will leave because they did not receive the leadership position in question. In practice some roles will likely yield a bench-strength index of zero while others might meet the goal of two- or even three-deep depending on the type of calculation. Once a baseline metric for bench coverage has been set, it is relatively easy to assess the impact of a succession planning process year over year by reviewing the impact of planned movement on the number of available talent to fill critical roles. The only concerns when working with this metric are ensuring that there is a consistent and transparent approach to allowing (or not allowing) the same individual to be "double counted" on more than one candidate slate list, and perhaps most importantly, ensuring that the individuals listed on the slating charts would indeed be considered as candidates for the position when it becomes open, versus just being listed on an HR process template because it needed to be completed.

Level 5: Bottom-Line Results (Return-on-Investment)

The fifth level of evaluation concerns the impact of talent movement on bottom-line results or return-on-investment. This is without a doubt the most complex level of measurement for a talent movement process. While this could in theory be measured by looking at the overall business outcomes of sales, market share, profit, and so forth (comparing the impact over time of new talent in critical roles versus other areas of the business with no change in leadership), it would be challenging to accurately link outcomes from the individual movement itself directly to these indices because there are so many other factors involved in the successful performance of a business overall.

One macro-level approach might be to determine the impact of a company's perceived weak or strong leadership on stock prices, and translate this into dollar figures. This would, however, require calibration across more than one organization to establish a true measurement model. Aside from this approach, dollar figures can be calculated from other actions related to talent movement (or misaligned placements), such as the negative cost to the organization of poor decisions, or movements resulting in turnover or terminations.

TM INITIATIVE MICRO SCORECARD

The discussion so far has covered a number of potential measures of the effectiveness of a succession planning and talent movement processes. Table 15-3 provides a summary scorecard of these measures of success.

Table 15-3. TM Initiative Micro Scorecard					
Talent Management Initiative: Succession Planning and Talent Movement					
Target Audience: Executives and Professionals					
Duration: Annual					
Business Objectives: Talent Movement Into New Roles to Build Leadership Bench Strength					
Planned Results					
Execution	Reaction	Learning	Application	Tangible Benefits	Intangible Benefits
Level 0	**Level 1**	**Level 2**	**Level 3**	**Level 4**	
Extent to Which Movement Plans Are Executed	Employee Survey Results Regarding Process Effectiveness (> 75% Favorable)	Degree to Which Individuals Are Exposed to Critical Experiences in New Roles	Performance of Talent in New Roles Improvements in Leadership Behaviors via 360-Degree Feedback Tools	Percentage of Bench Coverage for Senior/Key Roles ("3-deep bench") Internal vs. External Fill Rates	Perceived Strength of Senior Leadership in Role and Future Leadership Pipeline by External Stakeholders
Technique to Isolate Effects of Program: Multiple (plan execution, employee surveys, job-mapping performance and behavioral feedback, tracking)					
Technique to Convert Data to Monetary Value: N/A					
Fully-loaded Program Costs: N/A					
Barriers to Application of Skills: Unanticipated changes in positions following movement/placement					
Recommendations: Senior leader alignment on frameworks, measures, and outcomes					

Several factors will drive the determination of the most appropriate measures here. Aside from the conceptual aspects identified earlier, other factors include the timing and availability of data from HR processes, and the philosophical stance of senior leadership regarding which metrics are of most importance to them personally. While each metric will be linked to business outcomes in some way, different leaders bring their own perspectives and points of view to talent assessment. External stakeholders (boards of directors, customers, and suppliers) may also have a share in determining the right metrics for talent management-related outcomes.

CONCLUSIONS

The purpose of this chapter has been to review the key outcomes and measurement options associated with the talent movement component of a succession planning process. Although there is no best answer, it is possible to develop a robust set of measures that account for many different potential outcomes. The ultimate goal is to design a framework that effectively balances the needs of the business with some degree of acceptable rigor in the measurement model. Here are some final points to consider when building and evaluating an effective succession planning and talent movement process.

- As with most change initiatives, senior leader alignment on the frameworks, outcomes, and associated measures is critical to driving the successful implementation of any talent management scorecard. If the system does not speak to or meet the leaders' needs it will quickly be relegated to an administrative exercise.

- Data integrity and having the right systems to support a scorecard are very important as well. While having this infrastructure is foundational, many organizations today continue to struggle with the continuous reporting of quality data in the talent management area.

- By definition the role of any metric or scorecard is to provide feedback regarding the progress or outcome of a process. While such metrics are helpful for spotting trends and providing an indication of strength overall, they are far more useful at the function, business unit, or manager level. By measuring and comparing talent management results across groups where decisions are actually made (and linking these to performance ratings with pay-related outcomes), it is possible to drive an effective process.

- That said, the greater the link to individual performance measures, the more careful you need to be about exactly what you measure and reinforce. Be careful about unintended consequences, for example, measuring talent movement by itself across business units might drive high volume but low quality. Keep the measurement simple and focused on the behavioral outcomes you are trying to drive.

- Although linking talent management processes to the business strategy is critical, the strategy itself can and does sometimes change. If these changes occur too often it may result in an inconsistent (or even incorrect) approach to building future leadership bench. When an organization is undergoing rapid business-model changes, it may require more innovative and future-oriented thinking beyond the typical three to five-year planning horizon to maintain an effective long-term talent pipeline.

- Finally, it is important to establish as much stability in measurement and scorecard models as possible. While there are valid reasons for changing talent management processes and frameworks (for example, a new CEO, merger and acquisition, or a major cultural crisis), change for change's sake should be avoided as much as possible. The continual pursuit of what has been called that "shiny new penny" is not likely to result in a strong talent management process or set of outcomes for the long-term.

ABOUT THE AUTHOR

Allan H. Church is the vice president of organization development global groups and executive assessment and development at PepsiCo. He has been a leader of the talent management agenda there since 2000. Previously he spent nine years as an external OD consultant working for Warner Burke Associates, and several years at IBM. On the side, he has served as an adjunct professor at Columbia University, a visiting scholar at Benedictine University, and past chair of the Mayflower Group (a survey consortium). Allan received his PhD in organizational psychology from Columbia University. He is a Fellow of the Society for Industrial-Organizational Psychology, the American Psychological Association, and the Association for Psychological Science.

REFERENCES

Church, A.H., and J. Waclawski. (2010). "Take the Pepsi Challenge: Talent Development at PepsiCo." In *Strategy-Driven Talent Management: A Leadership Imperative*, eds. R. Silzer and B.E. Dowell. San Francisco, CA: Jossey-Bass.

London, M. (2001). "The Great Debate: Should 360 Be Used for Administration or Development Only?" In *The Handbook of Multisource Feedback*, eds. D.W. Bracken, C.W. Timmreck, and A.H. Church. San Francisco, CA: Jossey-Bass.

Phillips, J., P.P. Phillips, and R.L. Ray. (2012). *Measuring Leadership Development*. New York: McGraw-Hill.

Silzer, R., and A.H. Church. (2010). "Identifying and Assessing High-Potential Talent: Current Organizational Practices." In *Strategy-Driven Talent Management: A Leadership Imperative*, eds. R. Silzer and B.E. Dowell. San Francisco, CA: Jossey-Bass.

Silzer, R., and A.H. Church. (2009). "The Pearls and Perils of Identifying Potential." *Industrial and Organizational Psychology: Perspectives on Science and Practice* 2: 377-412.

16

THE REAL DOLLAR VALUE
OF EMPLOYEE ENGAGEMENT

Cliff Stevenson

INTRODUCTION

This case study provides an overview of how a national restaurant company tied employee engagement data to actual business outcomes. By measuring the ACE® scores (alignment, capabilities, engagement) of each store and comparing them with the sales and turnover figures for those stores, the correlation between the stores with higher ACE scores and high financial and customer satisfaction levels is quantifiable to dollars and cents.

BACKGROUND

Jack in the Box is a fast service restaurant with outlets located mostly in the western United States. Operating in a highly competitive industry, it has always been faced with the challenge of maintaining a competitive edge in the market. Although Jack in the Box had a few components that differentiated it from its competitors, such as quirky advertising campaigns, varied menu items, and a well-known brand, the company still needed to improve profit. This was accomplished in part by quantifying the business results of specific people programs designed to increase engagement, alignment, and employee skills.

This quantification was first initiated by Mark Blankenship, SVP and the Chief Administrative Officer of Jack in the Box, who noted that there was an opportunity for significant change when he first arrived at the company. With a common format used for pay, training, and so forth, Jack in the Box possessed a natural control group of stores that could be used to statistically validate the efficacy of experimental programs designed to increase employee engagement, alignment, and skills.

The ACE Model

These experimental programs utilized the ACE® model developed by the Metrus Group, a consulting company that Jack in the Box partnered with. By focusing on these three things (shown to have the highest correlation with financial success at the surveyed stores), Jack in the Box could not only show improvements in each area, but by comparing sales and turnover at the higher ACE-scoring stores to the stores in the control group, could also measure how its human capital efforts led to real business results in terms of dollars and cents.

As noted earlier, the three elements of the ACE scorecard are alignment, capabilities, and engagement. For the purposes of the metrics collected by Jack in the Box, each of these is defined in the following way:

- *Alignment* is a measure of how well employees understand the company's strategy and tactics, and how those strategies and tactics connect to what they do each day.

- *Capabilities* are defined as employees having the skills, resources, and information to execute their responsibilities.

- *Engagement* represents an employee's commitment, their advocacy for the brand, and the level of discretionary effort they are willing to put forth at work.

This program was begun as Jack in the Box underwent a large shift in how their business is operated. When this program was first instituted, Jack in the Box was 80 percent corporate-owned and 20 percent franchise-owned, a ratio that has since flipped—the company is now 80 percent franchise-owned and 20 percent corporate-owned. What this means logistically is that the company needed to prove that this engagement program worked before franchise owners would go along with it.

TALENT MANAGEMENT INITIATIVE

Jack in the Box's model for running restaurants is based on the service-profit chain. Briefly, the service-profit chain is a series of links between employee satisfaction and profit (Heskett, 1994). It shows how a framework of support and services provided to employees empowers them to deliver better service and value to customers. This perceived value on the part of the customers leads to greater satisfaction with the service and the brand, which in turn breeds stronger loyalty. Increased customer loyalty ultimately leads to greater profit and overall financial success.

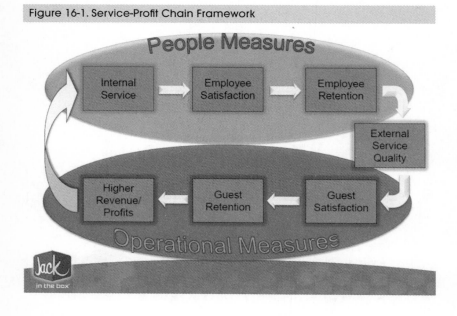

Figure 16-1. Service-Profit Chain Framework

Using this service-profit chain model, as depicted in Figure 16-1, the organization's leadership concluded that if they focused their efforts on hiring employees with greater skills and capabilities, this would drive positive growth along the chain. Logically, the more competent and happy employees were, the better the service they would provide, the happier their guests would be, and so on. This model permeated Jack in the Box's corporate philosophy.

In order to ensure that the service-profit chain was functioning, annual employee surveys were conducted with the objective of measuring employee engagement and satisfaction. In analyzing this data, Jack in the Box realized that the story emanating from the data stopped before reaching a conclusion. What was missing from the original data was the link between employee satisfaction and high-performing employees—merely scoring high on the employee satisfaction survey did not necessarily translate to a productive, engaged employee.

Now that Jack in the Box had an idea of what was missing, the annual satisfaction survey was supplemented with quarterly internal service surveys that measured each of the following eight dimensions:

- communication

- feedback

- interpersonal treatment

- leadership

- physical environment

- rewards and recognition

- staffing

- training and development.

Once the quarterly surveys were in use, Jack in the Box leaders had a wider spectrum of employee engagement and employee performance data points to analyze and correlate. They shared these results with the store managers and included them in their performance reviews as a means of reinforcing what was important for employee performance.

Although many of the managers were surprised by the results, the surveys were conclusive—the most important factor in driving engagement and performance was not compensation, as was commonly believed. Instead they showed that the key factors were consistency in training, staffing, and feedback.

This evaluation of employees across a number of different dimensions became known as the "people equity scorecard" (Blankenship, 2012). By examining the disparities in results across many different scorecards, the various areas that needed improvement in individual stores could be easily identified.

Figure 16-2. People Equity (ACE) Scorecard

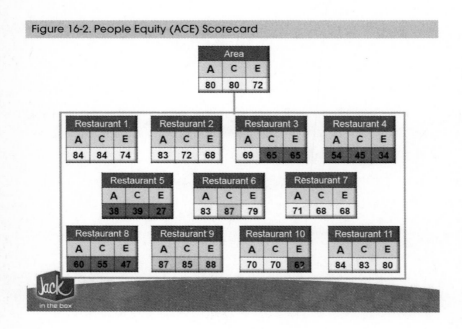

As seen in Figure 16-2, scores that fall within certain ranges are grouped on a "traffic light" model in which green is an overall positive score, yellow shows cause for concern, and red is an indicator that a particular area is in dire need of improvement. Only by optimizing all three aspects of the ACE model can a store truly be considered primed for financial success, and the correlation between those scores and the store's revenue has been shown to be statistically valid.

Jack in the Box franchise owners have embraced this approach (Blankenship, 2012). By surveying and collecting the data necessary for the program, it allows franchisees to gain a clearer understanding of not only what is making their stores successful, but also those areas that need work. Understandably, the greatest interest for the franchise owners is how to turn those opportunities for improvement into actions that lead to higher revenue-generating stores. In some cases this can mean improved communication—and usually more consistency in that communication—around areas such as compensation, equipment maintenance, and training. By giving the managers objective data on the problem areas, it shows not only how the managers can improve performance, but also the financial impact of those improvements.

Many store owners learned that by running this program at all of their sites, even those locations that had high scores could be improved. Often, those stores that scored "in the red" would receive the greatest attention; but even some stores that showed very high ACE scores could still find ways to improve and earn higher profits. This was especially true in high-volume stores.

Stores that have high scores in each of these three dimensions achieve consistently higher financial results over those restaurants that score high on one or even two of the ACE measurements. In addition, the ACE model allows for fascinating profiling of the many types of employees who score differently within the model. Just as with store data, where scoring high on all three components signifies full optimization, most employees in stores with optimized scores also score high in the three key areas.

In Figure 16-3, note that the top and bottom spots are those employees who score either very well or very poorly across all three dimensions. For those two types of employees, obvious categories are assigned. However, for those employees who score high in only one or two different dimensions, there are myriad ways in which sub-optimization can manifest itself. Only by understanding the various ways in which employees are under-utilized can managers provide the right type of guidance to get them back on track.

Figure 16-3. ACE Profiles: Are Leaders Optimizing Talent?

Alignment	Capabilities	Engagement	Profile	
⬆	⬆	⬆	Optimized Talent	
⬇	⬇	⬆	Misguided Enthusiasm	Sub-Optimization
⬇	⬆	⬆	Strategic Disconnect	
⬆	⬇	⬆	Under Equipped	
⬆	⬆	⬇	Disengaged	
⬆	⬇	⬇	Unable/Unwilling	
⬇	⬆	⬇	Wasted Talent	
⬇	⬇	⬇	High Risk	

⬆ High   ⬇ Low

Jack in the box®   **Metrus**Group

In order to implement such sweeping reforms at its many locations, technological upgrades were required to the system that gathered the results. In the late 1990s, the surveys and assessments were paper-based. Today, both the annual survey and the quarterly internal service surveys are computer-driven. Moving the surveys to an online format allows for efficient administration in both English and Spanish at computers provided at every store. An external partner is used for the survey and data collection, giving employees a greater sense of security in the information they provide. And shifting the time-consuming task of collecting and compiling the data to an external provider allows for more efficiency.

Many companies alternate between the use of quantitative and qualitative data. The benefits and detractions of both types of data are well documented, but there is still a dearth of research that shows the possible rewards of using both in a seamless fashion. This holistic approach is the goal of Jack in the Box's efforts with their assessment tools; they have created a methodology that captures the connection between employee data and financial data, and they also have identified strategies that show the individual employee benefits of a better quality work environment.

The commitment to consistency that is intrinsic to the ACE approach has been accepted throughout all levels of the organization. Job profiles, hiring tools, and performance management systems for managers and other leaders directly reflect the principles of that model. Also, as more data comes in, small refinements in the system can be made. For example, certain factors have recently begun to emerge as having more effect on employee performance than others (such as learning opportunities over preferred schedules).

One of the key takeaways is the knowledge that data work in two directions. People data can be used to make business decisions, but the business data can also be used to make people decisions. Two examples of this are programs created to help improve consistency and alignment at various Jack in the Box locations. First, 15-minute "crew huddles" were instituted to ensure that all the crew members are aligned with a central goal. Another is a series of programs to help employees with rudimentary English skills gain a higher level of competency with the language. This program, along with a few others, is shown to have a dramatically positive impact on turnover, as seen in Figure 16-4.

At the present time, not every franchisee has implemented all of these changes, but those that have are reporting positive results, and as the data continues to roll in, Jack in the Box continually finds more and more validation for its efforts.

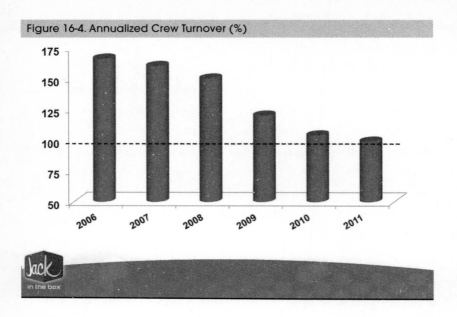

Figure 16-4. Annualized Crew Turnover (%)

EVALUATION METHODOLOGY AND RESULTS

Reaction

Before the ACE program, Jack in the Box was already using a home-grown survey to measure employee satisfaction and engagement. At the time, the survey was a paper-based measurement that gauged such factors as satisfaction with training and development, satisfaction with management, benefits, compensation, and so forth. Overall employee satisfaction was calculated and some correlations between the various factors measured.

As Jack in the Box transitioned to a computer-based system, they were able to gather data on other aspects of the evaluation process, although there were no explicit questions pertaining to satisfaction with the process itself. However, the current average completion rate is more than 90 percent, which can be considered an indication of satisfaction with the evaluation process.

Learning

After the survey scores are compiled and calculated, the store receives a score that falls into one of three distinct areas. When a store falls into the lowest subgroup, it is a clear indication that steps need to be taken to improve the identified problem area. Stores can also be classified in a middle warning category that indicates that there is room for improvement, but that only minor changes may need to be made. Finally, the A, C, or E score for a particular restaurant may be in the top third of scores, in which case it would be considered fully optimized, although even the best stores have shown that there is still some room for improvement.

The power of the data collected is that Jack in the Box can take the survey information and break it down to an individual store to show its strengths and weaknesses. Once this is done, work can begin in earnest with specific managers, focusing on their strengths and opportunities for improvement using proven techniques and strategies pulled from high-performing stores.

These strategies and methods have been collected over time by systematically gathering all of the data on the various high-performing stores and looking for consistent variables across those stores. For instance, if stores of equal size with similar local competitors and local economic conditions had differing ACE scores, yet one had managers with a distinctly different approach from the other, it removed the other extraneous possibilities for that variance in performance, and made it much more likely that those managers' approaches were the cause of their locations' success. Figure 16-5 shows the relationship between problems areas and satisfaction.

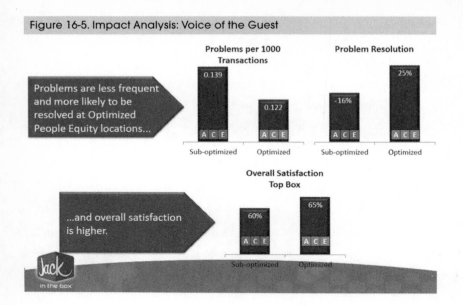

Figure 16-5. Impact Analysis: Voice of the Guest

Application

Part of the initial framework of this system was identifying where the greatest impact of the application of these principles could be had. Although there was most likely some benefit to improving all areas of employee capability, it was expected that there would be one or two areas that would show the greatest return-on-investment.

Jack in the Box found that the number-one driver of employee satisfaction was not pay, as was popularly supposed, but rather employees' perceptions of their managers. Most of the variance in employee satisfaction, and thus down the service-profit chain, could be accounted for by differences in supervisors. Figure 16-6 shows the impact of supervision on satisfaction.

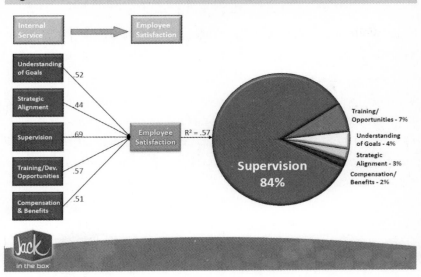

Figure 16-6. Validation of the Service Profit Chain at Jack In The Box

Armed with that knowledge, efforts were focused on improving managerial effectiveness at each store. Using survey data, such as the result that indicated that training opportunities had more effect on employee satisfaction than being able to work preferred schedules, gives managers the direction they need to properly reward their employees, and also lets them know where they should be focusing their attention and resources.

Jack in the Box set up focus groups, gathering those high-performing managers together and discussing what they were doing that made them stand out from the other stores. Unequivocally, they found that the star managers were using the techniques and strategies that had been suggested to them in their corporate training. The low-performing managers, on the other hand, had developed the habit of tweaking the system, or trying to work outside of the tools and capabilities that had been provided to them by corporate.

Using what they gleaned from these sessions, the organization put together a training program for all stores that provided a blueprint on being a good manager and rolled it out to other locations. This has enabled Jack in the Box to go into troubled stores, take additional quick-pulse surveys, and create action plans for the managers to hold them accountable. By doing so, they saw significant improvement in the engagement scores in those restaurants.

Also, by assessing the traits of successful managers at top-performing locations, Jack in the Box was able to create a manager profile that can be used in the job description, hiring, interviewing, and onboarding stages. The assessments did not uncover any new competencies that were missing before, but did allow Jack in the Box to prioritize the competencies that already existed within the framework. This supports the research that managers who view themselves as being part of a people business versus those who consider themselves to be working in a manufacturing plant have been shown to succeed more often (Blankenship, 2012). Prioritization of the competencies allowed Jack in the Box to customize all the hiring and training tools previously mentioned.

Business Impact

The real success story from using this program has been the company's ability to convert each of these measures into a dollar impact on the bottom line. This has been achieved by systematically comparing and contrasting the sales and turnover numbers at stores with lower ACE scores to stores with higher scores, and by evaluating those stores that had not yet participated in the program (the control group in a classical experimental setup) against those that had (the experimental group). By analyzing the data between these stores, and eliminating all other compounding variables such as local economic conditions, size of the store, average customers per day, time of year, and so forth, the only variance in sales that could be accounted for comes from the employee engagement, alignment, and capabilities scores. Drilling down further, in stores where all else is equal, and that also have matching alignment and capabilities scores, the engagement score alone can be shown to have real financial impact.

Figure 16-7. Impact Analysis: Top & Bottom Lines

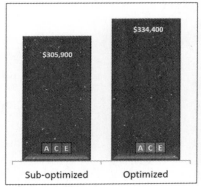

Sales 10% Higher in Qtr.

$334,400
$305,900

A C E   A C E

Sub-optimized   Optimized

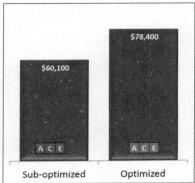

Profit 30% Higher in Qtr.

$78,400
$60,100

A C E   A C E

Sub-optimized   Optimized

In Figure 16-7, the sales and profits for both sub-optimized stores and optimized stores are shown. The differences are dramatic, and considering there are more than 2,200 Jack in the Box stores nationwide, even a small difference in the profit margins adds up to extremely significant increases in revenue.

The other component in determining the monetary impact of the program is turnover. In conjunction with other programs such as the English competency and fluency program, the push to facilitate better management has had an enormous effect on turnover. This is especially remarkable, considering the industry standard for turnover within fast-service restaurants is traditionally very high—well over 150 percent on average (Blankenship and Schiemann, 2012). Jack in the Box found that the ACE scores in their restaurants were highly correlated with turnover rates (r=0.70), accounting for half of all the variance in store-to-store turnover. Optimized stores have 21 percent less turnover than sub-optimized restaurants. In direct relationship to that is the labor cost as a percentage of sales, which are 10 percent more productive as a result.

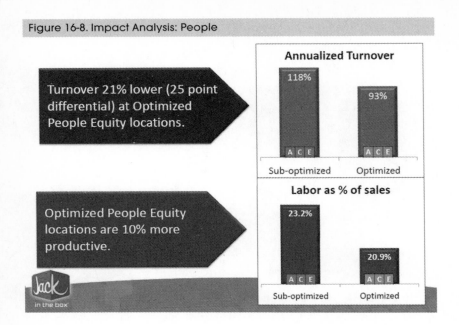

Figure 16-8. Impact Analysis: People

This business impact is likely to increase over time, as more efficient methods of assessing employees are developed. Figure 16-8 provides a sample of the impact data collected. In the future, fewer metrics will be used to evaluate staff. For example, the metric pertaining to the amount of training provided will be eliminated, as that is only an activity, and the idea is to measure outputs rather than activities. Within this framework, internal customers will provide feedback on the performance of the staff, and those performance numbers will be an indication of the effectiveness of the training.

In addition, the goal by 2014 is to have more of the incentive pay tied to functional measures that are tied directly to store success. Alignment of the corporate goals with the individual goals will help make the entire performance management and compensation system both more efficient and more aligned with the corporate goals.

Because the costs cannot be fully loaded, a true ROI analysis cannot be conducted. The partial estimated cost for the entire ACE program was around

$200,000. This estimate does not include the labor time needed for workers to complete the survey, but does include the cost of partnering for the design of the program, the data analysis, and the technology needed to implement the program.

However, financial impact can be seen. At stores that had top-tier scores in alignment, capabilities, and engagement, Q1 sales were an average of $28,500 more than those stores that only scored in the top tier in zero, one, or two of those measures. Similarly, fully-optimized scores in that same quarter had an average profit of $18,300 higher than sub-optimized stores. Given that this program was implemented in about 2,000 stores, total sales of $57 million and a total profit of $36,600,000 from having a fully engaged workforce could be realized in one quarter.

TM INITIATIVE MICRO SCORECARD

Table 16-1 illustrates how the results were compiled into the micro scorecard.

Table 16-1. TM Initiative Micro Scorecard				
Program title: ACE [Alignment, Capabilities, Engagement]				
Target audience: Front-line workers				
Number of attendees: 25,700 employees				
Duration: Three to five years				
Business objective: Higher engagement, capabilities, and alignment; higher profit by store				
Results				
Satisfaction	Learning	Application	Tangible Benefits	Intangible Benefits
Level 1	**Level 2**	**Level 3**	**Level 4**	
90% survey completion rate	N/A	Managers at fully-optimized store were using taught skills; those at sub-optimized stores were not	Increased sales and profitability Reduced turnover	Better experience for customers, resulting in a better brand

> **Technique to isolate effects of program:** Control group of stores that did not have higher scores on the three main categories
>
> **Technique to convert data to monetary value:** N/A
>
> **Fully-loaded program costs:** N/A
>
> **Barriers to application of skills:** Resistance from managers who may resent the changes
>
> **Recommendations:** Further work on finding ways to raise ACE scores at underperforming stores

CONCLUSIONS AND RECOMMENDATIONS

- The most significant takeaway from this study is also the one that seems the most obvious, or at least the simplest. Anything that is being measured must be measured for a reason—always start with the end in mind. If a program, initiative, or even data point cannot be tied to a specific business outcome (almost always a tangible monetary outcome), it rarely has a need to exist. Not every type of business lends itself as easily to creating control and experimental groups as the fast-service restaurant industry, but the difficulty in tying activities to business impact should not be an excuse. In actuality, if something can't be found to have a viable business impact, it should be evaluated for possible removal. What Jack in the Box has done is important because it shows the monetary impact of what used to be known as a "soft" variable—employee engagement. If something as fuzzy as engagement can be tied to a real dollar amount, then certainly a given program at most other organizations can as well.

- Every business that depends on people is likely to have a monetary connection of alignment, capabilities, or engagement to business performance; the challenge is finding and documenting it. Take note of the methodology involved in the prework leading up to implementation of the ACE program. Jack in the Box had evaluated its employees in different categories, including training, environment, and rewards. Only after further statistical analysis was Jack in the Box able to ferret out the key indicators of performance, which they accomplished by correlating the scores to the financials at a given store. For any business unit, results may vary—the lesson is to work with data sets that are large enough to create valid, statistically significant, and reliable findings.

- Managing and measuring engagement alone is not enough to optimize talent; Jack in the Box found that alignment and capabilities combined with engagement were a far better tool for prioritizing actions for improvement. No one metric, taken on its own, is typically enough to use for forecasting purposes. What Jack in the Box did was find three data points that interacted with each other in a statistically significant way and truly affected the business.

- Merely having the data is not enough. The most common lament heard from HR practitioners is in turning data into information (i4cp, 2012). Only by a thorough understanding of the metrics can actionable steps be created. Sometimes this is done through a more thorough statistical analysis, but don't be afraid to use qualitative methods as well. Find units that are outliers in terms of performance, and conduct interviews and follow-up studies to hear the actual stories from those units. Then, look back at the data for points that may correlate with or even predict those circumstances. This might help explain a blip in the data field.

ABOUT THE AUTHOR

Cliff Stevenson is a senior human capital researcher for the Institute for Corporate Productivity (i4cp). Prior to i4cp, Cliff worked as a freelance writer, and was the head of HR for a consulting firm in Boston. His undergraduate degree is in psychology from the University of South Florida, and he attended CSU-Long Beach for graduate work in industrial/organizational psychology and Suffolk University for organizational learning and development. He currently lives in St. Petersburg, Florida, and is an avid, if remarkably poor, sailor.

REFERENCES

Blankenship, M., and W. Schiemann. (2012). "How Jack in the Box Optimizes Its Talent." *QSR Magazine*, September.

Blankenship, M. (2012)."Happier Employees + Happier Customers = More Profit." *HR Magazine*, July.

Heskett, J.L., T.O. Jones, G.W. Loveman, W.E. Sasser, and L.A. Schelsinger. (1994)."Putting the Service Profit Chain to Work." *Harvard Business Review*, March-April.

Institute for Corporate Productivity. (2012). *Evidence-Based Human Resources in Action*. www.i4cp.com.

17

EMPLOYEE ENGAGEMENT AND RETENTION AT THE 2002 OLYMPIC WINTER GAMES

Darren Hughes and Lisa Wardle

INTRODUCTION

This case study describes an organization-wide initiative to retain a short-term, high-performing workforce staging the 2002 Olympic Winter Games. It shows how the organization's leaders overcame initial employee skepticism through good data collection and robust follow-up mechanisms that were put in place at the outset of the effort. It demonstrates how human resources (HR) and learning and development (L&D) initiatives can move beyond powerful motivators (such as association with the Olympic Games) to positively change business outcomes through partnership with employees and regular monitoring against stated objectives.

BACKGROUND

The Salt Lake Organizing Committee (SLOC) was a private corporation with an operating budget of $1.3 billion, formed for the purpose of staging the 2002 Winter Olympic and Paralympic Games. During 17 days in February 2002, more than three billion people watched the Games or attended sport and cultural events organized by 19,000 volunteers and 6,400 paid staff members—all recruited, trained, and managed by SLOC.

The successful presentation of the 2002 Olympic Winter Games depended on the engagement and retention of a core paid staff of 1,100 talented, highly motivated individuals. In past Games, employees in these specialty jobs had been offered jobs with other organizations anywhere from six months to six days away from Games time. When employees took those job offers, the organization suffered because their specialty skills were not easily replaced. SLOC had a lot of smart people in the top of their fields with transferable skills and a looming termination date, and it needed to retain them to mitigate the risk of attrition while staging successful Olympic Games.

An Organizing Committee is an unusual work environment—within hours of extinguishing the Olympic flame at the Closing Ceremony, most of the talented, specialized workforce members become jobless. With that, employees lose some of their identity, importance, purpose, connections, and, of course, their incomes. As with any project-based organization, staff members come into their employment arrangement knowing they will eventually lose their jobs, but the fear of an unknown future still affects them and causes a significant retention challenge. In SLOC's case, the retention challenge was exacerbated by a faltering U.S. economy and the uncertainty caused by the events of September 11th. In order to deliver great Games, SLOC addressed its challenges through a range of initiatives to engage and retain its workforce.

One of the most successful elements of the retention effort was SLOC's Job Transition Program (JTP), which is the subject of this analysis.

TALENT MANAGEMENT INITIATIVE

In order to host outstanding Olympic and Paralympic Winter Games in 2002, the Salt Lake Organizing Committee's HR team set as its mission to build the best Games workforce ever. As HR researched lessons learned from previous Games organizers, they discovered that retaining SLOC's talented full-time workforce would be important to achieving their goal.

As part of a multifaceted retention effort, SLOC developed an innovative program designed to provide peace of mind for staff members regarding their post-Games career opportunities and allow them to focus on their Games-time responsibilities. The Job Transition Program (JTP) aimed to assist the 1,200 full-time paid staff of the Salt Lake Organizing Committee in securing viable job offers prior to the Games. All of the leadership development efforts for the JTP were centered on keeping SLOC's workforce focused on executing great Games. The program was designed to ease the transition for employees and keep employees' minds on their Olympic jobs and not on unemployment or on potentially leaving the Games early in order to take that next job opportunity. Ed Eynon, SLOC Senior Vice President for Human Resources and International Relations said, "The whole idea is to aggressively pursue outplacement support that they can see and touch and feel" (Hinds, 2001).

SLOC started by doing extensive discovery interviews with current employees, employees who had worked more than one Games, and leadership from past Games. Many of the leaders from past Games gave an impassioned plea for SLOC to actively intervene on behalf of its employees. These interviews helped shape the project plan.

Evaluating the need for the HR team to deliver some type of retention program helped define the program scope and highlighted the need for data collection and measurement. It also shed light on the following realities:

- Staff had real fear regarding their future job loss.
- Staff disbelieved that the organization could do anything substantial to help with the problem.
- Employees don't have time to concentrate on the search for their next job, so unless there was training and support in place, nothing would happen.

Additionally, employees would begin to spend work time and attention on their post-Games opportunities rather than their immediate Games-related tasks.

Through the extensive needs assessment, SLOC reached every employee in a personal way. They were brought into the planning phase and began to buy in to the possibility that their own interests were being addressed.

The following table provides an overview of the needs assessment.

Table 17-1. Needs Assessment Overview	
Employee Survey	• Prepared job transition survey to determine interest in job transition. Employees were asked what training needs they had, what jobs they would want to pursue for post-Games employment, geographic preference, and companies for which they aspire to work. This survey was conducted a year and a half out (prior to the Games). • Distributed survey to all full-time paid staff. • Tallied results and used the data to further inform program design.
Interviews with former Olympic Games leaders and employees	• Interviewed senior human resources and operations leaders from the previous four Olympic Games including Lillehammer 1994, Atlanta 1996, Nagano 1998, and Sydney 2000. • Interviewed SLOC staff with previous Games experience.
Employee Interviews: follow-up to Employee Survey	• Team of four people interviewed all 1,200 SLOC full-time employees in 20-minute sessions. • Objective was meant to gain a deeper understanding of individuals' specific goals, plans, and needs of the program. • Employees were asked what they would want in a job coach/mentor. • Process took two months to complete.

"Workers who have taken posts with the Olympics know going in that the job will end with the Games," said Michael Bednarski, a psychologist specializing in career counseling. What SLOC's leadership didn't know was that the events of September 11, 2001, would change market dynamics and further disturb the economy in a way that left people feeling uncertain and even more fearful. Bednarski went on to say, "Now it's a whole different ball game. It's a time of reckoning" (Blake, 2001).

With a solid understanding of program needs, SLOC designed the program and developed an administrative system to collect data, and track and measure progress. Communicating the process, progress, and successes were instrumental in mitigating the employees' skepticism. This made collecting data that told a story the HR team's priority from the beginning. SLOC didn't set out to do a Level 5 evaluation (Phillips, 2005); it set out to meet its desired outcomes. The list of stakeholders was long and keeping them informed kept them committed.

To refine the design of the JTP concept, a retention and transition work group was formed to review the survey and interview results. With the high level of interest and a strong case for implementing the program, the program was approved for implementation and the structure and resources were discussed in detail. The preliminary design was left intact and minor adjustments were made to increase the number of consultants to teach and coach employees. The number was increased from two to four full-time consultants and educators.

The objective was clear: to retain SLOC's full-time workforce. The JTP's goal was to secure viable job offers for 90 percent of program participants who wanted them prior to the start of the Games (Horiuchi, 2002). In some cases, rather than a job offer, the JTP worked to accommodate the next career option—starting a business, going to graduate school, or long-term volunteer work.

Some of the highlights of the program included:

- Participation in the program was not mandatory, but the program enjoyed a 97 percent participation rate. Participation meant that employees were involved in all parts of the program.

- The JTP launched one year before the Olympic Games and continued for two months after the Paralympic Games to support those who did not yet have another job.

- A needs assessment was conducted at all levels of employees to determine training requirements.

- The training curriculum was designed, developed, and streamlined for a busy workforce; consisting of short incremental modules that would accommodate their schedules.

- The training program was implemented on site over a nine-month period, for all 1,100 employees.

- Relationships were established with more than 1,000 companies to facilitate pre-Games job offers to employees with post-Games start dates.

- Two hundred high-level business leaders were recruited, trained, and motivated to volunteer as mentors for the 1,100 Olympic employees.

All of the components of the program, as illustrated in Figure 17-1, were designed to work together to reach the one common goal of retaining and engaging SLOC's workforce.

Figure 17-1. Elements of the Job Transition Program

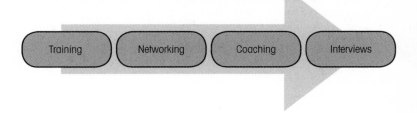

Training   Networking   Coaching   Interviews

The Job Transition Program consisted of:

- Development Workshops—learning programs to teach professional skills and provide opportunities for practice and application. Workshops were held on site in short two-hour sessions to accommodate the intense workload of the workforce.
    - » Approximately 350 workshops were taught over a 10-month period of time.
    - » Workshops ran from one year out up until two months out. At that point, the Games-time execution demands didn't allow much flexibility for staff members to attend training.
    - » JTP training topics included self-assessment, change transition, networking, building a résumé, interviewing skills, negotiating, communication, and entrepreneurship.

- Online Resources:
    - » iFair—online job fair was open for one year prior to Games.
    - » Job Search—a sponsor hosted an employment website for the SLOC staff. All members of their website were allowed to post jobs for free, maximizing the opportunities for staff.
    - » SLOC Message Board—SLOC employees could post their questions and comments, network, and communicate with each other on every aspect of looking for their next position.

- Job Search Consultant (JSC)—Each participant was assigned a Job Search Consultant who served as a mentor, coach, and employment representative for SLOC staff members.
    - » The team of Job Search Consultants was comprised of 200 volunteers supported by a small number of paid staff.
    - » Participants in the program were matched with Job Search Consultants to help in their job search. The match was based on the employee's interests, background, skills, and geographic preferences for future work.

> » The JSCs served as networking contacts; reviewed résumés, cover letters, and thank-you letters; helped research jobs and companies; and provided regular support to keep employees moving in the job search process.

- Employer and Sponsor Open-House Events—More than 1,000 companies were contacted on behalf of SLOC employees. A letter from the President and CEO of SLOC was sent to the CEOs of these companies, asking them to participate in the JTP program. Participation meant a couple of things:

  > » Preferential access to SLOC's highly skilled and talented staff. SLOC wanted these companies to recruit aggressively from SLOC's talent pool. Companies could view résumés, meet individuals, network, interview individuals, and make job offers.

  > » SLOC asked that companies offer positions contingent upon completion of individuals' Games assignments.

  > » Of the companies contacted, 391 of them posted jobs with SLOC. Most companies posted more than one position.

- Companies were invited on site to meet, interview, recruit, and hire SLOC employees. SLOC managers supported their employees in the process of interviewing for their next jobs, even while they carried out their current responsibilities.

- The Job Transition team set out to attract those organizations that most interested employees.

The benefits of this program to potential employers included access to a diverse, talented group of prospective employees.

The system SLOC used to track program-related data was a combination of a learning management system (LMS) and a database structure that kept a record of each employee's activity. SLOC was able to track exactly who was participating and who was not (and why). As SLOC gathered information from employees, it went into their records. That information was used to guide the selection process of coaches and mentors as they were assigned to employees.

All workshops were scheduled and tracked online. SLOC monitored each participant's progress in the program through a robust database. SLOC needed to see who was participating in what and when they were active.

To be considered a participant meant being involved in all parts of the program, from meeting with a Job Search Consultant, to attending workshops, completing an updated résumé, searching for jobs online, and interviewing for jobs. SLOC used the data tracked from these activities as they communicated with their many stakeholders, including employees, executives, the Job Search Consultant volunteers, the media, and future Organizing Committees.

The program was so successful that SLOC captured the attention and imagination of the International Olympic Committee (IOC), who lauded it as an innovative approach to deal with a reality that all Olympic Committees face. The IOC asked for interviews and reports from JTP leaders and managers to try to understand if this program was transferable to future organizing committees. However, transferability is difficult due mainly to the complexity of HR systems in the different countries around the world.

EVALUATION METHODOLOGY AND RESULTS

SLOC leadership and program sponsors invested in the JTP with the expectation that there would be a return on their investment and sponsorship contributions. They expected the monetary support would contribute to successful Games.

SLOC's approach was to be thoughtful and strategic about meeting its retention goals. SLOC wanted a strong connection between the needs and objectives. The connection was established during the design phase, with ongoing clarification of program objectives and measures of success.

SLOC kept good metrics throughout the process and have been connected to each Organizing Committee since the 2002 Olympic Winter Games for comparison and benchmarking. Even now the program is seen as perhaps the best implementation of a retention program that achieved dual goals of helping staff find their next career opportunity while maintaining their focus on their Games-time responsibilities.

A rear view of the JTP highlights the many levels of impact felt by the workforce and the organization. Data confirms the quality of the programmatic component, the impact on employees' job performance, and the impact the intervention had on the business goal of 100 percent retention.

The qualitative and quantitative data gathered made it clear that the JTP:

- contributed to the organization

- established priorities internally and externally

- focused on results

- managed stakeholder expectations and secured their support for the program

- achieved its goal of 100 percent retention.

Level 1: Reaction and Planned Action

Several measures provided evidence that the program was on track. Regarding the overall JTP itself, employees were initially skeptical but hopeful it would yield the promised results, and were willing to participate. Regarding the workshops:

- All sessions were full, indicating demand was high.

- Workshops consistently achieved evaluation scores of 4.5 to 4.9 (4.7 average) on a 5.0 scale. Participants were highly satisfied with all aspects of the workshops, specifically the opportunity to put their new skills to practice in the sessions and to participate in follow-up coaching with their mentors.

- Participants completed workshop requirements (such as completing an updated résumé, reviewing it with a coach, and submitting it to be viewed by recruiting organizations).

The JTP started in full inquiry mode, soliciting stakeholders and employees for input. Through the Level 1 data gathering, the JTP determined that the program supported the objectives. Data was collected using the following instruments:

- job transition survey

- job transition follow-up survey

- database for tracking program involvement

- workshop evaluations

- workshop roster and schedule.

Level 2: Learning

It was clear that momentum was building. Employees' attitudes about the program were positive. The discipline of preparing for the transition process so far in advance was building their confidence as well as their trust in the SLOC. Confirmation that the program was successful in Level 2 terms consisted of:

- participants putting skills from workshops to use to complete their résumés and engage in the résumé-posting process

- participants scheduling regular meetings with their Job Search Consultants

- participants becoming enthusiastic about the JTP and how it would help them.

Data was in the form of:

- Job Search Consultant feedback

- completed updated résumés from all participants in the system.

Level 3: Application and Implementation

The JTP objectives were coming to life as participants actively applied everything they had learned through the process. They were taking initiative in their job searches but remained fully connected to their consultants and mentors. Success stories materialized and created even more momentum. The following measures helped us evaluate Level 3 application and implementation.

- Participants were checking in daily with the JTP team.

- Employers were requesting résumés.

- Interviews were being requested.

- Job Search Consultants were meeting round the clock with participants, providing networking contacts, advice, mentoring, and feedback on résumés.

- Participants were applying what they learned in the workshops, presenting their best selves through their résumés, interviews, and salary negotiations.

Data tracked included:

- résumés submitted to employers, tracked by person, by company, and by posting

- interviews held (85 percent were tracked by SLOC; approximately half were scheduled by SLOC, half scheduled by the employer and individual)

- Job Search Consultant activity.

Level 4: Business Impact

The business impact of the JTP was obvious to Games leaders and all JTP stakeholders. Through the program, SLOC:

- retained 100 percent of its workforce (any attrition was through terminations)

- created goodwill and trust with employees

- established a standard for future organizing committees that has not been met yet.

Strong data was collected and submitted in support of Level 4 achievements, such as:

- HR systems

- interviews with leaders

- positive written feedback from 65 percent of participants

- tracked job offers—60 percent had their next career options lined up before the Games ended (the goal was 90 percent).

Level 5: Return-on-Investment

While it is easy to calculate the hard costs of the Job Transition Program, it is difficult to isolate the effects of the program. Many other sound HR practices were also in place to ensure the Games were staged effectively. Because data was tracked from the beginning, it was obvious at the end of the Games that the program was successful and had met the objectives.

TM INITIATIVE MICRO SCORECARD

Table 17-2 is the talent management scorecard that gives a snapshot look at the Job Transition Program and its outcomes. We measured Levels 1 through 4 but did not measure a Level 5. The actual program costs were estimated at about $900,000 and the Salt Lake 2002 Olympic Winter Games were successful. The costs of any one failure to execute at Games time would far outweigh the price tag of this program. Successful Games creates value for athletes, sponsors, communities, governments, media, organizing committees, and so on. Any failure to execute would destroy value for those stakeholders. History had informed SLOC to manage this risk and they did so successfully.

CONCLUSIONS

- The Salt Lake Organizing Committee successfully staged the 2002 Olympic Winter Games and is still held as a benchmark for organizing Winter Games. Improved retention and staff members' focus on their duties due to initiatives such as the Job Transition Program contributed to the success of the Games.

- Regular measurement of the initiative's success was a key contributor to staff-member confidence in the program and overcoming stakeholder skepticism.

- Strong data management and communication is recommended, regardless of whether a company is using an L&D framework for its workforce management activities.

- Prior to implementing L&D projects, an organization's HR leadership may benefit from an attempt to establish specific, objective measures tied to the desired outcomes of the initiative in order to help determine and communicate the project's success. In the case of Salt Lake 2002's retention efforts, that meant going beyond merely tracking attendance in outplacement courses to measuring outcomes (numbers of staff with post-Games employment, satisfaction with the employer's concern for staff members' futures, and so forth).

- Additional support may be gained for the project by ensuring that the objectives are agreed upon—that consensus is built around the objectives through staff-member participation in establishing the program. Salt

Table 17-2. TM Initiative Micro Scorecard

Talent Management Initiative: Employee Engagement and Retention
Target Audience: 1,100 employees of the SLOC, all full-time paid staff
Duration: 14 months
Business Objectives: 100% retention and a goal of 90% of full-time paid staff having their next career option (job offer, and so on) lined up before the Games' end

Reaction	Learning	Results		
		Application	Tangible Benefits	Intangible Benefits
Level 1	**Level 2**	**Level 3**	**Level 4**	• no attrition (other than necessary terminations) through the Paralympics
4.7 Average overall satisfaction rating (on a 5.0 scale).	85% of those attending learning programs increased skills and knowledge. Skills and knowledge assessed through JTP instructors and coaches.	Active application was supported through mentors and coaches. 70% of those who participated in the program applied and improved their job transition skills.	100% Retained Workforce	• high morale through eliminating fear of losing their jobs
	• skills to complete résumés, engage in posting résumés	• Checking in daily with the JTP team.	**Level 5**	• engaged workforce
	• regular meetings with Job Search Consultant (JSC)	• Employer requests for résumés; SLOC résumés sent.	N/A	• global networking
	• enthusiasm about the JTP	• Interview requests.		• positive PR and community relations for the organizing committee
	• skepticism no longer voiced.	• Job Search Consultants meeting around the clock with participants.		
		• Volunteer JSCs providing networking contacts, advice, mentoring, and feedback.		
		• Skills learned in workshops were affecting participants' performance in job searches.		
		• Skills applied were generating options for individuals.		

Technique to Isolate Effects of Program: Track and record the following data: participation in the Job Transition Program, attendance at each instructor-led program, content-based workshops, mentoring and coaching activity level, number of résumés submitted by company, job interviews conducted, and job offers extended. Qualitative feedback and comments captured and submitted throughout duration of program.

Technique to Convert Data to Monetary Value:

Fully-Loaded Program Costs: ~$900,000

Barriers to Application of Skills: Time was at a premium with this workforce. This guided our thinking on the design and integration of all components of the program.

Recommendations: IOC reviewed to recommend to other organizing committees.

Lake 2002 was able to do that through workshops and surveys gauging staff members' goals through the program.

- Finally, by nature of the project, Salt Lake 2002 was able to make the program time-bound and pragmatic (dimensions which help define any L&D initiative), creating a sense of urgency in achieving the project's objectives, a clear deadline for success, and realizing that the initiative will not address all of the retention challenges but can help in specific, realistic ways.

- Using the Phillips' evaluation framework to chart the formative data is a practical way to assess the results of the program.

- If no metrics had been in place and no data were gathered, there would have been no way to see the impact on the organization. Without going through Levels 1 through 3, we would not have known the impact the program had on the organization.

ABOUT THE AUTHORS

Darren Hughes is a U.S.-based human resources professional providing event consulting services to major sporting events. Darren has 15 years of experience in the event industry, supporting clients across a broad range of areas including event bidding, strategic and operational planning, event-time execution, event-owner governance, and all aspects of event workforce delivery.

Lisa Wardle is a managing director at Duke Corporate Education where she designs, develops, and delivers innovative leadership development solutions. Lisa has more than 18 years of experience in reward systems, transition and leadership, and strategic workforce planning. She has worked in various human capital and organizational development leadership roles and several large-scale organizational redesign projects. Lisa holds a master of arts from Columbia University.

REFERENCES

Phillips, J.J., and P.P. Phillips. (2005). *Measuring ROI*. Alexandria, VA: ASTD Press.

Hinds, G. (2001)."Salt Lake Organizing Committee for Olympics to Lose at Least 1,200 Workers," *Standard-Examiner*, December 28.

Blake, C. (2001)."Thousands of Olympic Workers Face Unemployment Come March," *The Associated Press*, December 29.

Horiuchi, V. (2002)."SLOC Workers Deal With Life After the Games," *The Salt Lake Tribune*, February 27.

18

IMPLEMENTING AN ORGANIZATION-WIDE PERFORMANCE AND TALENT MANAGEMENT SUITE

Dr. Sujaya Banerjee, Nishant Dangle, and Anand Justin Cherian

INTRODUCTION

This case study demonstrates how a diversified conglomerate approached the people and systemic challenges of a fast-growing enterprise, and went on to design, drive, and implement one of the most complex SaaS implementations to date in Asia. It also looks at the key criteria considered to evaluate the success and efficacy of the initiative thereafter.

BACKGROUND

The Essar Group is a global conglomerate and a leading player in the sectors of steel, oil and gas, power, shipping, ports, projects (EPC), and BPO services among others. Essar began as a construction company in 1969, and today it has operations in more than 25 countries across five continents, with employee strength of 75,000 people and Group revenues of over USD $27.3 billion.

In light of its fast-paced growth, Essar embarked on a transformational journey in early 2006 with a view to adopt and exceed industry best practices in key areas of strategic people management. Essential highlights of this agenda included the building of a learning organization (along the tenets propounded by Garvin, 2000), making people leaders out of essentially technocrat "supervisors," adopting a total-rewards approach that went beyond compensation and benefits, and enhancing the transparency and efficacy of the performance management system.

Performance management is a sensitive area in any organization, for natural reasons pertaining to employee aspirations, role clarity, goal alignment, transparency during appraisals, and of course, direct linkage to rewards. One of the fundamental challenges faced by Essar in the early years of its transformation journey was negating externalities affecting performance and ensuring objectivity of performance reviews. This included providing a defined structure in which performance could be managed and assessed, ensuring that employees had clearly defined key performance areas (KPAs) and a broad line of sight of overall business objectives. A basic first attempt at an online system for end-to-end performance management (2009), christened "MyPEP Trac," was plagued with usability, data integrity, and feature-constraint issues. Subsequently, in late 2010, there was a unanimous need for a more robust, better integrated, and user-friendly system that could standardize the process across disparate locations. Thus e-Compass was born.

TALENT MANAGEMENT INITIATIVE

Need Diagnosis

As discussed earlier, in the early stages of the organizational transformational journey, the organization found itself confronting several challenges associated with a people-management machinery still maturing to the demands of multiple fast-growing businesses. Some of the key challenges on this front included:

- providing employees a macro perspective of where the business was headed and ensuring that they remained focused on achieving their goals while remaining aligned with larger organizational objectives

- bringing in greater objectivity and transparency while assessing performance

- providing a mechanism for leaders to effectively track employees' progress toward achieving performance and development goals, thus feeding into the talent management agenda as well

- creating a successor pool of short-term, medium-term, and long-term successors for identified key critical positions, with customized developmental paths for each

- building capability via self-directed learning among the workforce, primarily comprising technocrats based in India and abroad.

Therefore an increasing need was felt by all stakeholders to revamp the existing performance management system and make it more robust, transparent, and user-friendly, with a special emphasis on goal alignment, ease of use, and process transparency.

In order to better crystallize the exact needs of the organization, an elaborate process was followed, summarized below:

- Detailed discussions were held, featuring the group president of HR, individual business HR heads (Essar being a diversified conglomerate) and the chief learning officer, on the essential challenges being faced on the performance and talent management front, and possible solutions for the same.

- Two independent performance management task forces were created; one composed entirely of HR managers from across the Group, and the other entirely of line managers from different businesses. Both taskforces adopted a "blue sky" approach to think freely and openly on what the ideal performance management system and the proposed application should be like. The views of both groups were consolidated and presented to the people's committee—the senior-most body on people management decisions in the Group, comprising promoter-directors, business heads and the group president of HR.

At the end of this exercise, there was reasonable clarity on the need for the envisioned system to integrate performance management, strategic talent management, and talent development, thus completing the cycle of sustained individual and organizational performance management and excellence. The idea of e-Compass, in the context of the organization, had multiple layers and dimensions pertaining to talent management and development, and organization design and development as well. This drive toward a robust, transparent, and integrated performance management system also encapsulated the delivery of "Anytime Anywhere Learning," with the provision of relevant learning solutions to users as and when needed.

With this elaborate brief and context in mind, a comprehensive search and comparative analysis was conducted of the different service providers who could cater to our unique needs. The key factors considered when assessing options included:

- Market Leadership: Proven expertise and leadership in the service area were essential prerequisites for vendors to be considered further.

- User Interface and Navigation: Learning from the experiences with the earlier system (MyPEP Trac), where the low user-friendliness of the interface and tedious navigation had severely impacted system usage and adoption, this was a key focus area at all times.

- Customizability: There was a clear understanding from the beginning that any system would need to be 'Essarized' adequately so as to enhance participation and adoption. This would entail customization in terms of both standard terms and nomenclatures, and key process flows and mechanisms.

- Features and Functionalities: While the team had a broad idea of the required system capabilities, it approached different systems with an open mind on how these capabilities would manifest themselves in the Essar context. The broad requirements included:

  » ease of use in setting goals with mechanisms to ensure alignment and "SMART-ness," as well as tracking and reviewing progress made to facilitate the achievement of business goals

  » talent profile where employees may post their professional and personal details, providing a holistic view on their areas of expertise, qualifications, certifications, achievements, and so forth, so as to facilitate better talent decisions

  » dashboards and analytics to empower leaders with the requisite data and insights to make informed talent decisions (mapping talent on the performance-potential matrix, promotion recommendations, successor nominations for critical positions, charting career paths, and so on)

  » tools to enable a focus on career progression and development opportunities within the Group; with career opportunities being acknowledged as the maximum driver of employee engagement, it was important that the solution provide employees greater access to career progression and professional development opportunities

> » active linkages to strategic manpower planning, talent management, and talent development.

- Web Access: Enhanced accessibility from out-of-office locations and mobile devices was another priority requirement.

After considerable effort, the task force zeroed in on SuccessFactors and Halogen as the two final choices. Eventually the decision tilted in favor of SuccessFactors, owing to their already strong presence with major organizations in India, and strong reference support. The proposed implementation would be one of the largest SaaS implementations in India, and would involve large-scale change management efforts to drive adoption and usage.

Implementation Phase 1

From the very outset, all key stakeholders were enlightened to the fact that this ambitious project was as much a strategic change initiative for Essar, as an ostensibly HR-driven agenda. Consequently, buy-in and active support from senior leadership and line managers was indispensable in bringing the performance management and talent and career development initiatives to life. In light of this, an elaborate cross-functional project implementation and governance team was instituted. This was comprised of specific task forces entrusted with key aspects of the project implementation, namely:

- project sponsors, including promoter-directors and the group president of HR, who acted as owners of the entire project

- steering committee, consisting of the Group CIO, senior business HR heads, chief talent officer, president of global markets and strategy, and vice president of corporate communications and intelligence, who were responsible for overall guidance and mobilization of teams and resources

- project managers, including the lead for performance management, central learning, and OD; the lead for e-Compass project management, and the support team from SuccessFactors, who were responsible for liaising with different stakeholders for the successful implementation of the project

- HR process team, made up of the performance management team from central learning and OD, business HR heads, and the international HR head, who were responsible for ensuring adherence of the system to decided processes, across businesses and locations

- data/SAP team, made up of the head of HR technology and the head of SAP services, who were responsible for integration of system with the SAP back-end already in place across the Group

- IT integration team, including the CIO of corporate services and international IT integration team, who were responsible for working with the SuccessFactors team on network integration and system compatibility issues

- change management and communication team, including the head of international HR, the lead for employee engagement and the lead for internal talent mobility, central learning, and OD, who were responsible for a detailed communication campaign and rolling out change.

Subsequently an Essar SuccessFactors Offsite was organized, attended by senior leaders from Essar as well as members of the product configuration and relationship management teams at SuccessFactors. This was perhaps the most significant chapter in the entire e-Compass implementation story, not least of all because the product was eventually christened "e-Compass" during this session. The sessions featured animated discussions on key people processes, looking at the desired "to be" variants vis-à-vis the "as is." The proactive onboarding of the SuccessFactors team at this early stage would prove critical in the iterative rounds of configuration and reconfiguration that would follow, as it helped bring all concerned to a shared understanding of the underlying process flows and mechanisms, and how the system would facilitate them.

After the conclusion of the off-site, detailed process flows were created and shared with the SuccessFactors project team, while the project implementation team at Essar prepared a phase-wise project plan, as follows:

- Phase 1—activation of four key modules—goal management, performance management, career planning and development, and talent profile—across 13,500 employees in India, Algoma (Canada), and London; go-live scheduled for October 2011

- Phase 2—extending existing implementations to international locations in 25 countries, covering 2,000 employees; go-live scheduled for March 2012

- Phase 3—balanced scorecard implementation for goal management and activation of succession management module, across all locations; go-lives scheduled for April and September 2012

- Phase 4—implementation of the social learning and collaboration module, "Jambok" (now SAP JAM), across all locations; go-live scheduled for December 2012 (currently underway).

A 16-week project plan was created for phase 1 go-live, with detailed role-wise and day-wise milestones. The orientation and training of a vast, dispersed employee base was a key focus area at the time, for which a comprehensive Four-Wave Training Plan was designed as follows:

- Wave 1—orientation and basic training to entire HR community across the Group; 260 HR managers covered

- Wave 2—certification train-the-trainer sessions for HR and line managers across the Group; 150 managers covered

- Wave 3—admin and reports cell training for dashboards and analytics support to leaders; 150 managers covered

- Wave 4—end-user training across businesses, conducted by trainers certified in wave 2; approximately 90 percent coverage of 13,500-strong target employee base.

Also among the key challenges which arose during the implementation of Project e-Compass was promoting adoption in an organization where leaders were not necessarily tech-savvy, even though the average age of the workforce was about 32 years. It was therefore decided that specialized one-to-one trainings would be conducted to secure the buy-in of the leadership team, for which key influencers were identified across businesses. Along with the Four-Wave Training Plan, this key influencer orientation was among the steps taken to proactively overcome the fundamental people barrier to change.

Another of the early challenges that Project e-Compass faced was ensuring data integrity and consistency, given that the project would go live across geographies. This was identified in the initial stages of the project and remained one of the key focus areas for the training, employee communication, and IT teams throughout its duration. Phase 1 go-live, which covered locations in India, London, and Algoma (Canada), and four modules of the SuccessFactors product, took place successfully on October 17, 2011; the project implementation and go-live was an unprecedented feat for the conglomerate. This phase saw the system being opened to a total of 13,500 employees.

Mid-way during the e-Compass phase 1 implementation, the team short-listed SkillSoft, world leaders in e-learning solutions, to power the learning management system. Efforts were made to integrate SkillSoft with the e-Compass platform, which would allow employees to select SkillSoft solutions at the time of creating development goals and help managers assign e-learning courses to employees at the single click of a button. This would empower Essarites to pursue self-directed learning from work or home. The repository of SkillSoft not only contained best-in-class e-modules but also a huge collection of e-books, executive summaries, executive blueprints, job aids, videos, and Quicktalks by subject matter experts. This proposed integration would be the first of its kind in Asia.

The central learning and OD team worked closely with the different taskforces at all stages of the implementation. The cohesiveness and direct-edness of the efforts were further enhanced by the inclusion of key members of the team in the different taskforces. Periodic user acceptance tests with attendees including HR representatives from different businesses, line managers, and IT taskforce members, were conducted since the inception of the project. Subsequently a demo sandbox link was released for all trainers to familiarize themselves with the product before initiating end-user training.

One of the critical aspects of the project was achieving a single sign-on from the existing company Intranet to access the SaaS-enabled product. The solution was generated and implemented by the Essar IT teams in Canada and India, and was part of end-user training and go-live communication content throughout the duration of the project. This remained one of the highlights for this mega cross-functional SaaS project. End-user training was critical in ensuring adoption and building awareness of the different functionalities of e-Compass and how they would fit in with the proposed quarterly perfor-mance review system.

What made Project e-Compass distinctive was the collective efforts in ensuring go-live in three major locations in India, the U.K., and Canada on the same date. Grand go-live movie premieres were hosted across locations, introducing e-Compass and how it would act as the true pathfinder for performance and careers within the Group. Externally, the project entailed intensive coordination and co-supported effort with SuccessFactors and SkillSoft, both of whom came together for among the most challenging project implementations accomplished to date.

The collective efforts of cross-functional teams from diverse functions like IT, HR, branding and communications, and line managers were critical to the successful implementation of Project e-Compass. The efforts were described as "exemplary" and "outstanding" and won the Essar Group the Best Project Implementation Award from SuccessFactors in 2011.

Implementation Phases 2 and 3

The second leg of Project e-Compass was initiated post go-live with the objective of introducing the product to all other international locations where Essar was currently operating (except Canada and the U.K., where the product had already gone live), and initiating work on the succession and career development modules. The locations covered 25 countries and more than 2000 employees. The period coincided with the annual performance review process, which would take place on e-Compass for the very first time at Essar, and was therefore extremely challenging. The method followed for ensuring adoption was similar to that deployed during the first leg of Project e-Compass with UATs and Four-Wave Training. Webinars and at-your-desk training were the preferred modes of delivering user training. Phase 2 went live successfully in March 2012. Subsequently the balanced scorecard implementation (April 2012) and succession management module (October 2012) were deployed as part of phase 3, following a similar approach. Phase 4 deployment is currently underway (December 2012).

EVALUATION METHODOLOGY AND RESULTS

The evaluation described on the next page follows the five-level evaluation methodology prescribed by Jack Phillips (2003).

E-Compass was by far the biggest HR delivery that Essar had ever embarked on. Naturally, all stakeholders, from the promoter-directors, to the people's committee and senior business and HR leaders, to the project implementation team, were conscious of the near-compulsive need for the system to successfully deliver on its value proposition; and as self-fulfilling prophesies often pan out, the deployment was indeed a resounding success.

At every stage of the implementation process, the project implementation team monitored the environment for advance signals of both successes and possible concerns—the former to bridge to realization, and the latter to preemptively address. What follows is a closer look at how the efficacy and overall success of this mammoth project was evaluated.

Level 1—Satisfaction

The involvement of line managers in the process and product design was expressly aimed at enhancing end-user experience and satisfaction. However, the project team did not invest in satisfaction surveys at any stage of the implementation, with the firm belief in actual ground-level adoption as being a better, more real indicator of satisfaction and buy-in. The path-breaking nature of the implementation and the features and functionalities being introduced therein further reinforced this belief. Some of the key highlights of the application, unprecedented in the working lives of Essarites thus far and seen to be strongly affecting satisfaction, included:

- Visibility of business plans and the CEO and business head scorecard, enabling greater alignment and a "sense of mattering" in the larger scheme of things.

- Smoother accessibility with single sign-on and a user-friendly interface. The earlier performance management system required an extra sign-in step, along with a more tedious and less intuitive system navigation. The welcome nature of these new features was evident at several touch-points, including the training programs, system trial kiosks, and end-user interactions.

- Comprehensive goal management coupled with seamless access to more than 20,000 e-learning resources, to help bring together the development and performance agenda for employees. This greatly enhanced the performance and development review discussions between managers and employees across businesses and locations.

The project team's stand was vindicated by the adoption levels achieved after system go-live, with 95 percent of employees having scorecards in place, with 75 percent goal alignment.

Level 2—Learning

Training a workforce of more than 13,500 employees was naturally one of the most daunting aspects of the project implementation plan, as well as immensely important for the successful adoption of the application. The aforementioned Four-Wave Training Plan was specifically designed keeping this in mind.

Wave 2 training focused on developing a cadre of certified trainers (including both HR and line managers) who would then be deployed to educate and acclimatize the entire workforce on the new application, the different process flows, and available features and functionalities. The train-the-trainer workshop designed for this purpose included an intensive half-day session where participants would train their respective groups on different system components. Under the observation of the session facilitators (members of the central learning and OD team), this session bridged many a gap between superficial understanding and the clarity required to deliver on the learning needs of employees down the line. The certification process involved a written test at the end of the training workshop, with a pass score of 70 percent. Additionally, certification also required the successful completion of e-modules with built-in quizzes, designed to test specifically on how employees and managers could make the most of the application. A total of 150 managers were successfully trained, tested, certified, and empanelled as part of the e-Compass trainers community at the end of Wave 2. This community of trainers formed the resource pool for businesses to conduct end-user training for employees down the line. To further ensure that the learning stuck, this community also sent periodic refreshers and learning aids to the central team.

Additionally, it was felt that the entire HR community must also be conversant on the essentials of the new system. With this in mind, the Train-the-Trainer workshops were preceded by sessions where all HR managers from across the Group were oriented on the top lines of the e-Compass online system (Wave 1), numbering 260 in all.

With a key component of the e-Compass value proposition being the in-depth dashboard and analytics made available to leaders, it was important also to have a specialized pool of HR and IT managers equipped with the requisite know-how to navigate the system's back-end as an administrator, and extract data and reports along desired parameters and drill-down levels. Therefore the Wave 3 training looked to develop this capability in a designated pool of employees, who would then partner with the central learning and OD team (custodian of performance and talent management, as well as e-Compass), and leaders across businesses and functions. More than 150 managers were trained on this specialized area of the e-Compass product. This training also included tests to ascertain proficiency.

Subsequently, Wave 4 training looked at the last leg of the training from a system-acceptance and usability perspective—the end-user training. This was driven in businesses by their respective business HR teams, and tracked by the central project implementation team. Approximately 90 percent of the workforce was successfully covered, which was a significant feat, given the fact that the employee base exceeded 13,500 and was spread across locations in India, Canada, and the U.K. The end-user training also concluded with a quiz to gauge the transfer and retention of the key concepts and insights related to the system and its application in the Essar context.

The entire training process was augmented with reinforcement and refresher mechanisms to enhance learning transfer and application in daily work activities. E-modules were created on different aspects of the e-Compass application (role of employee, role of manager, balanced scorecard, talent review, and so on), which were accessed by more than 1,500 employees across disparate locations. Leveraging the electronic medium to enhance retention and absorption of learning was an important cog in the overall learning plan for successful e-Compass deployment. Upon system go-live, the e-Compass film and user-aid videos that were made available on the Group Intranet portal received more than 100,000 hits, shortly after being uploaded. A dedicated helpline and IT channel were set up for handling user queries.

At the time the Level 2 measures were put into place, it was not antici-pated that the data would be used afterwards, and so they were not collected or analyzed further. However, as can be seen above, these Level 2 measures were emphasized throughout the four-wave training execution.

Level 3—Application

The ground-level implementation of any application, no matter how well designed, communicated, and driven, remains the proverbial "proof of the pudding." Even while planning and executing the intricate sequences prior to phase 1 go-live on October 17, 2011, the team was always aware of the need to anchor all activity and ideas in successful system adoption, where the combined efforts of the preceding 16 weeks would finally bear fruit.

This focus was translated to action with the configured product being first tested for adherence to agreed guidelines by the two initial taskforces. Feedback was collected to further configure and refine the product to Essar's needs. Subsequent User Acceptance Testing (UATs) also involved over 50 HR and line managers from across businesses and locations. This iterative and rigorous testing discipline (nearly 50 UAT sessions were conducted) ensured that all major features, functionalities, and data linkages were tested with diverse scenarios and combinations, leading to a robust final product. The extensive, phase-wise feedback helped assess the efficacy of the product for successful application going forward.

Upon system go-live, usage data was constantly tracked across locations with the aid of business HR SPOCs (single points of contact). The SPOCs also helped keep a pulse on any technological or awareness challenges that may have been faced at different locations. The IT, SAP data, business HR, and central learning and OD teams were all on high alert to nip any impediments in the bud. Externally, the teams at SuccessFactors and SkillSoft continued with their unstinting support for this big-bang system implementation. The system today has more than 15,000 users located across 22 countries. This was certainly among the most vindicating points in the entire e-Compass journey.

Among the first activities for users on e-Compass was the completion of their scorecards (then called "performance contracts"), which included detailed KPAs, KPIs, key initiatives, timelines, and other pertinent details. Directed communication from both the central and business HR teams helped drive closure, with a commendable 95 percent scorecard coverage, and 75 percent alignment of performance goals. This was undoubtedly among the most powerful results achieved on the e-Compass system, and a credible testimony of the ground-level application of the system across functions, businesses, and locations.

Our efforts toward ensuring adoption and application were further vindicated when SuccessFactors awarded us the "BizX Adoption Award" for best system adoption by the business, at SuccessConnect 2012. This award is given to customer organizations that have been successful in their change management and adoption efforts, specifically in the implementation and adoption of SuccessFactors tools. This external recognition of our efforts remained among the prized feathers in the decorated cap of the e-Compass project implementation team.

Level 4—Tangible Benefits

It is often instructive to reflect back on the key business drivers that mandated the design and deployment of an initiative. The essential business drivers for e-Compass included:

- aligning individual performance goals to the organizational business plan by providing employees a macro perspective of where the business was headed, and how their efforts contributed to it

- creating a high-performance culture by bringing in greater objectivity, transparency, and accuracy while assessing performance, and building capability with self-directed learning avenues

- putting metrics and decision tools in the hands of leaders for effective decision making on both performance management and strategic talent management fronts

- supporting the organization from a business continuity perspective, by enabling the identification of short-term, medium-term, and long-term successors for critical positions, with customized developmental paths for each.

As is evident, the essential nature of the desired organizational change and outcomes is long-term, and "evolution via revolution" in intent (evolving the organizational processes and mindsets through the provision of revolutionary, unprecedented transparency and enabling tools). The following are some of the areas where the organization expects significant tangible benefits in the coming years—a "Prospective Level 4," to be reviewed and measured over time:

- Greater alignment of goals with the larger business plan should result in increased efficiency and effectiveness of individual and team efforts. Reduced wastage of work hours and other resources and greater stream-lining of efforts would help teams and businesses capitalize on synergies. This should raise both the business bottom line (factoring in larger macro-environmental considerations of course) and productivity metrics such as earnings per employee.

- The formal documentation of the performance and development reviews on the system, along with greater transparency in goal setting, tracking and appraisal, would certainly have a positive impact on key engagement drivers such as career opportunities, performance management, immediate manager and training and development, among others. This should help raise engagement levels, and subsequently reduce attrition, thus saving costs of re-hire, re-orientation, and lost man-hours.

TM INITIATIVE MICRO SCORECARD

The scorecard shown in Table 18-1 summarizes the measures and results achieved, in line with the Phillips' model of learning evaluation. The results have been measured up to Level 4, with the last being "prospective" in nature.

Table 18-1. TM Initiative Micro Scorecard

Talent Management Initiative: Implementation of an organization-wide performance and talent management suite

Target Audience: Entire Essar Group (except Aegis, the BPO firm)

# of Participants: 15,000+ employees

Duration: Phase-wise deployment spread over 12 months

Business Objectives: Instating a performance-driven culture, greater alignment and rigor in performance and talent management

	Results			Intangible Benefits
Satisfaction	Learning	Application	Tangible Benefits	
Level 1[1]	**Level 2[2]**	**Level 3[3]**	**Prospective Level 4:**	Change agenda sponsored by CEOs and GP-HR, bringing into focus the need for a performance-driven culture
Visibility to business plans and CEO scorecards for the first time	150 HR and line managers trained, tested, certified and empanelled on e-Compass Trainers Community	15,000 users in 22 countries	Greater alignment of efforts enhancing both efficiency and effectiveness—positive impact expected on bottom line in the medium–long term	Enhanced focus on streamlined, aligned efforts across levels, facilitating strategy execution
High level of adoption of e-Compass across businesses, employee levels and geographies (95% have completed scorecards with 75% alignment)	>90% coverage of employees in End-user Training (with built-in quizzes) across businesses—essential to equip users to leverage the tool and positively influence adoption and buy-in	17,748 e-learning resources accessed, with 7,000+ unique users, in the first year itself	Greater rigour in performance and development reviews to positively affect employee engagement, reducing attrition, costs of re-hire, re-orientation, and man-hour loss	Greater transparency, credibility and buy-in for the PMS process contributing to a high-performance culture
Enhanced accessibility with single sign-on	e-Module usage: 1,500 employees accessed across locations	95% coverage of scorecards with 75% alignment		
Comprehensive goal management coupled with seamless access to over 20,000 e-learning resources brought together the development and performance agenda for employees		Best BizX Adoption in Asia Pac Award (2012) by SuccessFactors	**Level 5:** N/A	
Involvement of line managers in process and product design ensured well-rounded approach → enhanced satisfaction on PMS process & tool[1,1]				

[1] We have chosen to take system acceptance and adoption as proxies for satisfaction, instead of engaging in a separate satisfaction survey. External recognition has also been taken as conclusive evidence.

[1.1] Two PMS task forces were set up in the ideation phase: one comprising HR managers, and one comprising line managers. Both sets of inputs were considered when finalizing process and product design.

[2] The certification process (for HR Managers to train end-users in businesses) included a written test and e-Module completion (with in-built tests). Additionally, the Train-the-Trainer workshop itself included demo training sessions, to ensure the necessary assimilation of key concepts, and the context in which the process comes alive.

[3] The success of the e-Compass implementation (95% scorecard coverage, 75% alignment) would not have been possible without the buy-in and support of key influences, senior leaders, and the entire HR fraternity. We have taken this as evidence of gainful application of the online PMS implementation process.

Technique to Isolate Effects of Program: Level 3: Outcomes are direct results of the deployment exercise; external recognition from an objective third party. Level 4: Macro-economic and industry/cyclical externalities to be negated when determining impact; time-series/peer organization comparisons to be done for comparable business scenarios.

Technique to Convert Data to Monetary Value: N/A

Barriers to Application of Skills: IT infrastructure and readiness, data integrity and mindset toward performance management

Recommendations: Taking all key stakeholders on board at the very outset; involving end customers in initial need diagnosis and process/product design

CONCLUSIONS

- Involving the end customer in the initial need diagnosis phase enhances buy-in and acceptance moving forward, and also results in a more realistic assessment of both "as is" and "to be" states.

- Senior leadership and key influencer buy-in is a necessary prerequisite for the successful execution of any change initiative.

- It is imperative to have all key stakeholders on board from the very outset, to enable adequate support and coordination as required at different stages of the process.

- Roles need to be allocated and demarcated clearly, especially in complex projects such as e-Compass, to ensure accountability when driving the process against critical timelines, and to prevent things falling through gaps.

- When measuring or evaluating interventions and initiatives, it is important to consider both short-term and long-term impact on individuals, teams, and the organization as a whole.

- The outcomes of any intervention and initiative must be considered holistically, with a cognizance of linkages and spillovers to other seemingly disparate areas of people management.

ABOUT THE AUTHORS

Dr. Sujaya Banerjee, Chief Talent Officer and Senior Vice President of HR, Essar Group, has been a human resources professional for more than 22 years and has transformed the HR functions in several leading organizations during her career. She is an OD professional par-excellence, having set up world-class PMS and talent management programs and helped build learning organizations through her assignments at ADNOC, Lowe Lintas and Partners, British Gas, and the Essar Group. Sujaya has been listed among the top 40 HR professionals in Asia and has won the Youth Icon Award for 2009, besides bringing several international accolades to India, including the Learning Elite Award—CLO USA and Learning in Practice Award—among others.

Nishant Dangle, Joint General Manager and Head of Talent Management and Leadership Development, Essar Group, is a part of the Central Learning and OD Team at Essar, and brings more than 11 years of experience in the human resources function, having handled several strategic assignments in areas such as talent management, change management and OD, leadership development and human resources. An alumnus of Tata Institute of Social Sciences (TISS), Nishant is certified on various HR tools, including competency mapping and assessment, MBTI, and coaching using the appreciative coaching framework. Prior to the Essar Group, Nishant has worked with global and Indian organizations such as KPMG, PwC, Ambit RSM, and K.K Birla Group.

Anand Justin Cherian, Manager of Central Learning and OD, Essar Group, graduated from the Indian Institute of Management in Calcutta, and has been working as part of the Central Learning and OD Team at Essar for nearly three years. While he has worked in the areas of leadership development, talent management, and learning and development, his interests also include psychology, philosophy, writing, and painting.

REFERENCES

Garvin, D.A. (2000). *Learning in Action: A Guide to Putting the Learning Organization to Work.* Cambridge, MA: Harvard Business School Press.

Phillips, J.J. (2003). *Return on Investment in Training and Performance Improvement Programs,* 2nd edition. Butterworth–Heinemann.

19

TALENT MANAGEMENT FUNCTIONAL MACRO SCORECARDS

Toni DeTuncq

INTRODUCTION

This case study provides a look at how an international bank set up a learning and development (L&D) functional macro scorecard to track training programs throughout their organization. A system was established, used, and maintained to see, on any given day, how much training was being provided and how effective the L&D programs were in meeting individual as well as organizational quality drivers.

BACKGROUND

A large international bank, headquartered in Canada, has branches throughout the world. Many are English-as-a-second-language operations. The bank has a balanced scorecard that establishes goals for their profit, efficiency, customer satisfaction, and employee satisfaction. The L&D organization hired THD & Company, Inc. to help them set up a structure for seeing how the L&D organization was linked to these bank business objectives. The bank wanted its training organization to demonstrate the following:

- how much training was being conducted

- how many people were participating in the training programs

- how much was being spent on training

- what types of training were being provided

- what media was being used most often and most effectively.

They wanted this information broken out by business units (BUs), which for them were mainly different regions or parts of the world. In addition, they wanted to know how effective each program was within each BU and how each was helping the bank achieve its business objectives as mapped out in the Bank's balanced scorecard. They saw the audience for this information to be:

- the chief executive officer (CEO), the chief operating officer (COO), the chief financial officer (CFO) and the chief learning officer (CLO)

- each BU's operational manager (customers)

- each BU's learning managers.

TALENT MANAGEMENT INITIATIVE

The consultant recommended that an L&D functional macro scorecard be designed and built. The effort to meet the data goals for its intended audience required the scorecard contents to be conducted in a phased approach. Table 19-1 depicts the design and implementation phases proposed as well as the activities planned in each phase.

Table 19-1. Learning and Development (L&D) Macro Scorecard Roadmap

Design Phase		Implementation Phase		
Determine Fields to Populate	Design Initial Scorecard	Populate With Existing Data	Standardize Impact Tools and Populate	Share With Key Stakeholders
Determine Activity Data Fields Desired	THD and Co-Build	Send Activity Data To Repository	Level 1 Complete	Select Stakeholders
Determine Database Feeds for Activity Data	Task Team Review and Approve	Send Impact Data to Repository	Develop Level 2 Standard	Set Up Stakeholder Meeting for Initial Share

Define Impact Data Fields Desired	Determine Repository		Level 2 – Conduct Test Design Workshops	Conduct Ishare to Show Data and Offer Explanations
			Standardize Level 3 Ongoing Instrument	Gather Reaction Data
			Select Programs for L1 and L2 Reporting	Determine Revisions or Enhancements
			Select Programs for Impact Studies	
			Standardize Reporting Method	
			Send Data Into Repository	

TM FUNCTIONAL MACRO SCORECARD

A macro scorecard template was constructed using the Tier 1 and 2 structure described in chapter 2 of this book. It was decided to begin the effort using Excel, recognizing that as the database grew, a new database tool may be required. But it was seen as beneficial to begin with a tool that everyone could use as data collection began. Figure 19-1 provides the structure for the bank's L&D macro scorecard.

About the Learning Organization

This section of the scorecard provided information about the learning organization, its structure, and points of contact. The bank provided the consultant with two organizational charts, one for the entire bank and one for the L&D organization. This demonstrated how the learning organization was lined up within the bank as a whole. Then different BUs within the L&D organization were listed. The key people from each part of the charts were identified along with their contact information. These charts were updated monthly as needed. The bank's balanced scorecard areas were identified in this section as well.

Terms and Definitions

Key terms and their definitions populated this section. Business, performance, and learning objectives (DeTuncq, 2012) and the levels of evaluation (Phillips, 2003) were defined. It was hoped that if the intended audience ran into any difficulty understanding the measurement and evaluation jargon used in the scorecard, they could refer to this section.

Figure 19-1. L&D Macro Scorecard Components

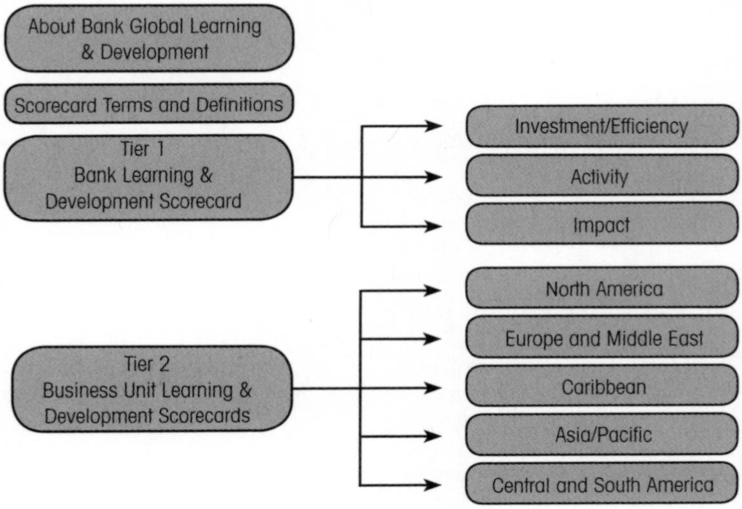

Tier 1 Data

Tier 1 data reflected all the metrics for all of the BUs, rolled up. Either totals or averages were used. They included three types of data: (1) investment/ efficiency, (2) activity, and (3) impact. For the investment/efficiency data, the following metrics were collected to populate the scorecard:

- dollar amount invested per employee
- L&D spending as percentage of overall operating expenditures
- training hours per employee per month
- cost per employee training day
- percentage of courses available via e-learning platforms.

The following monthly data were collected for the activity part of the scorecard:

- number of employees trained
- number of course completions (by category)
- number of courses available (by category)
- number of classroom sessions held monthly
- number of active courses (by category)
- number of monthly person hours of training.

For each of these types of data, the result, value, data sources for the metric, and the opportunity for the user to see the information in either a graph or table format was provided. Table 19-2 provides an example of an investment/efficiency scorecard.

Table 19-2. Example Investment/Efficiency Scorecard

Metric	Result	Value	Data Source	Detailed Results	
$ invested/ employee (trend over past 12 months)	$4,006	We are making good investments	SAP/ Hyperion	$ invested per employee Graph	$ invested per employee Table
L&D spend as % of overall operating expenditures (or as a % of payroll)	4.0%	We are funding L&D at the appropriate level	SAP/ Hyperion	L&D spend Graph	L&D spend Table
Training hours/ employee/month (trend over past 12 months; can we forecast forward?)	7.42	Our employees are spending enough/too much time in training	PeopleSoft	Training hours Graph	Training hours Table
Cost per employee training day	$949	We are spending too much/not enough per employee	SAP/ Hyperion/ PeopleSoft	Cost per employee Graph	Cost per employee Table
% of courses available via e-learning	28%	We have a proper mix of learning media types	PeopleSoft/ IntraLearn		

It is important to note that the value of each metric to the organization is decided upon by the training analysts and inserted in this part of the scorecard. The same value is made for the activity metrics. This value statement gives them an opportunity to quickly assess what each of these metrics means to the business. So the investment/efficiency and activity scorecards provide not only the "how much" but the "so what" information that most executives or decision makers need.

The levels of evaluation were used to collect and display impact (Phillips, 2003). Using a standard Level 1 instrument, the following average scores were provided:

- average rating for content
- average rating for the facilitators
- average rating for e-learning
- average overall rating.

For each of the areas, the number of participants and sessions that the scores represented were provided.

For Level 2 data, the test scores were provided as a percentage and the number of courses that average score represented was depicted. To be able to provide this data, the bank realized that their testing needed to be standardized so that scores could be compared. The consultant provided a "Test Construction and Validation Standard" to be used for test design and validation. It was envisioned that workshops could be provided to test design personnel to teach the standard principles and guidance.

For Level 3 data, the average percent ratings were provided. Some of the bank's learning professionals had been trained to conduct Level 3 analysis, but not in a standardized fashion, so the consultant provided standards for conducting various types of data collection to measure performance. But it was envisioned that the bank personnel skilled in conducting Levels 3 through 5 would design and conduct workshops for bank L&D staff and provide supporting material to them.

For Level 4 data, the average percent rating and the number of courses this rating represented was provided. To do this, decisions were made on the different metrics this data would represent and how to apply a rating to data collected. Ten standard metrics were selected when business objectives were developed or assigned to each program, such as productivity, efficiency (time savings), profit margins, or turnover. When data were collected using one or more of these metrics, the results provided a score of how well the objective had been met. For example, one program may receive a productivity rating of between 1 (lowest productivity rating) to 5 (highest productivity rating.)

Level 5 data recorded the average ROI percent received and how many programs evaluated at that level the percent represented.

Tier 2 Data

The Tier 2 part of the scorecard provided investment/efficiency and activity data the same way as the Tier 1 data only for each BU. The impact data were recorded as described for Tier 1, except that they were provided for each training program within that BU and included two new components. Each program's business objectives and its relationship to the bank's balanced scorecard components were listed. For example, if one program's business objective was to reduce turnover by 30 percent, that relationship would potentially impact employee satisfaction, a key indicator on the bank's balanced scorecard. That relationship was depicted on the scorecard. It was thought that this would be helpful to the executive audience because they could quickly see how many programs were focusing on the key metrics that they believed were important for the bank at that particular time. Table 19-3 depicts what the impact data for one BU might look like. Let's talk about this part of the TM functional macro scorecard as depicted in this table.

Although the data are fictional, this example provides the structure that was used for the impact data for one of the bank's business units. Each specific program is listed. One business objective is associated with each program. In reality there would likely be more than one business objective for each program. In the third column, the related bank objective(s) from the bank's balanced scorecard is listed. For the "Customer Relations" program, two related bank objectives are listed. Next to the Bank's related objectives are the scores for the different levels of evaluation. Level 1 was actually divided into four components: content, instruction, e-learning, and overall. In the example, there are shaded areas where no scores are provided. Many TM functional macro scorecards will look this way because not all programs are evaluated at all levels, particularly Levels 3 through 5. Conclusions about this business unit that can be drawn from this scorecard are:

- All the programs have business objectives, which is actually impressive. Many times programs are provided with no business objectives. If programs were listed with no business objectives, it would be painfully apparent that the L&D staff assigned to that program was falling short, particularly if all the other programs in that BU have them.

- Each program is aligned with at least one business metric from the bank's balanced scorecard.

- In this BU, two programs are aligned to Employee Satisfaction, three to Revenue, and three to Customer Satisfaction. The bank's other metric from the balanced scorecard, Efficiency, is not being addressed by any of this BU's programs. If the bank were particularly focused on efficiency measures in that particular year, the BU would need to justify why none of their programs were addressing them.

- The Customer Relations program looks like it is having difficulties. It received the lowest evaluation scores from Level 1 all the way to having a negative ROI. And the fact that this program is aligned to two related bank objectives makes it a program that should be investigated. If the Level 3, 4, and 5 studies were done comprehensively, they would show what the problems were and provided recommendations for its "cure." The L&D organization would need to be sure the recommendations were or are being addressed. For example, if it was recommended that the program be discontinued, is a plan in place to replace it?

- Only four programs out of the seven have Level 2 measures in place. What is important here is to make sure that the programs that do not have measures for learning in place do not have them because of a conscious decision not to have them, rather than some other reason. If, for example, the organization does not have the skill to do what is required according the test construction and validation standards the consultant put into place, they need to begin offering a workshop to teach the standards to staff.

- According to the guiding principles established for using the ROI Methodology (Phillips, 2003), when a higher-level evaluation is conducted, data must be collected at lower levels. The "Sales 101" program is evaluated at Levels 1, 3, 4, and 5. Fortunately the scores at these levels are positive. But if the Level 3 scores were not positive, without the Level 2 data, we would not know if the low score were due to the program or to something else. In a case like that, the training program would most likely be blamed for the lack of transfer. And if the ROI were negative, the organization would most likely be asking itself if it should keep investing money in sales training. Or they may wonder if

Table 19-3. Example of Impact Data From One Business Unit

Program	Business Objective(s)	Related Bank Objective(s)	Level 1	Number of Sessions	Number of Participants	Level 2	Number of Sessions	Number of Participants
Leadership 101	Reduce Turnover	Employee Satisfaction	4.2	10	130	85%	10	112
Sales 101	Increase Profit	Revenue	3.9	9	92			
Accounting 101	Increase Efficiency	Revenue	4.0	N/A Online	250	82%	N/A	250
Customer Relations	Increase Sales	1. Revenue 2.Customer Satisfaction	2.8	20	250	72%	18	120
System 1	Increase Efficiency	Customer Satisfaction	4.6	5	46			
System 2	Improve Quality	Customer Satisfaction	4.8	25	122			
System 3	Reduce Stress	Employee Satisfaction	3.8	3	15	86%	3	15

they should be looking for different design personnel for sales training. The L&D organization does not want to be put in that position.

- Four of the seven programs in this BU have evaluated up to Level 3. This is actually good from a percentage perspective. Level 3 evaluations require resources and should not be undertaken unless the organization believes it needs or wants to find out if transfer has taken place.

- This breakdown may create a sense of competition among the program designers or other stakeholders. Those with few or no scores would need

Level 3	Number of Sessions	Number of Participants	Level 4	Number of Sessions	Number of Participants	Level 5	Number of Sessions	Number of Participants
72%	2	25						
85%	3	48	75%	3	48	240%	3	48
60%	5	25	55%	5	25	-35%	5	25
88%	1	5						

to start conducting more evaluations for their programs. Such competition would be healthy.

Finally, the different users of the scorecard can quickly compare this BU's program progress with that of other BUs, by clicking on each BU's impact scorecards. Remember that all the BUs' training program impact data are rolled up and presented under the Tier 1 "Impact" tab of the macro scorecard database.

What wasn't considered at the bank, but could be considered in the future, is to have the macro scorecard provide the capability for the users to click on individual programs in the BUs' impact scorecards and be presented with the micro scorecard for that particular training program, such as those presented in chapters 3 through 18 of this book.

CONCLUSIONS

- This international bank started with a simple design for their L&D macro scorecard. The empty spaces seen on the macro scorecard serve as the placeholders for evaluations to come.

- The L&D macro scorecard will demonstrate to the bank's executives that the L&D organization is holding itself accountable for contributing to the bank's overall success, as measured by their balanced scorecard metrics.

- This scorecard generates healthy competition among the different BUs. The users can see how many programs each BU is providing, how they are aligned with key business metrics, and how successful they are. They will also be looking at how accountable each BU is, based on how much evaluation activity is taking place.

- Some foundational work had to take place to make this type of macro scorecard effective. The Level 1 evaluations needed to be standardized across the bank's BUs. This can best be done with a task force from each BU that ensures the final Level 1 instrument will work for each of them. A standard for designing and implementing Level 2 measures must be developed to make sure the Level 2 data are comparable. In this case, a standard was created by an expert in the field of test design, implementation, and analysis. Workshops may be needed to teach test designers the standard. Workshops and books galore exist for conducting evaluations at Levels 3, 4, and 5. The bank had several staff members within its design community who had attended workshops for this. They can put together a workshop for the rest of the L&D community, as well as webinars, job aids, and other helpful guidance. They may also want to establish an internal network for the purpose of helping one another as they conduct their impact studies.

A TM functional macro scorecard, such as the one built by this bank's L&D organization, will prove its ongoing value and demonstrate that the L&D organization is a key player in the bank's business.

REFERENCES

DeTuncq, T. (2012). "Demystifying Measurement and Evaluation." *Infoline*, no. 1211. Alexandria, VA: ASTD Press.

Phillips, J.J. (2003). *Return On Investment in Training and Performance Improvement Programs,* 2nd edition. Woburn, MA: Butterworth-Heinemann.

20

INTEGRATED TALENT MANAGEMENT THAT DRIVES ECONOMIC VALUE ADD

Karl-Heinz Oehler

INTRODUCTION

This chapter demonstrates how to move talent management (TM) measurement from concept to reality. It highlights the value of a systemic view in which talent management functions such as talent acquisition, workforce planning, learning and development, performance management, and succession and high-potential management are integrated into a TM service unit with financial TM measures to drive organizational effectiveness and market competitiveness. The chapter shows how a TM organizational macro scorecard can be used to demonstrate the value of an integrated TM organization. As integrated TM is not possible without an integrated human resources (HR) function, this chapter may use both terms interchangeably.

BACKGROUND

Hertz operates its car-rental business through the Hertz, Dollar, and Thrifty brands from approximately 10,400 corporate, licensee, and franchisee locations in North America, Europe, Latin America, Asia, Australia, Africa, the Middle East, and New Zealand. Hertz is the largest worldwide airport general-use car rental brand, operating from approximately 8,800 corporate and licensee locations in approximately 150 countries. Hertz is the number one airport car rental brand in the U.S. and has operations at 111 major airports in Europe. Dollar and Thrifty have approximately 1,580 corporate and franchisee locations in approximately 80 countries. Hertz is an inaugural member of *Travel + Leisure's* World's Best Awards Hall of Fame and was recently named, for the thirteenth time, by the magazine's readers as the Best Car Rental Agency. Hertz was also voted the Best Overall Car Rental Company in Zagat's 2012-13 U.S. Car Rental Survey, earning top honors in 14 additional categories, and the company swept the global awards for Best Rewards Program and Best Overall Benefits from FlyerTalk.com. Product and service initiatives such as Hertz Gold Plus Rewards, NeverLost®, and unique cars and SUVs offered through the company's Adrenaline, Prestige, and Green Traveler Collections, also set Hertz apart from the competition. Additionally, Hertz owns the vehicle leasing and fleet management leader Donlen Corporation and operates the Hertz On Demand car-sharing business. The company also owns a leading North American equipment rental business, Hertz Equipment Rental Corporation, which includes Hertz Entertainment Services.

Business Transformation Background

Hertz's change in ownership in 2006 from a privately owned company to a publically listed company and the subsequent stock-exchange listing resulted in a shift toward a centralized structure with global business processes. This transformation created the immediate need for a very different HR model in general, and for talent management specifically.

In July 2007, the shift to a fully integrated global HR structure was begun with the following steps:

1. Creating an HR matrix built on HR business partners, HR IT and operations, global total rewards, and a global talent management center of expertise (COE), all directly linked to and driven by business priorities.

2. Consolidating all talent processes such as talent acquisition, learning and development, performance and career management, succession and high-potential management, assessment services, change and culture, human capital measurement, HR due diligence, and post-merger integration into one unit, the global talent management center of expertise.

3. Positioning HR as a service organization to increase operational effectiveness to drive market competiveness, based on the concept "One Global HR—The people part of business."

"The people part of business" signifies a total commitment to become an integral part of the Hertz global value chain. Its sole focus is to relentlessly deliver both business-driven and integrated people solutions. It embodies an obsessive focus on the goal of becoming the employer of choice. In the case of global talent management, Hertz can draw on a seamless pool of expertise and competence to deliver specific people-oriented processes to Hertz businesses around the world.

Hertz defines talent as having "…employees at all organizational levels and locations who demonstrate sustained performance and proven potential." Talent is managed globally using a portfolio approach around an employee lifecycle model, which itself is integrated with business processes. Talent capability evaluation is an integral part of the annual strategy process, ensuring that critical talent needs are recognized and budgeted upstream. Thus, talent development is managed as an investment, not a cost. Figure 20-1 illustrates how TM was integrated into the business strategy.

Figure 20-1. Integration of Global Talent Management Into the Hertz Strategy Process

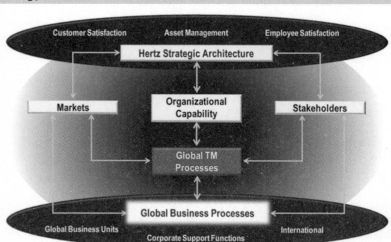

Today, TM must demonstrate its contribution to financial results. It must be prepared to answer questions such as: Which are the human drivers that affect key financial drivers? Which measures are relevant to the business? Where, by whom, and how is value created? TM must use data, facts, and analysis to improve business performance—and proactively implement corrective actions—to achieve both short-term results as well as sustained impact. In short, HR and TM must operate like a business.

INTEGRATED TALENT MANAGEMENT INITIATIVE

Consider this: The executive vice president of sales of a global manufacturing firm asks talent management to implement a three-day sales training program for 1,100 salespeople over three years. The total program investment is U.S. $1.1 million, including all expenses. The business driver for this decision is to increase sales effectiveness, which seems logical as company sales grew at a slower rate than the rest of the market for two consecutive years. In addition, although the company's product is the best on the market, and market demand is strong, competitor sales are growing faster. Upon first glance, it would appear that implementing the training program would be the legitimate next step for a reasonable investment, and one could have readily agreed to the VP's request. Now let's take a closer look. In this specific example the average revenue per salesman per day was $5,545. Conducting training for 1,100 salespeople over three days equals 3,300 days of missed sales opportunities. This represents revenue losses of $18.3 million over three years, or $6.1 million per year. The real investment per annum, therefore, is $7.2 million, including the training program cost, spread across three years.

Let's just focus on measuring TM impact. Shouldn't the question to the executive VP's request have been: How much incremental revenue will you commit to over the next two years to create an acceptable return on the training investment? HR's credibility as a business partner depends on its ability to ask business leaders the right questions. This skill makes the difference between being a business enabler and being a business differentiator.

How did this particular scenario conclude? Upon request, the finance department provided the standard measure of sales effectiveness in manufacturing ("asset turns"). Analysis showed the company's asset turn was 39 percent higher compared to their next biggest competitor. There was nothing wrong with sales effectiveness; the problem was elsewhere. Cooperation between TM and finance prevented cash from being spent, along with painful revenue loss. It also prevented the business from trying to fix the wrong problem.

So what's the point?

The point is that to earn credibility with the business, TM must become business savvy—understand the company's business model, define what constitutes value, and know where and how this value is created. Success depends on the ability to measure how much value TM creates for the business in terms of standard financial measures. In other words, TM needs to reinvent itself as a business function, fully integrated into the company's value-creation process.

Whichever financial models companies use to measure economic success, ultimately, cash is king. TM's (and HR's) formidable challenge and opportunity is to demonstrate how it contributes to improving the company's cash situation, and subsequently creates economic value for the enterprise. As employees are at the heart of every business, it's widely accepted that employee engagement and financial performance are strongly correlated.

The Hertz Transformation Process

The TM journey started when Hertz was floated on the New York Stock Exchange, evolving into a publicly traded organization running a global operating model. With a fresh eye on the economic challenges facing the corporation, Hertz adopted three strategic pillars named the Business Operating System:

- Customer Satisfaction
- Employee Satisfaction
- Asset Management.

Managing these three pillars, as shown in Figure 20-2, requires a fine balancing act of the entire Hertz organization, as all three are equally important. All TM initiatives needed to address at least one of these pillars. As a result, they became TM's guiding principles for conceiving and driving TM solutions. Looking back today, these three pillars drove a stronger partnership with the Hertz businesses, an integrated HR matrix structure, the need for financial and business acumen across TM, and the adoption of Lean Sigma methodologies.

Figure 20-2. The Hertz Transformation Process

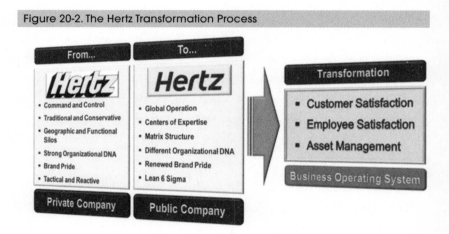

Building an Integrated Talent Management Structure

Organizational transformation, including culture change, was, and still is, the predominant priority for TM at Hertz. To be credible, HR had to take its own medicine first. Removing functional silos from the global HR organization itself was critical to integrating with the Hertz business operating system. Existing and related, yet independent, HR domains were selected and consolidated into one global TM organization. This was comprised of learning and development, talent acquisition, performance and career management, succession and high-potential management, operational excellence, and human capital management. Organization development and culture and change were also included.

The second and more challenging step was to identify internal HR talent with proven TM expertise, strong business and financial acumen, and with the subject matter expertise required to work effectively in a Center of Expertise. This challenge was addressed by blending Hertz experience with external talent, thus creating a diverse team of TM domain experts.

The new, global TM structure was positioned across Hertz as a business enabler, with the banner "the people part of business." TM's communication emphasized business-oriented values, including the vision to "Create economic value-add, delivering business-driven, integrated people solutions;" the mission to "Foster a culture of success by providing best-in-class HR leadership," and the value proposition to "Increase operational effectiveness to drive market competitiveness." The design of the integrated TM function quickly evolved into a service organization with clearly defined service-level agreements; it was evaluated and measured by its financial results, therefore demonstrating its economic value. Figure 20-3 shows how TM is integrated into the business planning cycle.

Figure 20-3. The Global Talent Management Planning Process

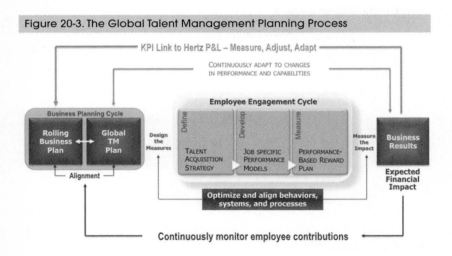

Execution With Discipline—The Key to Impact and Sustainability

With the global, integrated TM infrastructure in place, it was critical to implement and drive TM solutions with the greatest impact on financial results. After consulting with senior business leaders, we agreed to focus on the following deliverables:

- Transform the current TM activities into a systemic and integrative process built around Hertz's three strategic pillars.

- Expand the TM processes across the entire employee base to spot the most talented employees across the organization, irrespective of current level, position, or location, and ensure their development for future positions.

- Establish a strong link between TM and other key HR processes, namely selection and recruitment, to build a talent pipeline with employees who have the competencies critical for driving Hertz's growth imperatives.

- Make performance and career management the catalyst, not only for nomination to either the succession or talent management pool, but also for the decision to maintain or remove candidates from the respective pools or career tracks.

- Introduce a neutral and objective process to evaluate the ability of talent to successfully perform at the next level.

- Establish a dynamic, adaptable, and business-centric talent development process with regular reviews against defined milestones, to ensure that development plans are executed in a timely fashion.

- Enable employees to deliver an outstanding customer experience that meets Hertz's brand promises. This covered employer branding, employee engagement, harmonised recruitment and onboarding processes, as well as performance-based reward and recognition programs, measured biannually through an employee engagement survey.

- Establish value-stream maps linking Hertz TM processes to business processes to identify and remove waste.

- Align the strategic plan, TM plan, and financial plan to enable economic value-add for the Hertz business.

Combined, these initiatives evolved into a systemic process integrating TM and Lean Sigma methodologies to drive organizational effectiveness.

This resulted in reduced process waste, effectively measuring and correcting variability, quantifying economic impact, and strong alignment with company objectives.

As people manage processes and drive results, optimal employee profiles for the most critical positions were established. Furthermore, it was critical to understand key operational interdependencies and decide which HR processes made the biggest operational impact through these interdependencies. Finally, understanding the key operational interdependencies highlighted which HR development structures most affected business results. The connection between the interdependencies and processes is shown in Figure 20-4.

Figure 20-4. Connecting Business Process and Global TM Interdependencies

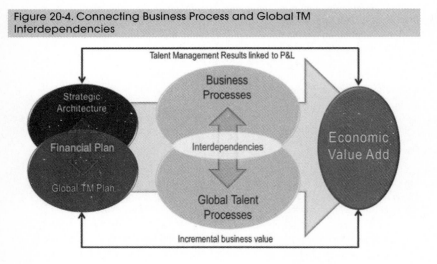

TM had to ensure value creation was the driver at every stage of the employee life cycle. Where there is recruitment there is a hiring cost; where there is onboarding there is an integration cost; where there is development there is a succession cost; where there is recognition there is compensation and benefits cost; and where there is progression there is a retention cost. It is a holistic view of the employee life cycle, as shown in Figure 20-5.

Figure 20-5. The Employee Lifecycle Investment Process

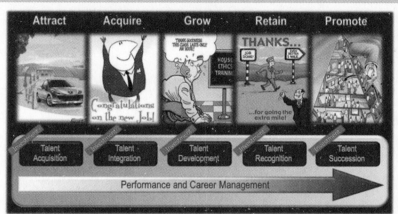

The Pivotal Role of Learning and Development

Integrating learning and development (L&D) into global TM is of paramount importance. It provides the glue that connects talent development structures spanning from talent acquisition to succession and high-potential management, consolidating vital development needs resulting from the performance and career management cycle.

A key decision was to outsource routine L&D work early on, to enable internal learning resources to deeply engage with the Hertz business leaders. The role of the global business-process outsourcing (BPO) partner was to provide training delivery resources, instructional design services, the learning management system (LMS), training administration, and reporting. The BPO partner also sourced specific programs at Hertz's request and facilitated program delivery as needed.

This approach led to a very different L&D model; a model of integration, adaptability, and flexibility, responding to rapid change driven by turbulent business environments. L&D was fully integrated into TM and hence into Hertz's value-creation chain. The proximity to the business enabled L&D to quickly prioritize learning solutions.

Why is this so important? As a business enabler, L&D must:

- Drive real-time learning and development for real-time results.
- Ensure transfer and application of knowledge to create sustainable business impact.
- Bridge the gap from individual learning to organizational learning.
- Deliver business-focused learning solutions, not training programs.
- Link compensation and rewards to changes driven through L&D.

The integrated L&D structure transformed the internal learning resources into a powerful team of subject matter experts working as learning business partners. Dedicated to the senior business unit and functional leaders, the learning business partners are integrated into the business. They understand both the day-to-day operational problems and the longer-term strategic issues, and work in partnership with the business leaders to build solutions. Their intimate business knowledge enables them to develop integrated learning solutions and define how to measure, compensate, and reward behavioral changes in the workplace.

Specific programs, such as change management programs, are kept in-house and delivered by internal trainers. These trainers also have a change-agent role. Thus, they represent the best of both worlds, (1) delivering training and (2) assisting the organization at large with transferring the knowledge back to the job.

Integrating L&D with TM is the way to go for many reasons. If the purpose of any business is to create value, it follows that unless L&D is fully integrated into the value-creation process, measuring the financial impact of L&D solutions is difficult. L&D must be aligned with market dynamics and therefore intrinsically linked to key company financial indicators. For L&D to add value, it must provide learning structures that enable knowledge transfer and application to achieve sustainable impact. And most importantly, L&D must be adaptable, resilient, and capable of responding quickly to rapid change in turbulent business environments. L&D has critical interdependencies with all other TM functions, and without being integrated with TM, L&D will not be able to maximize its business impact.

The decision to outsource parts of L&D proved to be the right move. Not only are the internal customer satisfaction ratings consistently very high, but the outsourcing arrangements saved Hertz in excess of $3 million per annum over the last four years.

Where We Are Today

As part of the strategic plan, pivotal roles with the biggest economic impact are identified. Position profiles, reward structures, business priorities, and cross-functional capabilities of these roles are part of selection, succession planning, and high-potential management processes.

The global TM organization provides robust tools and processes to manage turnover, increase retention, and standardize employee onboarding. Regional recruitment centers are in place to meet volume recruitment demands in a timely and effective way. A Hertz leadership model provides a strong foundation, describing job-specific core competencies and personality traits.

TM leads process-focused organizational design activities to establish more effective business structures. It also helps the organization capitalize on its talent, matching individual capabilities and career expectations with the competencies required for superior performance. Achieving this match provides a sound basis for maximizing job satisfaction, leading to sustained performance. Performance management is the catalyst for all Hertz talent processes.

Identifying, selecting, and promoting talent is part of ongoing career development and succession processes. Positions are preferably filled from within. Cross-functional and cross-geographical moves are encouraged, and wherever possible, actively implemented.

Focus on talent is critical for success in a more competitive and aggressive marketplace. The Hertz University provides comprehensive and targeted development programs globally. In addition, robust people evaluation processes (based on validated tools such as 360-degree instruments) and assessment methodologies are widely deployed.

MACRO EVALUATION METHODOLOGY AND RESULTS

It is rare that TM is incorporated into the strategic architecture of an organization to deliver the economic reasoning for top-level decision making. Hertz's 2010-2013 board-level strategic plan made the people component a potent element. It considers talent investments from a new angle: economic return. In other words, these investments are only made when analysis demonstrates the business impact and value add.

With the status of TM as a financial driver for the Hertz business, the key requirement for its implementation was to have a firm financial foundation. TM investments are directly linked to Hertz's profit and loss (P&L).

The approach to stakeholder management is dependent on stakeholder engagement driven by executive governance (the senior management team). The process of review and analysis is rigorous, backed by a series of stakeholder meetings and documentation. This includes quarterly board meetings where TM is a lead agenda item.

The relationship between finance and TM is particularly strong, and there are close links between TM and marketing (from a brand perspective) and corporate communication. These collaborations foster a productive environment that gives the business the capacity and ability to act; to be adaptable and to have the opportunity to experiment.

Achieving business results is a function of integration and alignment. It is about breaking corporate goals down into manageable and measurable units at the team and employee level. Hoshin-Kanri, a step-by-step planning, implementation, and review process for managed change, is an excellent way to ensure company goal alignment from the top down, while harmonizing the measurement process.

To move TM measurement from concept to reality, interdependencies between company objectives and TM objectives need to be recognized. This is often easier said than done. The art of measurement is in its simplification. In the case of TM, this means selecting only the financial key performance indicators (KPIs) that provide meaningful information for talent management and the business, and putting aside myriad indicators which have anecdotal value at best. With an almost indefinite number of measures to choose from, there is a real risk of selecting too many. And what appears to be a "key" performance indicator (KPI) may in fact not really be key.

For example, many TM functions still measure the average days of training per employee per annum. It is difficult, however, to explain how this particular KPI relates to financial contributions from TM without knowing how the business benefited in tangible terms. Selecting relevant TM KPIs is a prioritization exercise that requires discipline.

From an execution perspective, measuring TM's impact on financial results is a backward integration process. It starts with the company's financial plan. If, for example, adjusted pretax is a key financial measure, the question becomes how TM contributes to the improvement of adjusted pretax. Contributions can be manifold; such as addressing voluntary turnover with its secondary effects on succession, high-potential talent, or key functional expertise. Contributions could also be employee productivity or identifying training programs that do not create desired effects. Looking at measurement this way connects business strategy to the employee life cycle and provides a holistic view on human capital management, as depicted in Figure 20-6.

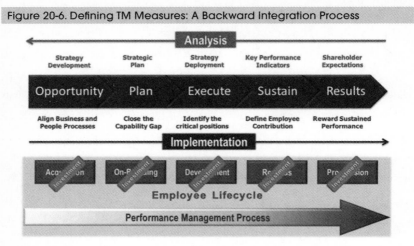

Figure 20-6. Defining TM Measures: A Backward Integration Process

Whatever the financial measure, and irrespective of process sophistication, talent and talent engagement is central to achieving desired financial goals. The question, "What is the most effective talent management strategy to improve organizational performance?" must remain on everybody's mind at all times. Mobilizing talent is the role of organizational leaders; providing clear direction for managing talent in a way that improves organizational performance is the role of TM in cooperation with the business. It is all about "human capital management," to use a more fashionable term.

All TM processes are systemic with multiple touch points across all businesses. Therefore, cooperation between TM and finance, and the business for that matter, is of paramount importance. TM must work with business leaders, and specifically finance, to raise awareness and knowledge about the impact of human capital on business performance. If successful, the outcome of this dialog will be a clear definition of human capital drivers for organizational success, and provide financial models that demonstrate the impact of human capital interventions on financial results. Human capital measurement or TM provides the glue for organizational performance.

Finally, there is a compelling need for finance and TM to find different and more creative ways to model financial impact of TM interventions. It is all about mindset—Is TM treated as a cost (constraint) or investment (possibility)? The answer to that question changes according to what is measured. Here is a simple example: Not many companies budget voluntary turnover cost in their annual plans. Yet this (hidden) cost often accounts for surprises resulting in budget overruns. Yes, turnover is a cost, but programs for turnover reduction are an investment.

It was recognized that the investment in the intellectual capital of Hertz needs to be in complete alignment with the business planning cycle, leading to an engagement model with the business. Each element in the model applies to both the business and TM, and includes:

- customer intimacy

- business-led solutions

- lean sigma principles

- seamless and innovative delivery model

- quality through continual improvement

- integrated cost/risk model linked to the Hertz P&L

- interlocked meetings to focus on continual improvement.

A systemic view of TM and the business is an absolute necessity. Business results and their measurements had to be designed at the front end, not as an afterthought, such that financial measures (adjusted pretax, for example) are linked to relevant TM initiatives to achieve the desired level of efficiency.

The starting point was the analysis of the strategic drivers, so that HR and business leaders could align, develop, and coordinate talent strategies that yield the desired financial outcomes. Implemented rigorously, this process makes the concept of "being business-focused" real for the senior leaders. It translates planning into execution and thus produces tangible results. Table 20-2 illustrates how TM was integrated with other functions to create value.

Table 20-1. Value Creation Through Functional Integration

Integrating Finance, TM, and Lean Sigma Concepts

Value Add	Impact Areas	TM Process Focus	Lean Sigma Application	Finance Impact
Improve Return	Positions with impact on: • Revenue • Customer Satisfaction • Cost	• Talent acquisition • Turnover management • Performance management	• Pareto • Value stream maps • 8D • FMEA • DMAIC	• Pre-tax • Revenues
Manage Risk	• Routine tasks • Volume transactions • Standard services	• Turnover management • On-boarding and integration • Development structures	• Pareto • Vakue stream maps • 8D • Frequency charts • Factor analysis	• Pre-tax • Revenues
Increase Liquidity	• Organizational change • Process management • Interdependencies • Span of control	• Process reengineering • Organization design • Functional interdependencies	• Work process design • Value stream maps • QFD	• Pre-tax • Revenues

Where Is the Money?

TM integration with the value-creation chain has delivered measurable, tangible benefits to the organization since 2007. Furthermore, each critical TM program must achieve a previously agreed-upon adjusted pretax contribution.

At Hertz, these success measures are directly linked to finance KPIs. Whether the KPI is to increase pretax profit by a defined percentage or to grow airport share by a defined percentage, there is an associated impact on human capital: turnover cost, talent acquisition investment, placement cycle time, and personal productivity. Financial results are tracked and vetted by the program management organization, and are linked directly to cost savings or incremental revenues—ultimately, to the bottom line. It is essential to break down the financial drivers by strategic objectives to demonstrate economic value add (EVA). For example, voluntary turnover is analysed since 2007, showing a cumulated cost saving of $27 million; and employee and customer satisfaction are at historic high levels, resulting in significant productivity increases over the past four years, as shown in Figures 20-7 and 20-8.

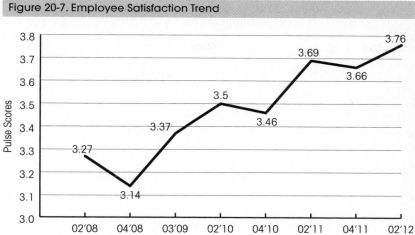

Figure 20-7. Employee Satisfaction Trend

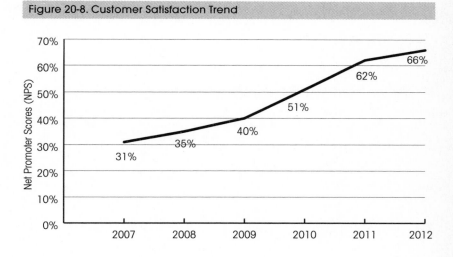

Figure 20-8. Customer Satisfaction Trend

The commitment of the Hertz CEO to the systemic approach to TM has led to a permanent increase of the HR budget, where elsewhere such budgets have typically faced cuts during and after the recession. Hertz can demonstrate that the investment (as a percentage of payroll and benefits) in employees at June 2012 is more than double the 2006 figure. Hertz also measures the financial risk of losing talent, which is crucial in the development of effective succession planning. Managing a succession pipeline avoided an incremental cost of $1.9 million as defined as first-year turnover.

The globalization of markets combined with ongoing economic uncertainties creates inherent risk. Acquiring, developing, and retaining talent capable of recognizing and proactively mitigating risk is critical to sustain organizational performance. Hertz engages talent with varied backgrounds to be more risk-aware. Hertz has evidence that the combination of a diverse talent portfolio and a corporate culture open to change will enable it to respond effectively to uncertainty and change.

Integrated TM is about organization effectiveness. Consequently, in the new HR world order, discrete TM functions must be merged into a systemic, interconnected unit. Hertz has established a unified TM organization with a high level of integration. This integrated structure operates as a center of expertise that continually improves internal effectiveness to enhance external competitiveness.

TM ORGANIZATIONAL MACRO SCORECARD

Progress against key performance indicators (KPIs) is continually measured and reviewed monthly by the senior leadership team. Trends are analyzed and corrective actions initiated as soon as trending information suggests that a specific KPI may be missed. Corrective actions may well be outside the responsibility of TM if, for example, business leaders suspend TM activities for cost-saving purposes. Having the TM scorecard fully integrated with the monthly business reviews leads to a more informed and objective dialog about the cause and effect of decisions made by senior leaders or the TM organization. To ensure utmost objectivity, TM scorecard information flows into the process improvement and program management organization, which presents an integrated view of all KPIs and their impact on business results.

Finally, TM KPIs are an integral part of the performance management process, affecting bonus payments both positively and negatively. Changes to TM KPIs caused by internal or external events need to be substantiated and approved by a senior leader. Having KPIs linked to the performance management process leads to disciplined execution of critical TM initiatives. Table 20-2 shows how the TM KPIs were integrated into the TM organizational macro scorecard to demonstrate impact.

Table 20-2. TM Organizational Macro Scorecard

Criteria	KPI (versus previous year)	P&L Impact	Status	Year-To-Date
Year 1 Turnover Reduction	-12%	Pre-Tax	■	Exceed +10%
Rcruitment Cycle Time (Volume Positions)	< 3 months	Revenues	▦	On par with previous year
Productivity gain	+10%	Pre-Tax	■	Eroding trend
Cost/Recruit (Volume Positions)	-7%	Pre-Tax	■	On par with 2010
Customer Satisfaction	+12%	Pre-Tax	■	+14%
Employee Engagement	+10%	Pre-Tax	▦	+6%

CONCLUSIONS

The systemic business approach to TM has been integrated into the company's value chain. It has delivered proven, tangible financial results for more than three years, with continuous and growing investment in the TM channel even through the recession. The concept has proven to deliver significant benefits to the bottom line. What have we learned?

- Implement a result-driven structure which makes TM not only accountable, but also a key driver for business performance. When evaluating TM success, the dialog should not merely be about the return-on-investment (ROI) of TM programs; rather, it's about their business impact.

- Define impact from TM initiatives as economic value add, which changes the way that the senior management team perceives its involvement and ownership.

- Build a strong internal governance group. At Hertz, business unit leaders meet quarterly to review key projects, remove barriers, work collaboratively, set priorities, and drive decision making in order to ensure alignment with the strategic direction.

- Ensure that TM initiatives provide a real-time response to business needs. This enables Hertz to respond quickly to volatile market conditions.

- Do not focus on "TM programs," but on planning and delivering integrated business solutions that deliver tangible results.

- Implemented rigorously, this process makes the concept of being business-focused real for the senior leaders. At Hertz, over the past four years they have started to "own" TM initiatives and set a global agenda and direction for the rest of the organization. Consequently, budget discussions have become less and less controversial.

- Communication between TM teams and senior decision makers maintain focus on business outcomes. Business leaders value predictability to mitigate risks in a timely fashion. Ongoing dialogue with the business at different levels about the status and impact of developmental initiatives on business performance is a major differentiator for maintaining awareness, knowledge, understanding, buy-in, and focus.

- Organizational effectiveness is never an after-thought, nor are quick fixes deemed appropriate. Review of shareholder value and identification of critical drivers, incorporating the Hoshin-Kanri planning processes, is part of a robust planning cycle.

- Integrate TM planning into the financial and strategic planning process to transfer responsibility for TM budget changes to the business. In other words, if the business requests a decrease in budget from TM, then previously agreed-upon TM-related outcomes need to be recalibrated in accordance with the new budget level. This situation fundamentally changes the dialogue between the business and TM.

At Hertz, all participants are equal partners in a fully-integrated, cross-functional approach, and the benefits of this process can only grow. The governance group members have become role models for change and transformation. Hertz is carefully analyzing the future that is indicative of this new corporate philosophy. The three-year predictions for continued investment, increased revenues, and increased productivity are based on sound data and linked directly to the work of HR professionals in Hertz. The TM organizational macro scorecard shows the value that the integrated TM organization at Hertz contributes to the business.

ABOUT THE AUTHOR

Karl-Heinz Oehler has pioneered leading-edge global talent management strategies at Hertz Corporation and other global companies. His work at Hertz has been recognized with the HR & Business Success Award and the overall winner's accolade, the Dave Ulrich Award of HCM Excellence, at the 2011 European HCM Excellence Awards. In addition, Karl-Heinz was conferred the Talent Leadership Award at the World HRD Congress of 2012. This is the organizer's most prestigious accolade of their "Global HR Excellence Awards for 2011-2012," and the highest honor which an individual can receive for his contribution to HR.

Karl-Heinz holds a masters degree in social psychology and economics. He is also a certified organizational auditor of the European Foundation for Quality Management (EFQM).

Karl-Heinz is based in Zurich, Switzerland, having previously lived and worked in Korea, Singapore, the United States, Finland, Sweden, France, and Germany.

ACKNOWLEDGMENTS

Writing a case study book involves the participation and expertise of many individuals working together over several months to create the final product. We greatly appreciate the contributions of everyone involved in the creation of this book. We received guidance, support, and assistance from friends, family, and professional acquaintances, and we say "Thank you" to all of them.

We want to extend our appreciation to each of the case study authors. They all stepped up to the challenge of aligning their case studies with the micro- and macro-scorecard formats required to illustrate our concept of integrated talent management. Each case study is unique and each author approached the evaluation of their programs creatively, often stretching their skill sets to meet the challenge of creating the scorecards. The quality of the written case studies attests to each author's in-depth knowledge and professionalism. We also want to thank the organizations that are represented in each case study. We appreciate the willingness of each organization to share its story with the world.

We greatly value the contributions made by the ASTD editors, and the magic they do by providing clarity and definition where needed. In particular, Stephanie Castellano worked closely with us to ensure each chapter was expertly written. Anthony Quintero made sure that our new concept of integrated talent management scorecards was positioned well in the community of human capital management. Ann Pace stepped in to help create and implement a marketing plan that guaranteed the book would be enthusiastically anticipated prior to publication, and well received after publication. We would also like to thank the graphic designers who worked with us to create a cover that best illustrates the concept.

In this age of social media we need to thank all of our virtual contacts who helped to refer potential case study authors. Individuals whom we had never met in person went out of their way to provide referrals and support. We couldn't have accomplished what we did, in the time frame that we did, without utilizing the many types of social media available today.

Toni Hodges DeTuncq

Lynn Schmidt, PhD

ABOUT THE AUTHORS

Toni Hodges DeTuncq is president of THD & Company, Inc. For the past 20 years, she has concentrated on measuring and managing human performance. Toni has managed operational, systems, and group evaluations for corporate, defense contracting, and government organizations. Her work has included the development of individual assessment tools as well as large organizational tracking tools, all aimed at measuring the performance and monetary value of human resource and systems intervention programs. Formerly, she managed measurement and evaluation for Verizon's Workforce Development group. At Bell Atlantic, she created and managed a measurement and evaluation program that, in 1999, was chosen as a best practice among more than 200 companies. Toni currently provides skill enhancement workshops and consulting services, helping organizations establish accountable and effective training and evaluation programs. She has conducted more than 50 impact assessments to include comprehensive return-on-investment (ROI) studies. Her clients include Bank of America, BMW Manufacturing, NASA, Raytheon, the United Nations, and Child and Family Services—Hawaii.

Toni was selected as one of nine "Training's New Guard—2001" by the American Society for Training & Development (ASTD), and was featured in the May 2001 issue of *T+D* magazine. In 2000, the ROI Network™ named her "Practitioner of the Year." She has published numerous articles, was the editor of the bestselling ASTD In Action series book *Measuring Learning and Performance*, and author of the recently published *Linking Learning and Performance: A Practical Guide to Measuring Learning and On-the-Job Application*. She was also co-author of *Make Training Evaluation Work*.

Toni is often sought after to speak at evaluation conferences and to publish articles about her work. Her work has been conducted in the United States, Canada, and Europe.

Lynn Schmidt, PhD has 26 years of experience as a talent management and organization development leader in large corporations. Currently, she is a talent management leader at Group Health Cooperative and has responsibility for succession management, leadership development, coaching, leader onboarding, and performance management. Prior to joining Group Health, Lynn was the director of talent management for Raytheon and had responsibility for implementing talent management and learning initiatives across the business.

In previous roles Lynn has created corporate universities and led enterprise-wide learning and development functions. She has had responsibility for strategic workforce planning, executive and high-potential leader development, diversity initiatives, employee engagement, and coaching and mentoring programs. Lynn is frequently asked to present at conferences and has presented at international conferences in Canada, the Netherlands, Jamaica, Japan, India, and Singapore. She has presented on topics such as leadership development, succession management, creating the corporate university, training scorecards, and measurement and evaluation.

Lynn has extensive experience evaluating the impact of talent management initiatives on the bottom line. She has received her certification in ROI evaluation, served as the chairperson of the ASTD ROI Network Advisory Committee for two years, and was a recipient of the ROI Practitioner of the Year Award. She was an adjunct professor at both Marymount University and Georgetown University in Washington, D.C. Lynn is the editor of the ASTD In Action series book *Implementing Training Scorecards*, co-author of *The Leadership Scorecard*, and has contributed to other books in the field.

Lynn has a BS in business administration, an MBA, an MA in human and organizational systems, and a PhD in human and organizational systems. In addition, she has received her ACC coaching credential from the International

Coaching Federation (ICF) and is currently the Director of Sponsorship on the ICF Washington State chapter board of directors. Lynn was awarded the Talent Leadership Award at the 2012 World HRD Congress, and the Global HR Excellence Awards in Mumbai, India.